CAUTION!!
COLORED PEOPLE
OF BOSTON, ONE & ALL,
You are hereby respectfully CAUTIONED and
advised, to avoid conversing with the
Watchmen and Police Officers
of Boston,
For since the recent ORDER OF THE MAYOR &
ALDERMEN, they are empowered to act as
KIDNAPPERS
AND
Slave Catchers,
And they have already been actually employed in
KIDNAPPING, CATCHING, AND KEEPING
SLAVES. Therefore, if you value your LIBERTY,
and the Welfare of the Fugitives among you, Shun
them in every possible manner, as so many HOUNDS
on the track of the most unfortunate of your race.
Keep a Sharp Look Out for
KIDNAPPERS, and have
TOP EYE open.
APRIL 24, 1851.

EQUALITY

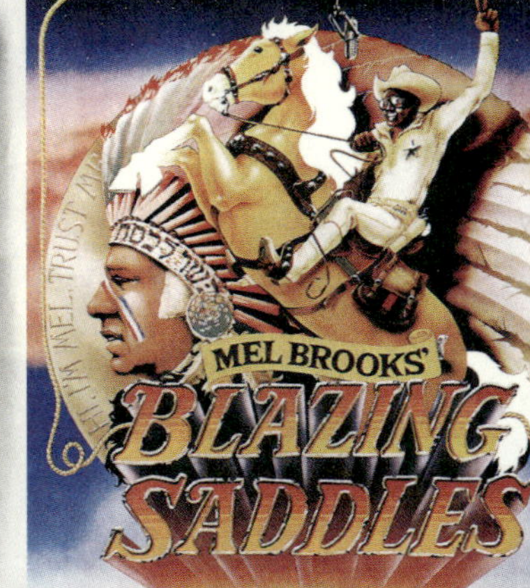
MEL BROOKS'
BLAZING
SADDLES

WATTSTAX
100,000
brothers
and sisters
turning on
to being
black...
telling
it like
it is!

37INK
SIMON & SCHUSTER

Something We Said

Richard Pryor,
a Notorious Word,
and Me

Elizabeth Stordeur Pryor

37INK

SIMON & SCHUSTER

New York   Amsterdam/Antwerp   London
Toronto   Sydney/Melbourne   New Delhi

37INK

SIMON &
SCHUSTER

An Imprint of Simon & Schuster, LLC
1230 Avenue of the Americas
New York, NY 10020

First 37 INK/Simon & Schuster hardcover edition June 2026

37 INK/SIMON & SCHUSTER and colophon are registered trademarks of Simon & Schuster, LLC

Simon & Schuster strongly believes in freedom of expression and stands against censorship in all its forms. For more information, visit BooksBelong.com.

For information about special discounts for bulk purchases, please contact Simon & Schuster Special Sales at 1-866-506-1949 or business@simonandschuster.com.

The Simon & Schuster Speakers Bureau can bring authors to your live event. For more information or to book an event, contact the Simon & Schuster Speakers Bureau at 1-866-248-3049 or visit our website at www.simonspeakers.com.

Interior design by Ruth Lee-Mui

Manufactured in the United States of America

1   3   5   7   9   10   8   6   4   2

Library of Congress Control Number is available.

ISBN 978-1-9821-5450-9
ISBN 978-1-9821-5452-3 (ebook)

Scan here to get book recommendations, exclusive offers, and more delivered to your inbox.

Some names and identifying characteristics have been changed. Some dialogue has been re-created.

For my father

A Note from the Author

I'm moments into writing my memoir, and I'm already stuck. My problem is not writer's block, but how to write a book about a word I don't want to put down on paper. I'm talking about the n-word. The word that symbolizes generations of racist violence and Black protest against it.

This book wasn't even meant to be a memoir. As a history professor, I set out to write a scholarly treatise on the n-word. But the further I got into my research, the more I realized how deeply entangled this word was in my own life, especially in my complicated relationship with my father, Richard Pryor. He was one of the first Black comedians to unapologetically use the n-word onstage and a key player in any conversation about the word in the twentieth century. Somehow in all my academic work, I'd missed that my obsession with the n-word had everything to do with him.

As soon as I made the connection, I knew I couldn't write about the word without writing about us. I pored over old photographs, scrapbooks, and journal entries and had long conversations with family and friends about what it meant to grow up as his daughter. I examined my personal history like a living archive, each encounter with the n-word a pin on a map that connected my life to his.

The result is a hybrid memoir and historical exploration of the n-word that moves between timelines: One story follows my coming of age as the mixed-race daughter of a comedic legend, from the first time I saw him onstage to the day he died. The other story tracks my adult reckoning with the n-word, from my father's funeral to the day I stepped onto a stage of my own. Interspersed throughout are historical interludes that reveal the powerful and unexpected ways the n-word has influenced the past, the present, and us all. Quotations from my dad's standup are at the top of each of these interludes, highlighting the connections I kept finding between the history, his comedy, and our relationship.

As the storylines weave together, the n-word emerges as an intellectual and emotional conduit between my father and me. He used the word to expose the inner workings of racism through laughter. I unearthed historical records to prove how deeply the n-word is embedded in American life. The word became our shared legacy and unlocked the love I had buried for years.

In the end, I decided not to spell out the n-word. When quoting someone who says the actual word, I'll use three asterisks to replace the three middle letters. Otherwise, I'll use the phrase "the n-word." How I reached this compromise is part of my story.

We ah gah-thered here today. On this sorrowful occasion.
To say goodbye to the dearly departed. He was dearly and
he has departed. . . . In other words, the n***er dead.
Richard Pryor,
. . . Is It Something I Said?,
1975

Prologue

December 17, 2005

Sitting in a chapel at Forest Lawn, I heard my dad's voice ring out like a song.

Ain't. This. Some. Shit.

Playful. Joking. Full of life. Which was funny, because this was his funeral.

Even before I slipped into my father's service five minutes late, I was sick to my stomach from dashed hopes and indigestion. For the last week, I'd spent hours sitting shiva at my sister Rain's house, stuffing my face with fried food and cornbread. I'd barely slept, my corkscrew curls were misbehaving—limp and frizzy at the same time—and an untreated sinus infection had me wiping my nose on my shirtsleeve like I did when I was a little girl.

I had hoped the funeral would be my chance to grieve and say a proper goodbye to my father. But from the moment I walked into the Church of the Hills, I couldn't feel him at all. The chapel was cold and sterile and monstrously hollow. Plain white pews, plain white walls, plain pine casket, plain glass windows. If Ikea did funerals, this would be it.

Where were all the Black people? The wailing women? The cries of "Lord" and "amen"? If it weren't for some familiar faces—my six siblings, a few of our mothers, a couple of well-known actors and comedians—I would have sworn I was in the wrong place.

The only sign that this was his funeral (and the only splash of color in the space) was a simple, blown-up photograph of him against a red backdrop from the 1970s. He looked healthy and full of life. A young man with round cheeks, a mustache, and a neat afro, making a silly face. But the picture was a staged promotional shot, as canned as a laugh track, and it had none of the wild kinetic energy of the flawed, fascinating, brilliant, earnest man he was in real life.

The funeral got even stranger when a miscast white woman stepped onto the podium to officiate. "Celebrant Kimberly" was a short, cheerful woman with long, red curls who kicked off the service with a cringy attempt at Black humor. "We ah gah-thered here today," she said, in my dad's booming preacher voice, "to say goodbye to the dearly departed."

She was quoting a bit from his stand-up called "eulogy." A few people shifted in their seats.

"Richard Pryor," she continued, snapping his name like a belt, "was a funny . . ."

My stomach dropped. Was this white woman about to call him a "funny n***er"? Even though the n-word was his comedic trademark and in the title of two of his most celebrated albums, I'd been uncomfortable with the word my whole life. The thought of hearing it at my father's funeral, especially from Celebrant Kimberly, made every muscle in my body tense.

". . . motherfucker," she said with a dramatic wink, punctuating the word with a crisp "er." She didn't say the n-word, but it felt as jarring as if she had.

I scanned the chapel for signs of like-minded outrage that this ceremony was a travesty of a mockery of a sham. Instead, everyone seemed appropriately lost in their grief. My daughter, Lilli, only seven at the time, squeezed my hand and leaned her head on my shoulder. My sister Rain was impenetrable in her sadness. With her perfectly coiffed ballet bun, fitted black dress, and Jackie O. sunglasses, she looked gorgeous and heartbroken. But tears refused to fall from my eyes.

Just as the impulse to stand up and walk out nearly overtook me, I heard my dad's throaty chuckle.

This shit is funny.

I looked around to make sure the voice was in my head, and almost laughed out loud. It felt like he was letting me know this whole event was a joke, the one about a dead Black comedian who accidentally ends up in white heaven (or maybe Black hell) and finds himself headlining a New Age, non-denominational funeral. Ba-dum-bum.

My breathing slowed and my shoulders started to relax. Even the smallest flicker of connection with my father loosened the confusion and shame at the heart of our relationship. My eyes filled with tears. At thirty-eight years old, I'd been searching for that connection my whole life. I had no idea I would eventually find it in the word that defined his career and would eventually define my own.

After the service, I dragged my exhausted husband, Jerry, and our two kids to my mom's, who'd finagled an invitation to the funeral. I was her only child and wanted to be with her to mourn the man she'd lived with in the 1960s and loved her whole life.

And to gossip.

"Quite frankly, Elizabeth," my mom said as soon as she opened the front door, "that funeral had no soul."

Together, we eased our heartache by reaching for the low-hanging fruit.

"Imagine," she said with her hands on her hips. "A white woman calling Richard Pryor a motherfucker at his own funeral." Even my white, Jewish mother knew that was totally out of line.

. . .

I was lying on my mom's bed, hoarding a plate of potato latkes, when she burst into the bedroom and tossed something heavy near my feet.

"Elizabeth," she said breathlessly as she struggled for air with ex-smoker's lungs, "this will explain everything."

She crossed her arms and waited.

At the foot of the bed, I saw a beat-up, brown leather briefcase I recognized because my mom had kept it in the bottom of the closet in every place we'd ever lived.

"Open it," she said.

Wiping my greasy fingers on my sweats, I unzipped the bag to see what treasure it held, but all I found were old brittle papers, receipts, matchbooks, dry-cleaning bills, a book of Canadian postage stamps, a yellow Kodak envelope with photographs of my mother, a Chase Manhattan bankbook, a hardly used 1967 At-a-Glance datebook, and a *MAD* magazine paperback that looked like it had never been read.

I raised an eyebrow.

"It was your father's," my mom said.

That got my attention. Maybe there was something inside that would reveal a few of his secrets. Or at least give me a hint about how he really felt about me. I dug a little deeper.

Turns out, the briefcase was a time capsule of the comings and goings of Richard Pryor from 1965 until April 1967, the month and year I was born. There were two different versions of his headshots, one with my dad's goofy smile and another with him dressed as a conservative-looking young man in a tie and jacket. There was also a Western Union telegram from a fan congratulating my parents on my impending birth; an invoice from The Apollo Theater; business cards with notes scribbled on the back from Budd Friedman's Improvisation Comedy Club on West Forty-fourth Street; a script for *A Time for Laughter: A Look at Negro Humor in America*, a television special produced by Harry Belafonte; memos from his theatrical agent; a love letter from a woman who was not my mother; and two three-subject, wide-ruled, spiral notebooks.

I pulled out the notebooks. One looked brand new and had only a few scribbles on the cover in my dad's telltale curve-and-loop handwriting. The cover of the other one was cracked and softened with use, shiny with a patina like aged, full-grain leather. He'd written all over it with phone numbers, a drawing of a stick figure, and thoughts, perhaps, of what he wanted to be called—Dick, Richie, Richard. There was also a phone number and a name on the top right of the notebook in my mom's lean, right-leaning cursive. But in case I doubted the notebook was my father's, he'd written his full name on the cover twice. More like a fifth grader gearing up for the first day of school than a comedian in his mid-twenties on the brink of stardom, living with my mom in New York City. "Richard Pryor," he wrote on the lines at the bottom. "Richard Pryor is . . ." he wrote again on the top.

I flipped open the well-used notebook to the middle. Each of his letters stood upright in black felt ink, surprisingly neat penmanship for a man who left school in the eighth grade. Page after page, all I saw was a collection of doodles, nonsensical couplets, and a series of set lists, hundreds of them.

One read:

Bowling pin
Weight Lifter
Skin Diver
Heart talking to Brain
Blood cells
Opera Singer's Laugh
Real Movies
War Movies
Sub captain
Can't understand drill master
Sambo

Home Life
People in NYC

Another:

School Play
The Gang
My Family
Super N***er
In God we trust
Breast
Drill Master
Army Life
Skin Diver
Maids and Hotels
Cabs and Subways
Play Boys
Weight Lifter
Blowing your Cool

One joke in particular leapt out at me. Super N***er. Slowly, I traced my finger over the n-word. Was it the first time he ever used the word onstage? In 1966, he was only twenty-five years old, and with a sleight of hand, he made a superhero out of a slur. Did he even suspect that in just a few years he would transform American culture with the word?

I put everything back in the briefcase as messily as I found it and zipped it up. The bag had none of the answers I wanted. It felt less like a memento than a stark reminder of how challenging and unpredictable my relationship with my father had always been: He struggled to show up as a parent, and I never felt funny enough, or creative enough, or Black enough to be his daughter.

"It's really special," I said to my mom, even though I didn't believe it was.

"Really, Liz," she said seriously, "this will mean the world to you one day."

That night, I tucked the briefcase away in a closet just like she always had, but as I lay in bed, the words from my father's notebook kept spinning in my head. Seeing the n-word written out in his handwriting touched me in an unexpected way. He'd been using the word onstage for as long as I'd been alive, and it was the same word I kept coming face to face with in my research as a Ph.D. student in nineteenth-century U.S. history. The Black people I studied were constantly called the n-word to dehumanize and humiliate them, no matter who they were or where they lived. A hundred years later, my dad took that same word, embraced it, tamed it like a lion in the ring, and invoked it to empower the very people it was meant to hurt.

And yet the word still had so much power. Even the possibility that Celebrant Kimberly was going to call my dad the n-word was so outrageous I couldn't stop replaying the moment in my mind.

For hours, I tossed and turned in bed, obsessing over the funeral and trying to make sense of everything. All I had ever wanted was to be close to my father. It took me another fifteen years to realize his notebooks and his beat-up leather briefcase held the key to our connection, and it all revolved around a single, complicated word.

One

Blazing Saddles

2010

"Get ready to get pissed off," I warned forty undergraduates as I launched into a lecture on the 1850 Fugitive Slave Act.

It had been five years since my father's funeral, and I was just hitting my stride as a history professor at Smith College, a liberal arts school in western Massachusetts. The students in my Civil War class leaned in and got quiet as I described how slave catchers and federal marshals hunted free Black people in the North, rounded them up, and forced them back into slavery.

Charlotte, a white student with long, wispy brown hair who sat in the front row, raised her hand. I liked her a lot. She was always ready for class and asked tough questions that generated meaningful conversations. We'd grown friendly since the semester started. About once a week after class, she walked me back to my office and told me private things about her life, about a student group she organized, and why being a college student sometimes felt hard.

"So, basically," Charlotte asked, "the fugitive slave law incentivized judges to find a Black person guilty of escaping slavery?"

"Yup," I said. "Judges got paid five bucks if they found someone not guilty and ten for guilty."

Five other hands shot up.

As the students sorted out painful truths about American history, I wrapped up the lecture with a presentation about anti-Chinese prejudice in California even among Black people.

Charlotte raised her hand so high she practically lifted herself out of her desk chair.

Beaming at her, I pointed and said, "Whatcha thinking?"

"Have you seen *Blazing Saddles*?" she asked.

My jaw dropped. *Blazing Saddles* was a satirical comedy my father wrote with Mel Brooks in the seventies about a Black sheriff who saves the white folks in an old West town.

Why was Charlotte bringing up my dad?

Until that moment, I was convinced my students had no idea who Richard Pryor was or that I was his daughter. I still felt raw and exposed when people asked overly familiar questions—"Did you know him?" "How often did you see him?" "Were you close?"— unwittingly cutting to the heart of my own insecurities about our relationship.

Now that sense of privacy crumbled. Charlotte, I felt certain, was about to put me on the spot by telling the whole class Richard Pryor was my father.

My warmth for her vanished in a snap.

"Yes," I answered curtly. "I have seen *Blazing Saddles*," instinctively claiming my authority as his daughter. The truth is, though, I hadn't. I was too young when the movie came out, and as I got older, not knowing my father as a public figure made me feel closer to him as a private man.

Desperate to change the subject, I made a big gesture, turned my back to the class, and clicked over to my final slide.

But Charlotte was just too eager, too engaged to contain herself.

She raised her hand again, and the words came flying out of her mouth before I even had a chance to call on her.

"'We'll take the ch*nks and the n***ers,'" she blurted, "'but we don't want the Irish.'"

She didn't say the phrase "the n-word." She said the actual word out loud.

Time stopped. The room started to spin.

All at once, multiple thoughts fired through my brain. A white student said the n-word in my classroom. She wasn't calling anyone a name. She was simply trying to connect to my lecture by repeating a funny line from *Blazing Saddles*. She was also quoting a joke that I had no doubt was written by my father. Somehow that made the situation even more disorienting.

I froze, and the energy in the classroom completely shifted.

Usually, my students paid attention. They listened carefully and nodded their heads. But when Charlotte said the n-word, their eyes darted to the floor or the clock, anywhere else in the room, but not to me.

The only person looking at me was Lori, a Black student about ten years older than her peers. Her big brown eyes looked pained. As the seconds ticked by, each of the four other Black students in the class turned to me too. Were they angry? Frustrated? Disappointed? Looking for answers? A surge of responsibility, like panic, rushed through my body in great swells.

I needed to do something, and do it quickly.

"Whoa, whoa, whoa," I said, holding up my hands, willing Charlotte to be quiet.

"No," she said, smiling and trying to reassure me. "It's a joke. From *Blazing Saddles*." Then she repeated it. "'We'll take the ch*nks and the n***ers, but we don't want the Irish!'"

And her Black professor did nothing to stop it.

The clock struck three. The period ended. For the first time since

I started teaching, not a single student waited while I packed up my laptop to ask me a question after class.

In a daze, I walked back to my office, trying to process what happened.

How could a group of six letters so easily throw me off my game?

As a Black professor of African American history, this was exactly the kind of racially charged moment I thought I should know how to handle. But instead of guiding the students and taking charge, I just stood there.

Growing up with my white Jewish mother and going to mostly white schools, I never felt comfortable saying the n-word. It dried up on my tongue like dirt, even though it was a mainstay of my father's comedy.

But in academia, there was an expectation to say the word for the sake of historical accuracy. Known as the "mention exception," teachers and legal scholars made a free speech argument that quoting the word from movies, literature, or history was necessary. Some even consider it disrespectful to Black authors like James Baldwin or Zora Neale Hurston not to quote their words verbatim.

The way Charlotte said the n-word was a textbook example of the mention exception, but her intention didn't matter. As soon as the word left her mouth, it sent a chill through the classroom and exposed something in me I'd been grappling with my entire life.

I sat down on a bench to catch my breath.

The n-word had a real-world impact. No matter how or why or in what context anyone said it, a single mention could open old wounds. Historical wounds like the brutality of slavery, the terror of lynching, the overt oppression of Jim Crow segregation, but also uniquely personal ones.

As I headed home, images populated my brain like the reboot of a computer, including memories of my father I hadn't thought about for decades. The n-word swirled around so many of the most awful, confusing, but also tender moments of my childhood.

It was so deeply entangled in every aspect of my life, and there was so much I didn't understand.

If I wanted to get to the bottom of what happened in my classroom and try to fix it, I had to go back to the beginning. Where did the word even come from? How had I missed the influence it had on my life? And why did it all seem connected to Richard Pryor?

Interlude One

You all know how Black humor started. It started in the slave ships. Cat was on his way over here, rowing. Dude say, "What you laughing about?" He say, "Yesterday, I was a king."

Richard Pryor,
*Bicentennial N***er*,
1976

In 1619, Portuguese mercenaries kidnapped three hundred and fifty people from the coast of Angola, forced them onto the slave ship *San Juan Bautista*, and set sail for the Americas. In the Gulf of Mexico, English pirates captured a few dozen who survived the terrifying journey and put them up for sale in Jamestown, Virginia. The governor of the colony bought the African captives for a few days' supply of food and beer. They were the first Africans sold in British North America, one hundred and fifty years before the colonies became the United States.

Those "20 & odd" men and women were called "n*gars." During the colonial period, the n-word was often spelled with a single "g" instead of two and an "a" instead of an "e."

In Captain John Smith's history of the colonies published in 1624, he wrote, ". . . a dutch man of warre . . . sold us twenty N*gars." Individuals who likely hailed from the royal West African capital of

Kabasa, including kings and queens, were reduced to a Latin word meaning "black" that marked them by the color of their skin.

When the governor who originally bought the men and women died in 1627, he left his heirs "goods debts chattles servants n*gars cattle or any other thynge." From the beginning, the word was used to position Black people as workers, as property, and as things to pass down.

The n-word wasn't yet a slur. But in just a few decades, it would become interchangeable with the word "slave," an idea that branded racial inequality into the heart of American culture.

Two

"This Is Your Daddy"

1974

I met my father for the first time when I was six years old.

My mom rapped on a hotel room door, and I gripped my right thumb with my left hand so I wouldn't be tempted to stick it in my mouth. A handsome man in his thirties answered, wearing nothing but a towel around his waist. Small coils of black hair sprouted from his chest. The hair on his head looked the same, only thicker. I wanted to touch it to see if his curls felt anything like mine. Glancing inside his room, I saw newspapers strewn across a queen-size bed and caught the familiar tang of coffee and cigarettes. Turning my attention back to the man, I was surprised by the twinkle in his deep, brown eyes, as if he and I shared a joke. My heart soared, but I felt bashful too. Looking only at him, I grabbed my mom's hand and hid myself inside her jacket.

She put her arm around me and held me tight. "Elizabeth," my mom said. "This is your daddy."

The man gave me a shy smile, and then pulled my mom and me into the room and closed the door.

"Hey, Lizzy," he said.

I looked straight up because he towered over me. "Hi," I said, stunned that this man was my father.

"Wow," he said to my mom, "she looks just like me." I closed my mouth and tucked in my lips, trying to hide a smile.

"I know," she said, and put her hand on her hip.

He stepped back and admired my mom from head to toe.

"Macky," he said, "you look good."

Hearing him use my mom's nickname gave me a little thrill. Her name was Maxine. Everyone outside of the family called her Max, but she let special people—my nana, my aunts, my uncle—call her Mac. I turned to see if she was happy too. She was.

"Richard," she said, and pecked him on the lips before she turned her head and touched her chin to her shoulder. A slight blush broke out on her cheeks, a shade darker than the pink rouge on her pale skin. She looked like Audrey Hepburn, with her straight, brown hair; rounded, oversized, tortoise-shell frames pushed up on her head; and blue jeans fitted to her thin body. To finish the look, a white-and-red fox fur coat hit right at her shapely hips.

Was she still in love with him? She never said it out loud. But she was always in love with the idea of him loving me.

My parents met in New York City in their early twenties, at a nightclub called Cafe Wha? in Greenwich Village. It was 1965, a time of great social and racial upheaval in the United States, when it was still illegal for a Black person to marry a white one in sixteen southern states. My dad was from Peoria, Illinois, a northern city that was segregated enough to make it feel like the South. My mom, Maxine Silverman, had just moved from Boston to New York City, a hotbed of the burgeoning counterculture movement. A rebel at heart, she didn't care that dating a Black man shocked her working-class Jewish parents. She was his first serious white girlfriend. My dad understood the risks involved and chased after her anyway.

Max so sweet and Max so true . . .
I will love you when the bigots come to take me away.
I'll love you when all is lost, save your love. I love you. I love you.

They were both ambitious and beautiful, gangly and vulnerable. On their first real date, he charmed her by singing "Moody's Mood for Love" as he said goodbye. A few weeks later, they moved in together.

Back then, my father was making a name for himself in the downtown nightclubs and appearing on network variety shows. While he was inspired by traditional comedians like Sid Caesar and Jonathan Winters, his material always explored the absurdity of racism in America.

My mother's Puerto Rican, and my father's Negro, and we lived
in a real big Jewish tenement building in an Italian neighborhood.
Every time I'd go outside, the kids'd say, "Get him! He's all of 'em!"

Granted, his mother wasn't Puerto Rican and he didn't grow up in a tenement, but he understood the nuance of American racism and called attention to it with humor. He even made fun of Black people. "I'm Negro," he wrote privately. "I'm probably one of the few people left that will admit it." At the time, he still called himself "Negro," while young activists like Stokely Carmichael and Huey P. Newton preferred what was then the more provocative term, "Black."

By 1967, my parents had moved to Los Angeles so my father could be closer to Hollywood, and he found himself caught between his ambition to be a star like Bill Cosby and his growing affinity for the burgeoning Black Power movement. He gravitated toward raunchier and more political Black comics like Dick Gregory and Redd Foxx, who confronted racism head-on in their acts. As the sixties came to a close, his ideas about what it meant to be a Black entertainer began to shift. He stopped straightening his hair and wearing conservative suits and started using the n-word onstage.

At the time, saying the word, especially in front of white audiences, was unheard of. Almost twenty years before hip-hop artists made the n-word a staple of their music, my father invented a Black superhero called "Super N***er."

As his onstage persona changed, so did his relationship with my mother. Their once playful dynamic became volatile and even physically violent. She'd yell and accuse him of cheating (which he was), and he'd drift away. On the night I was born in 1967, things had gotten so bad between them that he was hundreds of miles away, partying in Tijuana, and ended up in a Mexican jail on a marijuana charge. She went into labor alone in Los Angeles and drove herself to the hospital. A few weeks later, as hippies flocked to cities like San Francisco and New York to celebrate the Summer of Love, my parents broke up. My mom believed she had no choice but to leave her swanky life in Beverly Hills and move back to Boston to live with her parents.

Newly single and more driven than ever, my father fully immersed himself in radical Black politics. In the early seventies, he headed north to Berkeley, California, the heart of the Black Power movement. He made Marvin Gaye's political anthem "What's Going On" his personal soundtrack and hung out with members of the Black Panther Party. As he became more attuned to Black culture, his material became more authentic, and his career really started to take off.

On February 1, 1974, almost seven years after my parents broke up, my dad flew my mom and me from Boston to Newark, New Jersey, to watch him perform. Before the trip, I only knew him as a mythical creature who materialized once in a while on television, like a Black Loch Ness monster. Whenever he appeared on popular shows like "The Partridge Family," "The Merv Griffin Show," or "Soul Train," my mom would shout across the house in her thick Boston accent, "Elizabeeeeeth! Your father!" That was my cue to sprint across the living room as fast as I could to catch him before he vanished from the screen. The fast-talking characters he played, the funky clothes he wore, and the hip way he talked drew me in like nothing I'd ever seen on TV before. He made me feel connected to something and someone outside my tiny living room.

At school, I bragged at show-and-tell that my father was a Hollywood star because he was in a movie with Diana Ross called *Lady Sings the Blues*. The truth was a lot less glamorous. I had a photograph of him holding me over his shoulder when I was two weeks old, but didn't remember seeing him in the flesh until that day in his Newark hotel room.

From the moment I saw him, I struggled to believe he was real until he reached out and led me deeper into the cramped room. He stretched out his arms to take me in.

"Give me some sugar, baby," he said. For a moment, he seemed unsure.

I had never heard anyone use the phrase, "give me some sugar," but I understood exactly what he meant. As I reached up to kiss him, he met me halfway, touching my mouth with his moist lower lip. Part of me wanted to wipe away the wetness with the back of my hand, but the thought of hurting his feelings was out of the question. Besides, a sloppy kiss was worth it if I got to spend time with him.

A playful smile broke out on his face, his confidence back. "Booooooston Blackie," he said, stretching out the nickname like a Baptist preacher. It felt like he was inviting me into a private world. "Take off your coat," he said with a wink. "Stay awhile."

My mom stepped in and yanked gently on the pompom of my pink knitted cap, pulling it from my head. My dad hugged me again and invited me into the bathroom to watch him shave. Standing at the doorway, I stared at him in the mirror because I'd never seen a man shave before. Was the warm feeling in my chest what everyone felt when they got to spend time with their father?

Later that night, my mom shushed me as we stood together

backstage. I squirmed and wriggled in the wings while we watched him perform. His show was bursting with energy, titillating and naughty. Dressed in a windowpane-plaid suit and shiny brown shoes, he transformed from my young, sparkly father into an old wino who stumbled upon a vampire.

Say, n***er. You with the cape!
What your name, boy? Dracula? What kind a name is that for a n***er?

"N***er," he said, over and over like a magical incantation. It was the first time I'd ever heard the word. The audience roared. I didn't know exactly what the word meant, but every time he said it, a jolt of electricity shot through me. The word seemed to shock and mesmerize everyone in the theater. Even at six, and without the words to express it, I knew he was doing something daring and new.

When the wino finished telling off Dracula, he turned his back to the audience and pretended to unzip his pants and pee. I wanted to peek around the velvet curtains and tell everyone this guy belonged to me. Dizzy from the lights and the stage, I had a hard time keeping my Buster Browns firmly planted on the floor.

At the time, I didn't know how my mother worked behind the scenes to make that trip happen. Years later, in the bottom drawer of her hope chest, I found a copy of a letter she wrote to my dad a few months before we flew to Newark. The letter, filled with anguish, pleaded with him to do right by his daughter. My mom confessed how difficult it was for her to understand how he'd ignored me for the first six years of my life. "How is it possible for me to love a child so much," she wrote, "while her father feels nothing?" Appealing to his evolving sense of his own Blackness, she challenged him: If you really want to make a difference for the race, show up for your Black kid.

She was hyper-aware of his intellectual and creative shifts and followed his career like a spider eyeing a fly. On her bookshelf, she prominently displayed his first studio album, *Richard Pryor*, from 1968. I stared at that album for hours. My dad was on the cover staring back at me, wearing nothing but a loincloth and a huge ring in his nose, holding a bow and arrow. The album was bordered in yellow with a leafy design like my cousin's *National Geographic* magazines. As the years went on, my mom saved every mention of my father in envelopes and boxes, and tucked them away so I could have them when I was old enough to make sense of his career.

One night in early 1973, she went to see *Wattstax*, a documentary film about a Black music festival honoring the anniversary of the 1965 Watts uprisings in Los Angeles. Jesse Jackson was the MC, Isaac Hayes performed, and more than a hundred thousand mostly Black concertgoers filled the arena in funky seventies fashion. My father's comedy was interspersed throughout the documentary. He used the n-word in almost every single joke, and called out cops for abusing their power.

Every time you pick up a paper, n***er accidentally shot in the ass.
How do you accidentally shoot a n***er six times in the chest?

It was his coming-out party as the voice of a Black generation.

In her letter to my father, my mom reminded him there was a little girl in Boston who needed him as much as the movement did. "I saw *Wattstax*," she wrote, "and if you are going to do things for your Black brothers by way of identity, well . . . charity begins at home."

Soon after she mailed the letter, he sent for us to come to Newark, and we got to spend the night together at the Holiday Inn.

The morning after his show, we said our goodbyes in front of the Eastern Airlines ticketing counter at Newark Airport. I stared at him, hoping to memorize everything about him: the big mole on his chin, the pockmarks on his face, his bushy mustache, his felt fedora, and his long leather coat. My mom snapped a few dozen black and white photographs during our overnight stay, clicking away like the paparazzi with her prized 35 mm Canon. Later, she labeled the back of each blurry print—"Elizabeth & daddy 1974 Holiday Inn Newark," "Richard w/ Kool & The Gang & Gladys Knight Feb 1974," "Dressing room," and "Onstage." For years, I looked at those pictures every night before bed.

As we headed to the gate, my dad walked up to my mother to say a final goodbye.

"Mac," he said, kissing the top of her head, "you did good."

"I know," she said, letting slip a rare toothy smile. Then she paused, weighing whether or not to say anything more. "She's got so much love in her heart for you. Don't fuck it up."

"I won't," he said.

"I mean it," she said.

"I know." And he kissed her head again.

Then my mom took two more photographs of me and my dad, "Newark airport Feb 1974" and "The Last Goodbye Feb 1974 Newark Airport." In one, he gives me a sideways hug and leans on my head, goofily. In the other, he is in the background with his back to the camera, and I am facing my mom. My eyes are puffy with tears. I couldn't stop crying. I'd fallen madly in love and was sure I would never see him again.

Three

"Don't Let Nobody
Ever Call You That"

1974

"Richard, she can't stop looking at you," my mom said, with a big silly grin.

After only three months, my father was back in my life. And it was all because of the n-word.

"Can't stop looking at her either," he said.

My face heated up with delight. I pressed my cold fingertips against my hot cheeks.

Leaning back against the red leather booth, he seemed at ease in my favorite Boston restaurant. He opened a fortune cookie with one hand, his long fingers prying it apart. I savored his smell, a blend of sweet, citrusy cologne and the richness of tobacco smoke, and studied him like he was one of the seven wonders of the world, especially the crinkles under his eyes when he smiled.

The restaurant was bustling, but I saw only him, a girl in a fairy-tale blinded by her knight.

My mom broke the spell.

"Tell your father what happened at school."

Startled, I looked helplessly at my mother, her billowing cigarette smoke stinging my eyes. Failing to notice my distress, she demanded a full confession.

It all started on my seventh birthday when my mom told me to rush home after school for a surprise. Skipping all the way, I tried to guess what kind of present she'd gotten me. I knew it wasn't a usual treat—my nana's apple squares or pizza from Papa Gino's—because nothing like that made my mom so bouncy. As I turned the corner onto my block, the possibilities kept my mind so busy that I almost missed the Cadillac limousine parked against the flow of traffic in front of our house. The long white car was a stark contrast to the boxy, brown and blue Oldsmobile and Chevrolet sedans that lined Houston Avenue, a tidy working-class street just south of Boston.

Before I could inspect the car or its driver, my mother opened the storm door, flapping her hand to urge me along. "Hurry!" she said. "Come on!"

As I stepped inside, I saw him, a round-faced man peering over my mom's shoulder who looked a lot like my father, but I wasn't entirely sure. He had the same mustache, but a fuller afro. Dressed up in a white, three-piece suit with a brown silk handkerchief in his breast pocket, he looked too polished and too cool for our simple, shag-carpeted house. In the time since we'd first met, he'd recorded his third comedy album and had a new swagger.

"Look who's here!" my mom squealed. I was too shy to embrace him, too embarrassed to be wrong about recognizing my own father. Closing the distance between us, I walked to him, fawn-like on unsure legs. Something in his eyes reminded me of mine, but not until he crouched down and tapped my nose with his too-wet bottom lip was I certain it was him.

"Boston Blackie," he whispered, sounding just as shy as I felt.

He held out a gift in his hands, an offering. First, he gave me a huge stuffed dog, then a real gumball machine stuffed with jelly beans that worked with nickels, and finally, my first-ever doll with dark-brown skin. I'd never seen anything like it before.

Popping a jelly bean in my mouth, I noticed how extensively my mom and nana had prepared for his visit. The house smelled good, filled with the scent of all my nana's specialties, what my mom called Jewish food—sweet and savory stuffed cabbage, raspberry jam and lemon rind from Nana's famous jelly roll, mandel bread with red and green maraschino cherries, and the burnt smell of an almost-empty coffeepot still on the machine.

It didn't take long after opening gifts for my mom to put me on display like a contestant from the Miss America pageant.

"Elizabeth, read something for your father."

"Elizabeth, do your Mae West impression."

"Elizabeth, sing him that Stevie Wonder song." And I did.

"Can you teach me the words?" he asked.

"A boy is born in hard time Mississippi," I recited all the lyrics as slowly as I could. He repeated them back to me word for word.

"That's a good song," he said, and he meant it. He used it on his fourth album, 1975's . . . *Is It Something I Said?* Reading from what he called the "Book of Wonder," he preached the lyrics as if they were the holy gospel.

The next night we went out to dinner at my favorite restaurant. My parents chatted awkwardly about the weather and the next stop on his tour, and laughed when they weren't saying anything at all. Suddenly, my father seemed very interested to find out what happened at school. I'd tried to resist the pull of my thumb all night, but my resolve instantly evaporated. I snuck my thumb between my lips, hooked my pointer finger over my nose, and held the rest of my fingers tightly over my mouth like a shield.

My dad tilted his head and looked at me for a minute. Then,

angling his long, elegant fingers under the tips of my smaller ones, he moved my hand away from my face, tapping the palm of my hand to coax my thumb from my mouth.

"What happened?" he asked. I hoped to avoid the question, but I could not resist him.

"Two boys called me n***er at school."

I was dangling upside down on the monkey bars when Louis and Robert came up to me. Louis was Black; Robert was white. They'd teased me all of first grade. As the slight chill of spring smacked my face, I reminded myself that I hated Louis because he ate spaghetti with his mouth open, and I hated Robert because he was a follower. Whipping my head back and forth, I made myself dizzy wishing the boys away. But they did not go away.

"You're a n***er," Louis said. Just like that.

From the first day of kindergarten, Louis wanted to be my friend. He seemed to understand we had something in common. Maybe he noticed how I struggled with the kids at our mostly white school. They said I was adopted, that it was impossible for my white mom to be my real mother. I cried and told them it wasn't true. I was afraid that if I became friends with Louis, I'd no longer be able to ignore the gnawing feeling that my light-brown skin meant I was different from my mom, the rest of my family, and most of the other kids at school.

"Did you hear me?" Louis said. "You're a n***er."

He let me know no matter what my mother looked like, he and I were the same.

Tears started falling before I remembered to hold them back. How could the word be so magical when my dad used it onstage, and hurt so much when Louis said it at school?

The boys laughed as I tried to hide my tears and confusion.

I ran to my teachers to tell them what happened. The two young white women with long, straight hair hugged me and cooed and wiped my eyes. I waited for them to say something comforting like they always did when kids teased me—"You're not a baby," "You're not stupid," "You're not ugly,"—but the assurance, "You're not a n***er" never came.

Later, when I told my mom what happened, she didn't tell me I wasn't that word either. She was confident about all kinds of subjects—cross-stitching, taxi-licensing, chic outfits, Hollywood gossip, and who in the family made the best chopped liver. But when she sat me down on her lap and struggled for words, it was clear the situation was too complicated even for her. Before that day, kids called me a baby because I was a thumb-sucker and cried a lot. I hated it, but I figured it would stop when I grew up.

The n-word felt like it could last a lifetime.

When I finished telling my story, I struggled to look at my father, convinced he wouldn't see me the same way anymore. Slowly, I lifted up my head and couldn't believe he was looking back at me with as much love and affection as he had the whole night.

"Don't let nobody ever call you that," he said.

His voice was quiet, like a secret.

Since it first happened, I'd been waiting for someone to tell me what Louis said wasn't okay. My heart was wide open. With a single sentence, my father earned all the trust I had to give in the world.

He grabbed my hands, and told me something else.

"You are Black."

I am Black. I am Black. I am Black.

The meaning of his words was just out of reach, like when I had a mole removed and the doctor used ether to put me to sleep and for days afterward my thoughts were like fireflies I could not catch or hold on to. My father was telling me something vital, I knew, if only I could keep the essence of what it was from flitting away.

My mom sat back and smoked her cigarette, watching us like we were acting out a scene in a riveting TV show.

Did she know I was Black?

I thought I was just a Jewish girl, like my mom and my nana and my cousins, who loved lighting candles for Hanukkah and eating brisket at the Passover seder. As the news that I was Black sunk in, my mind buzzed. My dad and I were both Black, he said, a fact that tied us to each other and to other Black people too. I thought back to a day not too long before when a carload of brown-skinned teenagers called out to me as I walked to school. "Hey, Little Brother!" they shouted as they drove by, mistaking me for a boy, but not mistaking my Blackness.

Tenderly, my dad continued to talk to me without ever repeating what the boys said. "That word," he said. "It's a fighting word. Whenever anyone says it, you better knock them right out."

The warm feelings of just a moment before oozed out and left me ice cold.

The irony was, while my father was telling me I shouldn't let anybody call me that, he was also making the same word his creative calling card. Just before he visited me in Boston, he recorded his 1974 album *That N***er's Crazy*, a groundbreaking celebration of the very specific Black experience he knew from his childhood. It would go on to be the biggest-grossing comedy album of the year and cement his cultural influence forever.

His characters lived through all kinds of oppression—slavery, lynching, poverty, police violence, drug addiction—but came out the other side wiser and stronger for the trauma. Black people, my dad said, were resilient and powerful.

N***ers never get burnt up in buildings. They know how to get out of a motherfucking situation.

In the restaurant, my dad looked at me with the passionate conviction of a man who was confident in his Blackness and wanted nothing more than to pass it on. Turns out, my mom wanted that too.

When the boys at school called me the n-word, she knew she was out of her league and also knew my dad was coming to Boston to promote *That N***er's Crazy.* So she reached out, convinced that only a Black father could help a little Jewish girl from Boston understand the word. Gently, he told me I was Black, but not an n-word. He also said not to let anyone ever call me that. I had no idea how to stop that from happening, but I was willing to try because more than anything, I wanted him to be proud I was his daughter.

Four

A Subject Too Taboo

2010

When I finally made it home after Charlotte said the n-word in my classroom, I rushed right by my husband, Jerry, making dinner in the kitchen, and flipped open my laptop.

"Liz, what's wrong?" he asked as he squirted ketchup and placed chicken tenders on two plastic plates for our kids.

"A white student said the n-word in class," I said, eyes glued to the computer, searching for guidance on how to talk to students about the word. I couldn't find any.

"What? Why?" he asked.

"She was quoting a line from *Blazing Saddles*."

"Didn't your dad write that?"

"Yes." He was the only Black writer on the film.

"So what happened?" Jerry asked.

"I was talking about racism in nineteenth-century California, and she shouted out: 'We'll take the ch-words and the n-words, but we don't want the Irish.'"

"That's funny!"

"It wasn't! She said the actual word!"

According to Mel Brooks, he didn't want to use the n-word in the movie, but my father insisted.

"Your dad used the slurs on purpose. He was making fun of how ridiculous racism is. Don't you remember the scene?"

I didn't have the heart to tell him I hadn't seen the movie.

"It was a disaster," I said, laying my head on the table.

Jerry sat down next to me and put his arm around my shoulder.

"I really fucked up. I literally tried to stop the words from coming out of her mouth. I let all of the Black students down too. I didn't acknowledge how any of them must have felt when they heard the word. They probably think I don't have their backs."

What I didn't explain to Jerry was the depth of my misery. As the only Black professor in the history department, I was already self-conscious about being too soft to deal with the hard facts: there were ugly words in U.S. history that could cause enormous pain and sometimes people might repeat them. As a biracial person, I was also embarrassed by how I let the n-word derail me.

When my dad used the word onstage or onscreen, he tapped into something deep from his own experience. He made mixed-race audiences confront the racism of the n-word while they were laughing, even if they were uncomfortable doing it. If he'd been in my classroom, he might have seen the humor in what Charlotte said and chided her for saying it, all in one breath. Instead, I fumbled the ball. I owed my class an apology.

The night before our next class meeting, I drafted an email.

Dear Charlotte:

Just so you know, tomorrow I'm going to talk a little bit about what happened in class on Monday. I won't single you out or mention you by name, but I do need to address it.

Warmly, ESP

She responded immediately and apologized. She was open and receptive. But the next day in class, she looked broken and ashamed. Her usual seat in the front row was empty. Instead, she slumped at a desk in the third row. At the time, I didn't know that some of the Black students had gently pulled Charlotte aside after class. They told her hearing the word upset them. According to the students, Charlotte had listened and been very apologetic.

I didn't want her to feel any worse, but I needed to own up to my personal missteps as a teacher. This wasn't about her. It was about the word and about me.

"Hey, everyone," I said.

The room was perfectly quiet, and I heard my voice quiver.

"Something happened here on Monday. The n-word was said. I shouldn't have let that happen. I'm really sorry."

I took a deep breath.

"So, here's the deal. In the future, you will read the word in books and primary sources, and you will hear it in films. But I will never, ever say the word out loud in class.

"And, hey," I said, with more confidence than I felt, "I don't want any of you to say it either."

I looked around, waiting for someone to challenge me. In theory, by asking them not to say the word, I was violating their free speech. But not one person pushed back.

Banning the students from saying the n-word seemed like the best way to prevent another classroom incident. But censoring it just created more tension. For the rest of the semester, the room was no longer filled with comradery and curiosity. Despite my best efforts, I hadn't solved anything. Charlotte never walked me back to my office again.

Had I made the n-word into a subject too taboo to discuss openly? Every great teacher I'd ever had encouraged their students to hash out hard topics. I shut the conversation down.

It was time for me to be brave and face the n-word head-on. If I wanted to do that, I had to understand more about it, like how the word got all the way from Jamestown to my classroom.

Interlude Two

They stole the cream of the crop from Africa . . . and God put us all together and called us one tribe. N***er.

Richard Pryor,
Wattstax, 1973

In the early 1830s, a white actor in New York City named Thomas Dartmouth Rice rubbed burnt cork on his face, danced a funny jig onstage, and pretended to be Black. It was the height of blackface minstrelsy, and he called the character Jim Crow.

New York had abolished slavery a few years earlier, on July 4, 1827. To most white Northerners, the newly free men and women posed a threat to democracy and public safety. As Black people tried to exercise their equal rights—to go to school, buy property, use public transportation—white people from all walks of life fought to deny them. During an Emancipation Day celebration, angry white New Yorkers put up flyers around the city, issuing a warning in blackface mockery: "Ven de n***er all free, do as he please."

White people insisted that Black freedom would lead to chaos and must be contained.

Jim Crow quickly became the emblem of white fear and supremacy. He was a caricature of a free Black man who wore raggedy clothes; spoke in dialect; chased after women, especially white women; got into fights; refused to work; got drunk; gambled; swore; and most dangerously, was free to go anywhere he pleased. The character became an international sensation and created an enduring stereotype that Black people were ignorant, dishonest, and would never be equal to white Americans.

The Jim Crow performance also used the n-word in a new and damning way: "Do what you will / The n***er will be a n***er still." The meaning was clear. There was nothing Black people could do to rise up and free themselves from their slave roots. While millions of enslaved men, women, and children had long been called the n-word, Jim Crow made sure the word applied to every Black person, no matter their status or success.

The word became a degrading slur that shackled all Black people together into a single, inescapable tribe.

Five

Mulatto, Oreo, Redbone, Sister

1974

"Elizabeth," my mom said before I boarded the DC10 to Los Angeles. "Follow Daddy's rules. Don't cry too much. And don't forget to clean up after yourself." She twirled one of my braids around her finger. "Promise?"

"Promise," I said, and stuck my thumb in my mouth. It had been two months since I'd seen my father, and I couldn't wait to be with him again.

My mother hugged me goodbye and handed me off to a pretty flight attendant who took my hand and walked me through the gate.

"Elizabeth," my mom called out. "Don't forget to do your Bette Midler for Daddy!"

I could tell she was nervous, but I had one week to make my father love me, and I planned to pull out all the stops to do it, including singing "Delta Dawn."

When the pilot came over the loudspeaker and told us to prepare for landing, I fidgeted with the silver wings pinned to my chest and pressed my nose against the cold oval window. Ever since my father left Boston, I'd fantasized about visiting him in Los Angeles. I imagined stepping off the plane, leaping into his arms, and burying my head in the crook of his neck like the women in the made-for-TV movies I watched with my mom.

That's not what happened.

Instead, when he met me at the gate, my father looked exhausted. And he wasn't alone. On his arm was Patricia, a white woman in stylish clothes and big dark sunglasses who spoke with an accent like a 1940s movie star.

"Hello, Miss Elizabeth," Patricia said. "I've heard a lot about you."

I looked over at my dad, puzzled. I hadn't heard anything about her.

"Give me some sugar," was all he said, his voice groggy and his smile weary.

He held my hand as I skipped through the terminal, and when we climbed into a huge black limousine. I felt like a princess sitting between my dad and Patricia, even though he was quiet. Leaning his head against the window, he closed his eyes.

As we wound our way closer to the creviced hills of West Hollywood, stacked with more houses than I'd ever seen before, we reached a steep road called Sunset Plaza Drive, and then an even steeper one called Belfast.

We stopped in front of a house that looked sturdy from the front, but as I walked through it, the whole house seemed to be floating on air.

"It's on stilts," Patricia said.

I turned around to ask my dad, "Like clowns?" But he and Patricia were gone. A door closed before I could see what was behind it.

Alone in a huge living room, surrounded by two black leather couches and a grand piano, I sat down on the floor next to a stack of albums leaning against the wall. Each record had my dad's face on the cover, and Richard Pryor: *"That N***er's Crazy"* written across the top. The album had just topped the Billboard R&B charts at #1. I crouched down to get a better look at the cover. He was making a funny face and pointing at himself like he was the n-word.

Why was he calling himself that word? He told me to never let anybody call me that.

I wanted to ask him all about it, but I didn't know where he was. Just then, Patricia appeared out of nowhere and interrupted my thoughts. Her expression was sour.

"That's our bedroom," she said, pointing to the same door they had just closed behind them. "Knock before you come in. Yours is off the kitchen."

She disappeared down a short hallway, and I had to run to keep up. On the way, we passed another bedroom where two teenagers sat on a bed, a round-faced boy who looked about twelve and a beautiful older teenage girl. They were both Black but had much darker skin than mine. Patricia was moving so quickly I only saw them for a second.

When we reached my bedroom, I asked, "Who was that?"

Patricia slammed the closet door and said, "Renee and Richard Jr.! Your sister and brother!"

I have a sister and brother? My brain went into overdrive. How were two complete strangers related to me? I had begged my mom for siblings, but she never mentioned Renee or Richard.

"Unpack your bags. Then you can come out," Patricia said.

I put everything away as fast as I could, but by the time I got to my siblings' room, Patricia was making the bed. They were gone.

"Where'd they go?" I asked.

"They left," she said, like it was obvious. "They went home. To their mothers."

Disappointment landed in my stomach with a thud. I missed out on my new family before I even got a chance to meet them.

"Are they coming back?"

"No," she said, her face softening when she saw how sad I was. "But don't worry. You'll meet Rain this week."

"Who?"

"Jesus! Didn't anyone tell you anything? Rain is your little sister. She lives with her mother, Shelley, in Beverly Hills."

It was too much information to process on my own. I wanted to ask my father about my brother and sisters. I wanted to ask why Patricia was so grouchy. I wanted to ask about the n-word on the cover of his album. But I didn't see him for the rest of the afternoon or the day after. He didn't come out of his room, not for dinner or to kiss me goodnight or to help me understand what was going on and where I fit into his life.

It was years before I learned he'd had a heart attack on the ride back from the airport.

Three days after I got to L.A., my father finally came out of his room. Patricia had arranged for a swim coach to give me private lessons in the small kidney-shaped swimming pool in the backyard. My dad never got in the pool while I swam, but every day he sat on his perch—a set of three concrete steps between the upper patio and the pool—and watched me splash, kick, and do my strokes.

Whenever I tried out a new skill, I turned to see if he was watching. He always was. Day one, I learned how to doggy paddle.

"Did you see?" I called from the water, showing off and splashing my way to the side of the pool.

"Yes! Yessssssss! I see. I see."

Climbing up the steel ladder, my pigtails flopping in my face, I padded to the side of the pool and gripped my toes on the edge.

"Guess what?" I said.

"Chicken butt," he responded in his throaty chuckle. I wasn't quite sure why the joke was funny, but it made me giggle anyway.

Putting my hand on my hip, I said, "I can dive!"

I looked for confirmation from my pretty young teacher, who watched our conversation as she treaded water. "She's a natural," she said.

"A fish," he agreed, smiling at her with lingering eyes.

Patricia told me years later that my dad was having sex with my swim teacher. Turns out he had a lifelong inability to stay faithful to any woman, no matter how much he loved her. The richer and more famous he got, the more women flocked to him, and the more difficult it was for him to resist his demons of all kinds.

All I knew was he always watched me in the pool. Having him around was worth staying in the water until my toes were pruned and my eyes, soaked in chlorine, were as red as blood. Whenever I looked up, he was there.

Patricia captured all the joy of that moment in a black and white photograph, him fully dressed and me in a swimsuit, sitting together on the concrete steps by the pool. Just as she snapped the picture, he kissed me on the nose with his moist lower lip. I scrunched up my face to receive it. Patricia blew up the photo to the size of a poster, and my father kept it framed and on display in every home he ever had.

When I wasn't with my dad, I spent most of my time with Patricia. We darted around West Hollywood in her dark-green Mercedes sedan, food shopping daily at Chalet Gourmet, a market so fancy the butcher capped the lamb chops with white paper crowns. She took me to buy clothes at Saks Fifth Avenue, and I stood by as she bought top-shelf liquor at Gil Turner's Fine Wines and Spirits.

One day, we had just finished sifting through jazz albums at Tower Records on the Sunset Strip when she ran into someone she knew on our way to the car.

"Oh, look," she said. "There's Rain and Shelley."

My pulse sped up. I saw a little girl, hanging on a tall, blonde woman's elbow. Using her mother's arm like a jungle gym, Rain lifted her feet off the ground and swung.

As I got closer, I saw her skin was even lighter than mine and she had a few freckles on her nose. Her hair was thicker and frizzier than mine too, and could barely be contained by an elastic band. She landed on her feet and perked up.

"Hey, there," Shelley said with a big smile on her face.

Tall with pale skin and honey-colored hair all the way down her back, she looked so unlike my tiny, brown-haired mother, whose traditional good looks made her seem less ferocious than she was. Shelley was an obvious force, who carried her body fluidly, grandly, like a prima ballerina or Cher. Even though she was a white Jewish woman like my mom, she sounded like a Black beat poet from Oakland, her voice cool and nasal, like someone who raised her fist in protest to the man. "All power," she might say, "to the people." As it turned out, she was also the woman my dad left my mom for. Apparently, his racial awakening didn't apply to his taste in women.

"Hey, Mama," she said to Patricia. Then she put her hands on Rain's shoulders and pushed her gently toward me. "Baby girl," she said, "this is your big sister. Elizabeth."

Patricia crouched down between us, held each of our hands, and said to me, "Elizabeth, this is your baby sister Rain."

Rain and I stood about a foot apart, studying each other. She examined me with deep brown eyes so much like my own. In an instant, I knew that I loved her.

Until I met Rain, I thought I was the only person like me—a little bit Black, a little bit Jewish, a light-brown–skinned kid with a very white mom. Later, I would hear people use all kinds of terms to describe girls like us: *mulatto, Oreo, redbone, high yellow, best of both worlds, half and half.* But in that moment, my heart shouted, "sister."

Rain's barely brown cheeks started to turn pink, and she opened her mouth to speak. "Pussy!" she yelled at the top of her lungs. "Motherfucker!" she screamed, dancing around her mother. "Bitch!" she said right to my face. "Asshole! Banana Face! Cocksucker!"

As Rain wiggled and shouted, my fingers tightly grasped Patricia's hand while she and Shelley chatted as if it were perfectly normal for a little girl to raise hell in a parking lot.

Rain was hardly the first person I'd ever heard swear, but she was the first to do it with such gusto. My mom used profanity as punctuation and let loose when she was really mad, but she always did it with a little smirk on her face, like she was letting me know she was doing something wrong.

The way Rain cussed was unapologetic. She didn't say the n-word, but she swore with the same confidence my dad did onstage. Was that something they shared? Did a real Pryor speak their mind and demand to be heard? Maybe Rain didn't like Patricia or maybe she needed a nap. Either way I could tell she was saying something important: Move over sister, there's a line. If you want to get close to Daddy, you better learn his language.

On my last day in California, I was desperate to squeeze in all the time I could with my father. I didn't know when I'd see him again and wanted to make sure I left a lasting impression. The pool was the place to do it. I asked Patricia if I could go swimming, but she said no because she was too busy to supervise.

I went to my dad's bedroom to find him. He was sitting on the edge of his bed smoking a cigarette.

"Daddy?" I asked.

"Daughter?" he asked back, his voice teasing.

"Can I go swimming?"

"Yes, daughter," he said with playful formality.

Excited, I ran through the house, into my room, put on my purple seersucker bathing suit, and skipped outside through a small opening in the sliding glass door. Smacking my bare feet against the scorching-hot concrete, I scraped my soft toes on the rough ground, leaving little bloody toe prints behind me. I saw my dad sitting in his usual spot, so I plopped down next to him and showed him my injured feet.

He grabbed one of my toes. "This little piggy did something," he said, and grabbed another, "and that little piggy did something else." He pretended to kiss each of them one by one.

"Hey," I screeched.

"Hay is for horses," he said, and kept on tickling me.

I couldn't stop giggling. In that single moment, I felt more safe, more loved, more cherished, than I had the whole time I'd been in Los Angeles. It was exactly what I'd been waiting for. All the questions I'd wanted to ask were about to pour out of me.

That's when Patricia found us.

"You're manipulative!" she yelled, her face so angry and red I thought it might explode. She tapped her black clogs against the patio.

I turned to my dad with questioning eyes. Is she talking to me?

"God damn it, Richard! Can't you tell when you're being manipulated?"

Suddenly, the look on his face changed.

He spoke in his quiet voice and asked, "Did Patricia say no about you swimming before you asked me?"

"Yes," I said, shyly, not sure what I'd done wrong.

"See!" Patricia snapped.

A look of resignation I came to recognize all too well appeared on my father's face. It said, "I'm sorry, my dear. I wish I could do something to help, but I have no control over the women in my life. And," as he often said when things weren't fair, "dems the breaks."

Deferring to the women he loved was a habit he picked up as a little boy. He was raised by his grandmother in a Peoria brothel. Mama, as he called her, was the madam who ran the business and everyone in it. He feared and revered her in equal measure. "Her face was so soft and beautiful, you could cry from the tenderness of its glow," he once explained, but most of the time she was ruthless, like "a man who killed apes bare-handed for a living." He never questioned Mama's authority, or that of any of the women in his life. At least not until he cheated or broke their heart.

The real measure of my father's love was how completely he ceded his power. That day at the pool, he gave it all to Patricia.

She grabbed me by the wrist so tightly it burned. Stumbling, I tried to keep up as she dragged me through the backyard, through the sliding glass door, down the hallway, and to my bedroom off the kitchen. She used my arm like a lever to push me onto the bed. My eyes filled with tears.

"Don't come out of this room until I say so!" she yelled, and slammed the door.

Years later, Patricia told me she'd reacted out of terror. My father did not know how to swim and had no business watching a child at the pool. But at the time, as I rubbed my tender wrists, I blamed her for coming between us and stopping the conversation I'd dreamt about having since I had arrived in L.A. I felt even more disappointed that my dad hadn't stood up for me. The first time we really talked, he told me being Black meant you had to be brave. But it didn't seem like he was following his own advice. I crawled under the covers, yanked my bathing suit out of my crack, and stuck my thumb in my mouth.

After crying into my pillow for an hour, I calmed down and wondered if this was how people showed love in a two-parent home. In Boston, I always felt jealous when my friends said they had the world's strictest mom. My mom and nana had no rules—no bedtime, no chores, no need for permission to be excused from the dinner table. Maybe getting punished was a sign of how much a parent really loved their child.

But lunchtime came and went, and being sent to my room was not playing out as I'd hoped. My father did not slip into my room while I pouted. The bed didn't creak under his weight as he put his hand on my back and gently asked if I'd learned my lesson. I waited and waited for him to come and save me. He never did.

As I watched the sky grow dusky outside my bedroom window, the digital clock on the nightstand read 8:00 p.m. I'd been there since 10:00 a.m. I was so lonely and bored and hungry my stomach felt like it was squeezing my insides. I hadn't eaten all day.

Suddenly, a door squeaked outside my room. I sat up on the bed and listened as high-heel shoes stomped into the kitchen. Paper crinkled. Metal clanked against metal and then something sizzled.

Patricia was making dinner. The smell of grease and onions wafted throughout the house.

If I wanted something to eat, I was going to have to be brave, speak up, and summon all the Pryor I could to walk out of the room. Rain might have had the words, sharp and sure. All I could do was push the door all the way open. It creaked.

Patricia looked startled.

"Oh!" she said, as if she'd forgotten I was there. "I thought you were with your father?"

"I'm hungry," I said, and reached down to adjust the bathing suit I was still wearing from the morning.

"Want some French fries?" she asked, laying out shoestring potatoes on an oily pan. I nodded.

"They'll be ready in a few minutes," she said. I wasn't sure I could wait, but I wandered through the house, hoping to catch one last glimpse of my dad. He wasn't around and his bedroom door was closed. The only light in the living room was from a street lamp, but I could still see the stack of his albums, *That N***er's Crazy*, leaning against the wall. I picked one up. His face looked so handsome and inviting underneath the magnetic word, stamped in bold letters across the cover.

Would anyone notice if I took it?

I didn't just want the album, I wanted access to the power the n-word commanded. Somehow I could tell the person who took charge of that word at the right moment was a force to be reckoned with. Staring at my father's smile, I wondered how I would ever become that person. I thought about tucking the record into my bathing suit, slipping into my room, and hiding it in my floral suitcase underneath my coloring book and crayons.

Before I had a chance to decide, Patricia called me.

"Miss Elizabeth, fries are ready." I put the album back and ran to the kitchen as fast as I could. She handed me a steaming French fry that glistened with oil. It burned my fingertips, but I was starving, so

I shoved it in my mouth. The fry's hot weight dropped into the pit of my stomach like a rock. A second later, I threw up onto the kitchen floor. And then I threw up again. Patricia brought me back to my room and my private bathroom. I cried when I saw yellow-greenish bile land in the toilet. I cried again when my stomach heaved into the wee hours of the morning but nothing came out at all.

Nobody held back my hair. Nobody even came to check on me. As much as I wanted to be close to my father, living with him wasn't easy. At seven years old, clawing my way into his inner sanctum required a muscle I hadn't yet developed, and maybe never would. I was ready to go home.

Six

"Black Is Beautiful"

1974

"What's Patricia like? Is she pretty?"

On the way home from the Boston airport, my mom leaned over the front seat of a yellow cab and peppered me with questions.

"Did she say how cute you were?"

"Yes," I said, as the wind pushed smoke from my mom's cigarette back through the open window and into my face.

"Was it hot in California?"

"Mm hmm," I said, sticking my thumb deep into my mouth and leaning my head against the car door.

"Did your father ask about me?"

"I think so."

There were so many things I wanted to tell my mom about the trip—about my little sister, about the pool, about my punishment, about the n-word on the album I wanted to bring home. We were so close, I usually told her everything, but she didn't ask anything about me so I kept it all to myself.

Later that night, as soon as my mom tucked me in and I could

51

hear the TV blaring in her room, I snuck downstairs to grab her copy of *That N***er's Crazy* that I had found in her record collection when I got home. I tiptoed back upstairs, opened my red plastic record player, took my copy of *Free to Be . . . You and Me* off the turntable, and carefully placed the needle on my dad's record.

> Thank you. Good evening. Hope I'm funny. Yah, cause I know
> n***ers are ready to kick ass.

I wasn't sure what he meant, but it sounded like he was saying being an n-word wasn't a bad thing at all. His voice lulled me to sleep, even though I tried my hardest to keep my eyes open and listen to every word. When I woke up a little later, the needle was scratching against the record label. I slid the album back into the jacket and pushed it as far as I could under my bed.

The annual Franklin Park Kite Festival in the Dorchester section of Boston was my favorite event of the summer. The warm air was fragrant with hot dogs and cotton candy, and a good breeze blew as different-sized kites fluttered and dipped in the sky above. Lying next to my mom on a blanket, I looked up at the clear blue sky as a diamond-shaped kite rose high on a big gust of air.

Suddenly, my mother jumped up and started shouting at three skinny, dark-skinned teenage boys.

"You give it back right now, you little shits!" my mom said, adjusting her striped tube top so it didn't fall down while she screamed. She was only 5 feet tall and weighed 90 pounds, but she took the boys on with the confidence of a man three times her size.

It took several minutes for me to figure out what was happening. My mom was accusing them of stealing her wallet.

The boys seemed unfazed and danced around our blanket, laughing at the tiny, wild-eyed lady cussing them out.

They taunted her with a rhyme. "Black is beautiful. White is pitiful." "Black is beautiful" was a chant rooted in the civil rights movement. "White is pitiful" wasn't.

As soon as I heard the song, I loved it. The poetry of it made my heart fly as high as a kite. So, I sang it too. "Black is beautiful. White is pitiful."

The words shot a surge of energy through my body, like when I saw my dad onstage. By singing the words aloud, I felt as if I was proving to everyone that I was his daughter. I knew my mom couldn't sing the song because she wasn't Black like we were. But I also thought she would be proud of me for being brave about my Blackness like my dad told me to be. I sang the song again and joined the boys, dancing around the blanket. I felt carefree and bold.

My mom didn't say a word, but I watched as a kernel of anger, like a sty, formed in her dark-brown eyes. She had never looked at me that way before.

A few nights later, shooting pains seized my chest.

"I'm having a heart attack!" I screamed across the second-floor landing.

"Mac, come quick," my nana yelled, unsure what to do.

When the pain came over me like sharp currents of electricity, my nana was curling my hair in finger ringlets like Shirley Temple. My mom charged out of her room with a cigarette between her lips, barefoot and wearing her long pale-yellow nightgown. Smoke surrounded her like a halo and light from the TV flickered behind her. I wanted to run into her arms. But I stayed in place, sure that if I moved, I would die.

"Elizabeth," my mom said, getting down on her knees and holding me. I caught a whiff of her sweet shampoo and her cigarettes. We stayed that way until the sharpness in my chest stopped stinging. She wiped away my tears.

But it kept happening. Every few days, my heart clenched, pains so sudden and strong I cried and gasped for air. After three weeks, my mom took me downtown to visit a psychiatrist, a woman with long black hair; clear, white skin; and a clean, square office. She invited us to sit on a leather love seat. After a while, my mom left the room. The doctor took my hand, and we sat down at a child-sized table and chair set low to the ground. We put together a wooden puzzle and played Chutes and Ladders.

"Do you miss your daddy?" she asked.

"Yes," I said, feeling a little embarrassed about telling her something so private.

"What kinds of things do you do when you're together?"

I told her about the swimming pool and my sister Rain, but not about the punishment. "He didn't come out of his room a lot," I admitted. "His house was too big, and I was lonely there." I fidgeted with a puzzle piece until I figured out where it went. "Now I feel lonely at home too."

On the drive back from the appointment, my mom said, "It's an anxiety attack. Not a problem with your heart."

I looked at her, confused.

"Now that you've met your father and said goodbye, you're worried you won't ever see him again. You're not having a heart attack. You're afraid."

It was true, I was worried about my relationship with him. I hadn't seen him as much as I wanted to in L.A., he had three other kids who I assumed knew him better than I did, and everyone was vying for his love and affection. But as my mom stepped on the gas, I couldn't stop thinking about the boys in the park and my father's album under my bed. I couldn't stop thinking about how I was Black and she wasn't and how she looked at me when I sang the words "Black is beautiful." I put my arm out the window and let the wind lift my hand up like a kite.

A few weeks after visiting the psychiatrist, I sat in my nana's kitchen, waiting for a pan of *kichel*—puffy Jewish sugar cookies—to cool.

"Guess what?" my mom said.

"Chicken butt!" I said, very proud of my joke. She rolled her eyes and kept talking.

"We're moving to California!" she said.

"Right now?" I asked.

She tickled my stomach. "No. Not right now."

"I don't want to live in California."

"Daddy's in Los Angeles," my mom said. "You'll get to see him all the time. Isn't that what you want?"

"Yes," I said, sticking my thumb in my mouth and flicking my eyelashes with my finger. She held my face in her hands.

"Lizzy, I want you to have a relationship with him."

I wanted a relationship with him too, but I worried getting close to him would be harder on both of us than she realized.

"Are we gonna live with him and Patricia?"

"Don't be ridiculous!" she said without smiling.

I saw the same angry look in her eye I had seen in the park. A twinge of pain stabbed my chest.

Seven

The Voldemort Theory

2011

"We're gonna talk about the n-word," I said, facing a brand-new crop of students at the start of the fall semester.

In the aftermath of the *Blazing Saddles* incident, I was left with a series of gnawing questions. Why had I lost my cool when I heard the n-word? Why had censoring it made the classroom even more uncomfortable? And why was I suddenly thinking about my dad all the time?

"Last year," I told the students, "when I taught this course, someone said the actual n-word in class."

A few people opened their mouths in shock.

"The real problem wasn't her. It was me. The moment she said it, instead of trying to help everyone process what happened, I panicked. I banned the word from the classroom without explaining why I made the decision, and missed an opportunity for all of us to learn.

"So, the word is going to come up in this class—in slave narratives, in pro-slavery writings, in the films we watch. I want us to work together to come up with the best way to handle it when it does. Do we quote it? Should we never say it? Are we obligated to say it for the sake of historical accuracy?"

I explained how we would work our way up to the conversation and spend the first half of the semester building trust and rapport.

"About six weeks into the semester," I said, "we will have a debate about whether to use the actual word in class or not. Until then, please stick with the phrase 'the n-word.' It's imperfect, I know. But it's the best we have until we decide what to do."

I paused to look around. "Sound okay?"

A few students nodded.

The first half of the semester went off without a hitch. The students were prepared and engaged. Everyone spoke up in class and asked great questions. When the n-word came up, the students used the phrase "the n-word" without complaint.

But three full minutes into the debate about whether or not to say the word in class, the room was not just silent, it was still. Nobody raised their hand or shuffled their papers or kicked over a water bottle or even got up to pee.

"Anyone have an opinion?" I said, jumping into the quiet.

A white student named Amelie lifted her hand noncommittally. "I don't think any white person should ever say it," she said. I wasn't entirely surprised by her comment. Seventy percent of all adults believe there are no circumstances in which a white person should ever say the n-word, according to a 2019 Pew Research poll.

"Why not?" I asked.

Bella, an activist student with huge blue eyes and straight brown hair, answered. "Because of its violent history. How it's used against Black people. How it's really a way to give racists power."

Throughout the classroom, the energy started churning. Students opened their laptops or pulled out pen and paper to take notes.

"The fact that racists use the word shouldn't be a reason to censor it," said a student with spiky red hair named Tamara. Her brows were furrowed, like she was trying to work something out. "It reminds me of *Harry Potter*."

Several of her classmates snickered, but Tamara forged ahead.

"Everyone at Hogwarts called Voldemort 'He Who Must Not Be Named' or 'You Know Who.' Harry and Professor Dumbledore were the only ones brave enough to say the evil wizard's name out loud. The point was, not speaking Voldemort's name made him more powerful, not less." She paused and looked around the room before she cautiously concluded, "Doesn't it make the n-word more powerful not to say it?"

Hands popped up all over the place.

The students passionately debated both sides of what I've come to call "the Voldemort theory," the idea that it's important to say the word out loud in order to defang it. On one hand, Black artists like my father had tried to do just that. He used the word in his album titles, movies, and stand-up to speak out against racism. But white people had been saying the word for hundreds of years, and it hadn't taken the sting out at all. The students didn't resolve anything, but the conversation finally began to flow. Talking about a fictional villain was easier than talking about the actual n-word.

As they got more comfortable with the subject, the tenor of the discussion started to shift. Courtney, a shy student, tall and slender, made a surprising confession.

"I'm from a mostly white part of New Jersey," she said. "There was only one Black kid in my grade." She paused and wrapped one leg all the way around the other like stripes on a candy cane. "In my junior year of high school, these three football players made fun of this kid. The Black kid. And they called him the n-word all the time."

"The actual n-word?" I asked.

"The actual n-word," she said. "And I was there, standing at the lockers one time, and I didn't do anything. The next year, that kid didn't come back to school."

Everyone in the room was quiet, yet alert. The nervous anticipation was palpable, like in the middle of the night when a strange sound shakes me out of sleep, and I sit up and lean forward, holding my body taut, hoping and not hoping to hear the sound again.

My heart hurt for the boy in Courtney's story. But it was also a revelation to learn how this experience stayed with Courtney and how she carried the shame for all these years.

Paige, a white student from Connecticut, squirmed in her seat and took a deep breath. "I haven't talked to my dad in a few years," she said. "He always called our neighbor 'that n-word next door.' I told him I wouldn't talk to him if he said that word again, but he wouldn't stop."

As Paige fought back tears, Courtney reached out to hold her hand.

One after another after another, the students opened up and told heartbreaking stories about the n-word, and their shame, outrage, and confusion. This wasn't just an academic discussion about when it was and wasn't okay to say the actual word, but a deeply personal outpouring of emotion that showed the lasting impact of the n-word. It was the conversation I hadn't realized we needed to have, and it was gut wrenching. Throughout history and even today, the n-word demoralized people and divided them.

When had the word gained enough strength and momentum to do so much damage?

Interlude Three

They got all the Vietnamese in the army camps and shit, learning how to say "n***er" so they can become good citizens.

Richard Pryor,

. . . Is It Something I Said?,

1975

On September 28, 1841, Frederick Douglass bought a first-class railroad ticket in Lynn, Massachusetts, and boarded a northbound train. As he sat down in his seat, an enraged conductor ordered Douglass to leave the first-class car and go to a small, dirty "cage" called the "Jim Crow car." It was one of the first recorded times the term "Jim Crow"—derived from the minstrel show—was used to describe a physical, segregated space for Black people. When Douglass refused to move, five or six Eastern Railroad workers grabbed the well-dressed, twenty-three-year-old Black abolitionist by the head, arms, and legs.

"Snake out the damned n***er!" yelled one of the railroad men as they tossed him off the train.

As more free Black people traveled in the North, the n-word became more than just a slur. White people used the word as a gatekeeping mechanism to keep free Black people separate. This was the birth of Jim Crow segregation, a system of racial discrimination that established white dominance over Black people, and would eventually become law across the post-Emancipation South.

Douglass described the n-word as a constant onslaught. White people used it to segregate Black people in cities and towns as they tried to cross the threshold of public spaces and go about their daily lives—in churches, museums, zoos, libraries, taverns, steamships, railroads, and stagecoaches.

Wherever he went, he heard the "fiendish hate" of his white countrymen.

"We don't allow n***ers in here!"

The n-word had become the rallying cry of the good citizens of the United States.

Eight

"A White Woman Raising a Black Child"

1974–1975

"I'm a white woman raising a Black child," my mom said, shouting over the wind and the radio as we drove her yellow '73 Mustang convertible, top down, along Little Santa Monica Boulevard. She'd said that a lot since we moved to West L.A. a few months ago. She said it when she sprawled out on our blue velvet couch and listened to Earth, Wind & Fire in the two-bedroom apartment we rented; and in the Mustang, where she blasted the R&B radio station KJLH. She said it after she brushed out my dry hair and laughed at herself when it got too frizzy. She said it after she pressured my elementary school's principal to transfer me into another classroom because my second-grade teacher yelled at me and refused to believe a kid who looked like me belonged in the gifted-students' program.

And she said it now, when she talked about how much better it was for me to grow up in L.A. than in Boston.

"What they're doing in Boston is disgusting!" my mom said, as she explained the 1974 Boston busing crisis. When a federal court ordered Boston public school officials to bus inner-city Black children to white suburban neighborhoods, the city exploded in protest. White people did not want to integrate.

I listened on full alert. "Disgusting" was a word my mother only used when she talked about a white person doing something awful to a Black person. When she said it, she put the "gusting" in the back of her throat like she was gearing up to spit it out of her mouth. Every time she said it, a drop of spittle formed on the left side of her bottom lip.

"Boston is like a small town," she said, shaking her head. She bent down close to the steering wheel to get out of the wind and take a puff of her cigarette. "Did you know it's more dangerous for Black kids to walk through South Boston than it is for them to live in Mississippi?"

I shook my head no.

"You know what's happening there right now? What the whites are doing? Grown men and women are dragging Black kids off buses and yelling at them."

I looked at my mom in horror as strands of hair blew out of my ponytail and whipped my face. Gnawing on the callus on my thumb, I tried to figure out the best places to hide if a grownup started screaming at me on the way to school. The thought of angry people holding picket signs and screeching in the streets made me scared to go back to Boston, even though I missed my family.

Most of the time when my mom called herself "a white woman raising a Black child," it made me happy, like instead of her being white and me being Black, she and I were in a group of our own. She was like a hero who put on a cape, rescued me from the racism of Boston, and set me down gently in a safer place. In the process, she sacrificed so much that was important to her, leaving behind her friends, her family, and the shrimp and lobster sauce from China Sails restaurant. But other times, hearing her talk about being a special kind of white woman made me feel itchy, like the welts that bloomed on my arms and legs whenever I played in the grass. Sometimes, when she described herself that way, she made me feel bad about myself in a way she never did before I knew I was Black.

One night, my mom took me to Tito's Tacos and we ate saucy beef tacos in homemade shells at a picnic table in front of the restaurant. I could tell she was working her way up to tell me something upsetting because her pretty face looked ugly, like she was sucking on her teeth with her mouth closed. A sourpuss, or *farbissina punim*, as my nana called it. The muscles in my neck got tense, and I could feel a bite of taco get caught in my throat.

"Aunty Paula makes me so mad!" she said. I felt my body relax. My mom always complained about her sister. "She's disgusting!"

Uh oh. I wasn't sure I wanted to know the reason, but I asked.

"How come?" I said, shoving too much taco into my mouth as beef juice dripped between my fingers and into the palm of my hand.

My mom blew out a big cloud of smoke. "Yesterday Aunty called me," she said, leaning in, checking to see if anybody sitting around us was listening. Then she lowered her voice. "She asked me why all Black people sound the same."

I put my taco down, wondering what my aunt meant.

My mom put her hand on her hip. "I said, 'Does Elizabeth sound like that?'" Then she leaned in again. "And Aunty said, 'I don't know, I'm too close to her to tell.'"

Questions popped into my head. *Do all Black people sound the same? Do I sound that way too? Could people tell I was Black from the sound of my voice? Was having a Black voice like having bad breath, a thing I wouldn't notice until someone else pointed it out?*

My stomach filled with acid, and I felt ashamed. I wasn't hungry anymore. All I could think about was running home, recording my voice on my tape recorder, and playing it back to hear myself.

"Cousin Enid is disgusting too!" she said. "She told Nana she refuses to drive through Mattapan because of the '*schvartzes.*'"

Mattapan was a neighborhood in Boston with lots of Black people. *Schvartze* is Yiddish for the n-word. I heard the word growing up, but my mom told me it was a bad word and yelled at anyone in the family who said it.

Crumpling a soggy napkin, I stood up to toss the rest of my taco in the trash.

"Elizabeth," my mom said, grabbing my sticky hand. "I couldn't in good conscience raise a Black child there."

She was talking about Boston, but I wondered if she was also talking about her family. My nana and my aunty both treated me like I was their favorite. But since we moved to California, my mom started telling me stories that painted a different picture. To me, they were *mishpachah*, family, the center of my world. But maybe to them, I was my skin color first, and only my mother's daughter and their family second.

Every few weeks, my dad picked me up at our apartment on Camden Avenue—a street lined with squat beige-and-pink–stucco apartment buildings—and took me out to dinner. The first time we were supposed to go out, my mom told me it was okay to wear jeans, but I wanted to dress up. I wore a plaid dress with long sleeves and a white Peter Pan collar, and I made my mom pull my hair back into a tight bun with lots of bobby pins to hold the stray hairs in place.

When he knocked on the door, I was so excited, I ran from the living room to my mom's bedroom to my bedroom and back into the living room before I calmed down enough to answer the door.

"Dizzy Liz," my dad said, stepping into our kitchen and using my new California nickname.

"Daddy," I said, wrapping him in a huge hug.

"Hm, hm, hm," he said, admiring my outfit. My mom stood with her hands on her hips and acted like she was too cool to be impressed with my father, but I could see a hint of a smile on her face. Maybe she acted nonchalant because she got to see him all the time.

Since we'd moved to L.A., she spent several days a week at his house helping him type up a film script for a Black version of *Cyrano de Bergerac*, a movie that never got made. But for me, seeing him was always a special occasion. Getting all of his attention made me feel like a movie star. He looked handsome in tight blue jeans and a silky button-down shirt. He smelled delicious and sweet too.

As we left my apartment, he held my hand. "You like Italian?" he asked. I shrugged. I didn't know.

He drove us to a small restaurant in Hollywood with red-and-white–checkered tablecloths and Chianti bottles wrapped in dried vines hanging from the beams. Then he showed me how to put my napkin on my lap and ordered an appetizer, a block of deep-fried mozzarella that was crunchy even though it was smothered in red sauce.

"You making friends in school?" he said when our spaghetti came.

"Sort of," I said. The kids at school teased me because of my Boston accent. I couldn't say my "r"s. I said, "pahk," "cah" and "yahd." On the walk to school, the kids made a game of it.

"Say that," said a boy who lived in the apartment building next to me as he pointed at the giant sign of a car dealership that we passed every day on the walk.

"Jaguahhhhh," I said, trying my hardest to get it right.

All of the kids imitated me, and I burst into tears. Another second grader, Abby, who was half Japanese, half Jewish, came up with a nickname for me. "Pryor Cryer." It stuck.

I told my dad about Abby and the nickname.

"You give her a right hook?" he asked.

"No," I said, wondering if he was disappointed.

"Maybe she's jealous?" he asked.

"No. She's popular. She has the best handwriting in class."

He leaned back in his chair and thought about that. "Maybe she thinks you going after her man," he said.

"Her boyfriend's name is Calvin," I said, trying to play it cool, but like every time I tried to hide my feelings, a little smile boxed its way out of the corners of my lips.

"Oh, Dizzy!" my dad said, his voice delighted. "Is Calvin fine?"

I smiled again. My cheeks felt hot.

"He a white boy?"

I shook my head no.

He cupped his ear. "Can't hear you." He liked it better when I spoke.

"No," I said. "He's Black."

"Go ahead with your bad self, Dizzy Liz," he said, reaching over and tickling the top of my hand. "Tomorrow, you walk up to this girl and ask her does she want to play."

He always had good advice and took my feelings seriously; he never treated me like a silly kid. The next day I felt confident enough to walk up to Abby and ask her how she got her letters so rounded and straight. From that moment, she and I became good friends and sat next to each other for the rest of second grade.

On the way home from dinner, he pointed up at the moon, which was full, bright orange, and low in the sky.

"You were born on a harvest moon, Dizzy," he said. "The moon looked exactly like that one."

It was the first time he ever said anything to me about the night I was born. He looked at me and smiled, his face wide open. I felt so loved and safe, I wanted to ask if he thought my voice sounded Black. But I didn't want to break the spell.

Just like my dad guessed, Calvin was the boy I had a crush on. He was handsome and tall like Weird Harold from my favorite animated TV show, *Fat Albert*. He was also the handball champion of Westwood Elementary School. Everyone liked and envied him and lined up during recess to try to beat him.

One day, a third grader named Bryce, who was skinny and white and had a squarish head like Frankenstein, accused Calvin of cheating.

"No Americans!" Bryce yelled. "Americans" were when you hit the handball without letting it bounce on the ground first.

"I didn't do Americans!" Calvin yelled back.

Bryce shoved Calvin. Calvin shoved Bryce. Then the rest of the kids—the white ones, the Black ones, the Mexican ones, the Japanese ones—gathered around and chanted a song as casually as if it were a nursery rhyme.

*It's a fight, it's a fight, 'tween a n***er and a white.*
*The n***er's all right, but the white can't fight.*

Hearing everyone sing the n-word in unison was unnerving. It sounded like the kids were rooting for Calvin, but if they were, why did they call him that name? As more and more students joined in, the teachers came over to break up the fight, but they didn't stop anyone from saying the n-word. Usually, the teachers dragged anyone who swore to the principal's office. Second and third graders got suspended for saying "fuck" and "shit" and "asshole." Wasn't the n-word a swear word too? Was it okay to use during a schoolyard fight? Or was it okay as long as it meant the Black kid was a better athlete than the white one?

Every couple of weeks, I got to sleep over at my dad's house.

Patricia wasn't around anymore. Sometimes when I visited, he had a different lady or two hanging around, but the night I brought home the class rat, he was all alone. My teacher Miss Marlowe assigned me as rat monitor because I was the new kid in the school. I was nervous about taking on the responsibility. There was so much to remember: keep the rat in the cage, feed him special pellets, and refill his water bottle. Most important, never stick your fingers in the cage.

"He will bite!" Miss Marlowe told me when I lifted the cage to bring him home. With dark-brown hair, tiny red eyes, and two giant front teeth, the rat did look pretty vicious.

My dad picked me up from school and brought me back to his house, where we ate peppery hamburgers at the kitchen table, and he taught me how to play backgammon. At bedtime, he helped me get ready and promised to come in and tell me a story before I went to sleep. While I brushed my teeth, he made a phone call. By the time he walked back into my bedroom, he looked tense and swirled a golden-brown liquid slowly in his glass while he smoked a cigarette. He noticed the rat, seemingly for the first time.

"What should we feed him?" he asked, putting down his glass and lifting the rat's cage from its spot on my dresser. He held it up to his face and took a closer look.

"Miss Marlowe said only pellets."

"Is that so," he said with a frown, like he was thinking of a better snack for the poor, unfortunate rat.

"It has to be the pellets," I said again, feeling a spike of anxiety.

He didn't like me correcting him. Instead, he made a clanging sound as he ran his middle finger back and forth along the cage and stuck his pointer finger between the bars.

"Daddy, no," I said.

"He likes it," he said, wiggling his finger.

Suddenly, the rat leapt across the cage and bit him.

"Motherfucker!" My dad yanked his hand away.

Shaking his finger to ease the sting of the bite, his eyes narrowed, his lips pursed, and with a cruel look on his face, he stuck his lit cigarette into the cage.

"How do you like that, motherfucker?"

The rat bit the tip of the burning ember and then banged its body against the cage in pain. I screamed and cried the whole time.

"Help him! Help him!" I begged.

"You saying it's okay he bit me?" He looked at me with a scowl.

"No!" I said, sobbing. "But the teacher said—"

"Fuck the teacher!" He held the rat's cage in one hand and the cigarette in the other. "That motherfucker bit your father! You should be begging *him* to stop!"

I couldn't hold back any longer. Shaking in fear and feeling defeated, I had to suck my thumb.

Back at home the next week, a note arrived in my mailbox.

I think your father yells at you because he's jealous. Your father can't suck his thumb like you do. Your father loves you, though, he told me so. And he wouldn't lie to me. You see, I am he.

I read it out loud to my mom.

"Your father," she said. "He sure does have a way with words."

My mom and I had just finished watching an episode of *Good Times*, a sitcom about a working-class Black family trying to make ends meet. We were cuddling on her bed when she let out a giggle.

"What?" I asked.

"I was just thinking about the show." I waited for her to finish her thought. I knew there was more coming. "The way J.J. says 'ignorant.' It's so funny."

J.J., the main character of the show, was very silly, but I didn't understand what she was laughing at.

She turned and faced me.

"Okay. There are two words Black people can never say. 'Ask,' and 'ignorant.'"

Even though her voice sounded playful, her words seemed unkind.

"Your father can only say 'ax.' And no Black person can ever say the 'g' in 'ignorant.'" She had a twinkle in her eye.

It was true that my dad said "ax" instead of "ask," but I knew exactly what he meant when he said it. It didn't sound wrong or different to me at all. Did I say "ax" too? Was my mom pointing out how different we were from each other? Or was she saying I was more like her than other Black people because she was a white woman raising a Black child?

I didn't want to take any chances. The next day before school, I stood in my bathroom in front of the mirror and practiced one word over and over—"Ig-norant. Ig-norant." I was careful to pronounce the "g" and not blend the letters together. Then I said it the other way to see how it felt in my mouth. "In-orant. In-orant." Speaking the right way was important, no matter who I was talking to, whether it was my mom or my dad. For weeks, I practiced other words too, saying them every day before school. Never again would anyone hear me over the phone and know I was from Boston. Never again would they be able to hear the color of my skin.

Nine

Parthenia Street

1975

The moment I opened the back door to the Parthenia house, I heard the smack of tiles against a table and roars of laughter coming from the kitchen.

"This n***er think he a motherfucking preacher," said my great-uncle Dickie, rolls of fat shaking his stomach as he played dominoes with my dad and a few other men.

"That's Reverend N***er to you, motherfucker," said my dad's friend and record producer David Banks, using his right hand to slick back his glistening, straightened hair as he slapped another domino on the table. Their words sounded mean, but their voices were warm and teasing.

By the time I started the third grade, my dad was so famous even my friends at school had heard of him. His second Grammy sat on a table in the living room, and he was filming *Silver Streak*, a blockbuster that would make him a superstar, and the first of many he would make with funnyman Gene Wilder.

More fame meant more money, more people hanging around,

and the purchase of a sprawling two-acre estate in the San Fernando Valley. There was always a party at my dad's new house on Parthenia Street: friends, exes, his latest girlfriend, family visiting from Peoria, and other people who didn't seem to know him well at all. Black men, loud and laughing, were some of the regulars, including Banks; the painter Prophet Jennings, whose provocative artwork decorated the house; and the comedy writer Paul Mooney. Mama, my dad's grandmother who raised him, came from Peoria and stayed for months at a time. So did her daughter, Aunt Mexcine, and her son, Uncle Dickie. Dickie traveled with an entourage of his own: his wife, Betty, and also his girlfriend, a sex worker named White Velvet. Dickie's ex-wife, Aunt Dee, was there too, but not with Dickie.

The house was huge but everyone hung out in the kitchen, sitting around an unfinished pine table, eating, drinking, smoking, and talking smack, trying to get my dad's attention.

"E-liz-a-be-th!" Uncle Dickie was the first to see me and called me over, stretching out my name into five syllables, like a celebration. He was tall and overweight with dark-brown skin and a white goatee, his voice so raspy and deep that when he spoke, the vibration tickled the inside of my ears. "Come over and let me holler at you!"

I paused for a second, unsure what to do. Whenever my nana hollered at me, it meant I was in trouble. But Uncle Dickie's arms were wide open, and he gave me a big smile. So, I ran over and hugged him.

He squeezed me tight and turned to David. "I'm done with you, Reverend N***er. I've got my baby niece here now."

"She pretty like her momma," David said.

"She is," my dad agreed and looked at me with so much love, I wanted to jump into the middle of the kitchen and do pirouettes across the floor. He pulled me over for a kiss.

Cozy in his arms, I wanted to ask why it was okay for Uncle Dickie and David to call each other the n-word. *Were men allowed to say it to each other? Were friends and family allowed to say it too?* The way they said it made the word sound like an inside joke I didn't understand.

Before I could ask, my dad put me to work. "Dizzy. Make me a tequila sunrise."

"What's that?" I asked. The name sounded made up.

"A drink. For your daddy. To drink." He looked at me with a serious face, but with a smile in his eyes. "Don't ask so many questions."

He sent me to the pantry and shouted instructions. Gathering all the ingredients, I filled a tall glass with tequila and a splash of juice without spilling a drop.

David doubled over in laughter. "Richard, this girl trying to fuck you up!" My dad looked over at the drink, which was 90 percent tequila, and couldn't keep a straight face. I slipped my thumb into my mouth, hoping my father wouldn't notice.

"Baby," he said, gently tugging on my thumb. "That's too strong for your daddy. Pour that one out. Let's start over." And then he showed me how to measure two fingers of tequila at the bottom of the glass and fill the rest with juice.

He sipped the drink. "Perfect," he said. I stood up a little straighter and felt as proud of myself as when I got straight As in school.

Gracefully, my dad put a homemade cigarette to his lips, flipped open his lighter with a metallic jangle, and inhaled. The tip lit up while tiny pieces of paper crackled and floated in the air.

An awful stink smacked me in the face.

"Ew. What's that smell?" I said, fanning my nose.

The room got quiet.

Then Uncle Dickie said in his deepest voice, "It's reefer, baby."

Everyone exploded in giggles.

I couldn't tell if they thought I was funny or if it was funny that I didn't know what reefer was, but I loved that I was finally in on the joke.

"Is Rain here?" I asked.

Rain and I had grown close since the day she introduced me to an array of new curse words at Tower Records. Our moms didn't speak to each other, and they didn't plan our visits together, but I was happiest when we ended up at our father's house at the same time. Every few months, we got to have sleepovers together in our shared bedroom at Parthenia Street, and my dad usually bought us new dresses and took us out for fancy dinners in Beverly Hills.

"Your old man not good enough for you?" my dad teased. Before I could protest, Rain came barreling into the kitchen wearing muddy overalls with no T-shirt underneath. I felt a little thrill of satisfaction knowing my jeans and T-shirt were clean and tidy, and she was in disarray, especially her hair. One side of her head was tucked neatly into a ponytail, the other side was a loose afro, with thick, kinky curls that stood at attention.

"Hm, hm, hm," Mama said, wrangling Rain into a chair. Everyone called my great-grandmother "Mama," even David Banks, who wasn't a relative at all. I didn't think the name fit. "Mama" sounded like a name for someone cute and sweet like my nana, who knitted me pink slippers and baked fudgy brownies. My father's grandmother was tall and imposing, with light-brown skin and long white hair; her face sagged at her cheeks; and she had a permanent scowl that made her look strict. She was the boss of everyone, even my dad.

"Sit still, baby," Mama said to my sister, as the men continued to smack their dominoes against the pine table and Mercy, my dad's housekeeper, stood by the stove, stirring a big pot of her honey-sweetened Salvadoran lemonade.

"Okay, Mama," Rain said, trying not to squirm as our great-grandmother started fixing her hair. When Rain was three years old, her mother dropped her off in Peoria for a few months to live with Mama. They'd been close ever since. Rain was also close to her Jewish grandma, who, unlike my nana, kept kosher and observed Shabbat every Friday night. Rain knew all of the Hebrew prayers. She was a Black Jewish girl, just like I was, but she was a lot more Jewish and Blacker too.

"Why don't this baby have good hair like Elizabeth?" Mama asked.

By "good hair," she meant curly hair that was also a little bit straight and smooth. But as she tugged on Rain's hair and tried to shove the kinks into a ponytail, she did it with so much satisfaction, it felt like having good hair wasn't exactly a compliment. When my hair was down, it fell into soft curls that were easy to put into a neat ponytail. My hair was like me. It followed the rules. Rain was wild and free and let it all hang out, even her hair.

When Mama was done, she kissed the top of Rain's head and said, "Take your booty and your sister booty out to play."

Rain grabbed my hand, pulling me to the back door. "Let's pretend . . ." she said, the same way she started all of her made-up games.

"Elizabeth," my dad called out, stopping me in my tracks. "Tell everybody how many books you read this summer."

All the men at the pine table got quiet, waiting to hear what I had to say.

"Three!" I said, pleased with myself, since summer had just started. But when I peeked over to see if Mama heard me, it didn't seem like the news impressed her at all.

Rain and I spent most holidays with our dad and every single Christmas. We usually got the same presents in different styles or colors. I got a diamond and ruby bracelet, and she got diamond and ruby earrings. I got red silk pajamas, and she got blue silk pajamas. The gifts were always picked out by his current wife or girlfriend, who never really knew us or understood how different we were.

This Christmas, though, my dad was in between women so it was just the three of us.

"I picked out the presents myself!" he bragged. After he handed Rain her gift, he struggled to place mine on the floor at my feet.

"Heavy," he said, and smiled at me shyly.

I sucked in my cheeks to hide my glee.

Rain and I sat across from each other on the white couches in the living room as she tossed aside our father's handwritten card. His notes were always hard to decipher. He had dyslexia and drew his letters backward and mixed up the order of letters in his words. His learning disability made school almost impossible for him, and he'd dropped out in the eighth grade.

"I'm a terrible reader," Rain said, as she meticulously unwrapped her present, savoring every minute of our father's attention. It seemed like she wanted to bond with him about how they both struggled in school.

I picked up the card. Making sense of his handwriting took a little extra concentration. "To Rain. Love, your father, Richard," I read aloud.

She looked at me with a smile. "Elizabeth is the smartest person I know," she said.

"She most certainly is," our dad said. If Rain hadn't been there, it would have felt like he was giving me a compliment. Now it felt like being smart created a barrier between me and them.

My little sister pulled a big rainbow-colored afro wig and a palette of oil-based clown makeup out of the box. The gift was so unique and seemed like a recognition that she was funny and silly and embodied the spirit of a clown. Rain was so clearly touched, a teardrop fell from her eye.

Now, our dad turned all of his attention to me. "Whatcha waiting for?" he said, with a big goofy grin on his face.

I dropped to the floor and ripped open the brick-heavy present. But as soon as I tore off a sliver of paper, my heart sank. It was books. *The Annotated Shakespeare* by A.L. Rowse. A giant, hardcover, three-volume set including almost everything Shakespeare ever wrote. The set came in its own case for easy storage.

My shoulders slumped, even though I tried to smile.

"You're learning about Shakespeare in school," he said, looking a little hurt. "And you love to read."

"Yes," I said, and gave him a hug even though it ached inside that he thought only Rain was a comedian like he was. I loved to be funny, and creative too. I spent hours sitting at an IBM typewriter on a desk in his guest house, writing stories and poems. I felt like an artist and wanted him to see it.

Later, I asked Rain if I could try on her makeup. He overheard and interrupted. "I don't want you wearing makeup," he yelled from the other room. "You're not old enough." Even though I was older than Rain, and he was the one who gave her the makeup in the first place.

I couldn't understand at the time, but by giving me the Shakespeare collection, he was trying to expand my world, like he did when I was in high school and he took me to see Federico Fellini's *8½* and Akira Kurasawa's *Ran*, and when he gave me his marked-up copy of Richard Leakey's *Origins*, an anthropological study of Africa and early man. But what I heard was *you are not funny, you're smart. You are different from me.* What I didn't understand was that my father's comedy only existed because of his voracious appetite for learning, including his love of books and movies and theater. He wasn't pushing me away, he was showing me the intellectual connection we shared.

All these years later, I still have the Shakespeare books. They bookend my record collection, holding them upright so they don't fall off the shelf.

Whenever Rain and I visited the Parthenia house together we spent the whole day splashing in the swimming pool, playing in the life-sized dollhouse, exploring the huge yard with forty fruit trees, and running in and out of the main house making up games. Our favorite was "The Wizard of Oz." Rain always played Dorothy, and I was the Wicked Witch of the West.

"I'll get you, my pretty!" I said, making my voice sound witchy and chasing after her, my hands shaped like claws. I ran through the kitchen and into the living room, where we circled the white couches, giggling. I tried to catch her by changing course and running in the opposite direction, but when I turned suddenly, I knocked over a

delicate vase that sat on an end table. It shattered into a hundred jag-
ged little pieces.

"I told that little n***er not to run in this house!" Mama said to
my dad as I tried to pick up the broken pieces of glass with my fingers. She didn't say the n-word with the teasing, playful tone of the
men at the pine table. She spit it out of her mouth like it was poison.

I looked over at my father, sure he was going to give Mama a
piece of his mind, but he didn't say a word. He hung his head low as
if he were a little boy in big trouble.

His relationship with Mama was complicated. He rarely stood up
to her. When he was a child, she protected him fiercely, but also hit
him frequently to keep him in line. He used the beatings as fodder for
his comedy, telling stories about how she whipped him with a thin tree
branch he called a "switch," and how she'd make him pick it off the tree
himself. "That was a hell of a psychology," he said, "to make you get a
switch to beat your own ass with." His ideas about physical discipline
were shaped by his early experiences with his grandmother. So were his
ideas about women and sex because the family business was prostitu-
tion. In one of his bits, he imitated the pinched voices of Mama's white
customers who stopped him on the street when he played outside:

Hello, little boy, is your mother home? I'd like a blowjob.

Everyone in the family worked for Mama. His father, Buck, and
Uncle Dickie were both pimps at her brothel until they started their
own businesses selling sex. In 1968, Buck died at fifty-seven years old
in the arms of a woman a third of his age. My dad made a joke about
that too.

My father died fucking. He came and went at the same time.

Turning his trauma into comedy was the only way he knew how to
deal with the effects of his childhood. Privately it had a more profound

impact on his life. As vocal and vulnerable as he was onstage, at home he struggled to speak up for himself when it came to his grandmother. Still, I was certain when Mama called me the n-word, he would never let her get away with it because he told me not to let anybody call me that. I knew he was going to defend me.

"You need to whoop that ass," Mama said. I knew an ass was the same as a tushy, and I definitely didn't want anyone to whip mine.

My dad answered her with a flat voice like a robot. "Yes, Mama," he said.

Shaking with fear, I suddenly felt like I had to go to the bathroom. I clenched my muscles to hold it in. He held his body rigid like he didn't know me and he didn't want to. My eyes filled with tears. I'd never had a spanking before.

We stepped into his bedroom, and for a moment, he relaxed and patted the bed for me to jump up. Relief washed over me. My mom always threatened to hit me, or take away a trip to the zoo, or when she was really mad, kick me out of the house. Though in the end, she never did. I hoped this was the same, that together we were going to trick Mama and put on an ass-whooping show.

But it didn't happen that way. He turned to me coldly and said, "Pull down your pants."

I cried in heavy, hiccoughing sobs as he lifted me up and laid me across his lap.

"This is going to hurt me more than it's going to hurt you." He said it like he meant it. The stiff way he held his hand made that impossible. I braced myself as he alternated between blaming me and making excuses every time he hit me.

"Why did you make me do this?" *Smack.*

"I never wanted to hit you." *Smack.*

"You know you're supposed to listen to Mama." *Smack.*

"How else you gonna learn?" *Smack.*

When he was done with the spanking, he sat me up and tried to dry my eyes with the back of his hand, but the tears refused to stop. I thought running around the house wildly like Rain did would make Mama love me. Instead, my bottom hurt as much as my heart and my sense of pride. And I was angry too.

Why didn't he stick up for me when she called me the n-word?

"Stop," he said about my bitter tears. "You want me to give you another ass whooping?"

"No." My voice cracked as I tried to hold in my feelings.

"Then you go outside and put a smile on your face. You go outside and play."

After that, I was the only one in the family who never called his grandmother "Mama."

Ten

Points of Encounter

2011

For the entire summer after my students revealed their painful sto-ries about the n-word, I thought about how to continue the dialogue with a new class. The next semester, I set aside time for my students to share their personal experiences with the word. The confessions tumbled out.

Clara, a white student from New York City, said her eighth-grade teacher wanted everybody to experience firsthand the word's racist venom, so she insisted they all say the n-word out loud when they read *To Kill a Mockingbird*. When it was Clara's turn to read, she hid in the bathroom until the end of the period so she wouldn't have to say the n-word at all.

Sylvie, a Latina student from Los Angeles, shared her frustration over the n-word "pass" or "badge." I had no idea what she was talk-ing about, but most of the students did. The "pass" was when a Black friend gave permission to a friend who wasn't Black to say the word. Sylvie wasn't mad at the Black kids who handed out the pass, but furious at her non-Black friends for accepting it.

As the conversation became deeper and more fraught, I found myself increasingly uncomfortable. The feeling reminded me of how Black literary scholar Emily Bernard described teaching African American novels, chock full of the n-word, in an all-white classroom at the University of Vermont. She urged her students to say the word to foster discussion, but she hadn't anticipated the personal impact of being the only Black person in the room when they did.

And then I realized something. None of my Black students had said anything. I suspected they were feeling tender and raw because of their own experiences with the word. Were they quiet because the conversation was too painful? Or because I wasn't facilitating the right conversation? I made eye contact with each of them and smiled softly, trying to encourage them to participate.

Finally, Ife, a Black first-year student I'd known since she toured Smith the year before, leaned forward. A quiet student from the South, she was so shy that on the rare occasions when she did speak up, she tried to do it without showing her teeth.

On this topic, however, she had plenty to say. "I don't get the big deal. I'm from South Carolina. Everyone at my high school said it. Like, administrators and everything. Whenever they got annoyed with a student, they called them the n-word."

A white student from Virginia nodded her head in recognition, but I was shocked.

"White administrators?" I asked.

"White administrators. Black administrators. Teachers. Everyone," she said.

Were there really educators who thought it was okay to call their students the n-word?

A few days later, Ife came to my office hours with another Black student from my class. Sometimes, when students are in turmoil, they bring a buddy with them for moral support. The space was small, so I pulled up a chair for each of them and I sat on a leather footstool my mom had given me a few years before.

"About the conversation," she said, "I don't like it."

"You didn't like that we talked about the n-word?" I asked, concerned I had offended her.

"Not that," she said, and shook her head. Then she inhaled deeply, sat up straighter, and held her face still to hold back tears. "I don't like that people at my school called us that word."

At first, I'd believed Ife's claim that she was unaffected by the n-word and immune to its power to hurt. Now, as her eyes filled with tears, and her hands shook while she tried to control her emotions, I could see she wasn't immune at all. As I reached over and put her hands in mine, I realized the truth. She had never paused to untangle how she really felt about the word.

There were so many unexpected ways for young people to be confronted by the n-word: in the classroom, in books, in American history, in music, poetry, movies, and museums. Not to mention personal interactions with family, friends, and, on occasion, an ugly episode with a random stranger. It left a deep impression.

These were "points of encounter," as I came to call them, the emotional fallout of coming face-to-face with the n-word.

I thought my reaction to the *Blazing Saddles* incident was about my own complicated identity as a Black, Jewish woman raised in white neighborhoods who was the daughter of Richard Pryor. That I was uniquely squeamish about the n-word because of the mixed messages I got as a child—from my mother, my father, the men at Parthenia Street, and Mama.

But I was wrong.

The n-word was most destructive to African Americans, but it affected everyone who encountered it, no matter their background—Black people, white people, other people of color. It encapsulated the anti-Black racism of the nation and was deeply woven into the fabric of American history.

The impact was so far reaching and devastating, even white people could get killed for it.

Interlude Four

It's great how we think we can all sit in the same club together. White and Black. And not understand each other.

> Richard Pryor,
> *"Craps" (After Hours)*,
> 1971

On April 11, 1865, President Abraham Lincoln leaned out of a second-story window at the White House and gave an impromptu victory speech to thousands of Americans who flooded the grounds to celebrate the Union's defeat of the South.

He hailed the end of the Civil War and charted his hopes for the future, calling for national unity after so many years of violence and bloodshed. It was essential, he said, that former Confederates feel welcomed back into the United States as if they had never left, a radical idea at the time.

Lincoln also took a courageous stance when it came to African Americans. During the war, the president authorized Black men to carry arms for the Union Army and recognized their bravery as soldiers. Now, he said not only should all white men have the right to vote, but for the sake of creating harmony in the country, Black men should have that right too. "The colored man," he said, "in seeing all united for him, is inspired with vigilance, and energy, and daring."

Many in the audience vehemently disagreed with Lincoln's vision. One of them was a white actor named John Wilkes Booth, who cried out in response, "That means n***er citizenship!" The idea of Black equality terrified men like Booth who believed it would destroy the very foundation of America.

"That is the last speech he will ever make!" he shouted.

And it was.

Three days later, Booth entered President Lincoln's state box at Ford's Theater, shot him in the back of the head, and killed him.

Eleven

"Catfish It Is"

1976

"This is where you're staying," my dad's assistant Bobby said, as the car tires crunched on a gravel driveway.

On the way from the Atlanta airport to the rental house near Madison, Georgia, Bobby and I passed a five-and-dime, a hardware store, a brick-front department store, and a quaint diner. I couldn't wait to see my father, who was filming a new movie called *Greased Lightning*, about Wendell Scott, the first Black person to win a race at NASCAR's highest level. The role was my father's biggest to date and his first dramatic lead. He'd also just signed a multimillion-dollar contract with Universal Pictures to produce, write, and star in six movies over three years—the first of its kind for a Black actor. The future of Black filmmaking seemed to rest on his shoulders.

Deeply segregated Madison was a stark contrast to the Hollywood studios where my father was becoming a major player. Plantation-style homes right out of *Gone with the Wind* lined Dixie Avenue in the white part of town, while Black people lived in a working-class neighborhood called Canaan, built on the site of a former plantation. The vestiges of slavery and Jim Crow segregation were still ingrained in Madison. When the film's mostly Black cast and crew descended on the town, they were not welcomed. At one point, the town's sheriff had to intervene when local whites tried to disrupt filming by whistling and shouting every time the director yelled, "Action!" Townspeople also called members of the cast and crew the n-word. It must have been a rude awakening for my dad, who had just finished recording *Bicentennial N***er*, a deeply political album that called out American racism. He was a long way from the Sunset Strip.

As we drove through town, big houses with giant white pillars whipped by, and my excitement started to build. For a nine-year-old, visiting a movie set on a faraway location was thrilling, but the idea of spending the whole week with my dad without my brother and sisters was almost impossible to imagine. Instead of having us all visit at once like he had on a recent trip to Jamaica, he invited each of his kids to Georgia separately for a chance to bond one-on-one.

As my father became more famous, he experimented with ways of bringing together his fractured family and even explored the topic in his comedy. In *Bicentennial N***er*, he focused on the lasting tragedy of slavery and how it tore Black families apart. In one of the most innovative routines on the album, he created a character he called the "bicentennial n***er," a two-hundred-year-old man in obvious distress who guffawed while recounting the horrors he'd endured.

> They split us all up. Took my mom over that way, took my wife that way, took my kids over yonder. . . . I don't know where my own mama is now.

It was my father's critique of the false narrative that enslaved people were happy.

We pulled into a long driveway, and the screen door to a large ranch house banged. Mama waved and smiled from the stoop.

"Elizabeth!" she sang out. The last time I'd seen Mama, she called me the n-word and made me feel like I wasn't part of the family. Now, she seemed excited to see me. Bobby put the car in park, and I opened the door and ran into her arms. If she wanted to treat me like her favorite great-grandchild, it was okay by me.

"Baby," Mama said, and squeezed me tight. "Get inside," she said, "your daddy's still at work."

Like Parthenia Street, the house in Georgia was filled with people. Mama and several other family members were visiting from Peoria to make it feel like home. Stylishly dressed people were chatting at the dining room table and sprawled across a black leather couch. Mercy, my father's housekeeper from Los Angeles, was in the kitchen, flipping fish in a big cast-iron pan. There were two dead fish with their heads cut off on the counter next to the sink, waiting to be seasoned and fried. Blood and fish guts were smeared on the kitchen cabinets. Mama pointed it out to Mercy, who washed away the guts. The sight of the dead fish turned my stomach.

Aunt Mexcine, Mama's daughter, was sitting at the dining table organizing a blue-and-white tackle box. She gave me a big hug.

"How's your momma?" she asked.

"Good. She said 'Hi,'" I said.

"Aww," she said. "You know the best people are always named Maxine," she said, joking about how they both had the same name, though they spelled it differently.

I hugged her and scanned the couches for familiar faces.

"They're movie people," she said, which explained why I didn't know anyone.

A skinny white lady I did recognize snapped pictures of me with her Polaroid. It was Lucy Saroyan, my dad's latest girlfriend, who had a small role in the film. She always carried her leather-cased camera and let me take pictures with it.

I was shaking a Polaroid of Aunt Mexcine when my father came in, still wearing his costume from the movie: vintage Levis, a white

T-shirt, short-cropped hair, and his face cleanly shaven. I gasped. He looked so different. I'd never seen him without a mustache.

"Dizzy Liz!" he said. I ran to him and rubbed his face with both of my hands. He swept me up in a hug. Next to him was a very pretty Black lady, also dressed in a costume from the fifties. She smiled widely, like she was overjoyed to see me.

"Pam," my dad said to her, "this is my baby, Elizabeth."

"Nice to meet you, Elizabeth," she said, and shook my hand. "I bet everybody tells you that you look just like your daddy."

I nodded my head because they did.

"Don't she, though?" Mama said with a smile, which made me feel warm all over.

"This is Pam Grier," my dad said, with his arm wrapped around her. Pam was a famous actress best known for her starring role in the seventies blaxploitation film *Foxy Brown*. I had never seen Mama hug a stranger before, but she opened her arms and embraced Pam.

The movie set was a magical time machine that sent us all back to mid-century America—the cars were old and the clothes were too. All the actors in the movie looked like they came from the fifties. The set designers made a dirt road look like a racetrack. There were trucks and lights and trailers. All in, there were about a hundred people, mostly Black, working on the movie, including the director, a man with light-brown skin and bright-green eyes, who let me sit in his director's chair.

My first day on set, my father gave me an Instamatic camera, and he asked various members of the crew to take our picture—me sitting on his lap, me leaning over him while he sat in his chair reading his script, and us doing funny poses on the road. It was hot and dry and dusty and there were a lot of bugs, but it didn't matter because being on the set with my dad made it the best day of my entire life.

The second day on set, I said, "hi" to everyone, and everyone knew my name. One of the camera assistants let me snap the clapperboard and pretend I worked on the movie. I sat in a director's chair with Richard Pryor stitched across the back and watched them film.

I had paid attention to everything on my first day and knew how important it was to sit perfectly still while the camera rolled.

Right before lunch, the director called, "Action!"

The scene they were filming was all the way across the dirt road. It was too far away to hear anything the actors said. My stomach rumbled with hunger. The sun just kept getting hotter and hotter. I wore the lightest clothes I had, but I was still sweating. That's when a bee started buzzing around my head. It landed on the wooden arm of the chair.

"Ahhhh," I screamed and hopped up.

"Cut," yelled the director. I'd ruined the shot. My face heated up, and I slunk underneath my chair to hide.

"Baby," my father said, pulling me up, "it happens to everyone." He held me and let me cry until I was all cried out.

The movie broke for lunch and we all sat at picnic tables and had fried chicken and greens together. After lunch, the crew went back to filming, but Bobby said it was time for me to go back to the house. I left before I could even say goodbye.

I spent the whole next day with Mama. She and Aunt Mexcine stayed in a house in Canaan, the Black part of town. I'd never been in a neighborhood with only Black people. My mom and dad both lived in neighborhoods with mostly white people, and I'd never been to the family house in Peoria. In Canaan, every person I saw who drove a car, walked by, and fanned themselves for relief from the heat looked like me and Mama.

She invited me over to help cook, and afterward we were going to take food back to the ranch house to feed everyone.

"Baby, stand over by the table," she said, filling a cast-iron pan with heaping spoonfuls of shortening and putting lots of seasoning into the flour for the fish.

I went over to the table in the tiny kitchen but knocked the tub of Crisco on the floor.

Mama tsked. "Baby, get over by the sink."

My nose tickled, so I sneezed.

"Baby. You're underfoot. We need to get you outside."

Then she led me to a patch of grass in front of the house and said, "Stay here and don't go anywhere."

Out front in Mama's yard, I played with the grass, studied ants, and searched for a four-leaf clover until a police car turned the corner onto our block. The officer was white and leaned his head out of the black-and-white cruiser like he was looking for something. He drove more slowly than I ever saw anyone drive a car before. My body shivered when I realized I was the only person standing out on the street.

Every once in a while, I heard my dad and Uncle Dickie and even Mama talk about the police. They laughed when they shared their stories, but it sounded like the cops were the bad guys.

That made sense because in my favorite old movies, the cops were the bad guys too. My second-best impression, after Mae West, was my impression of James Cagney, who played a gangster fighting with the police: "You dirty rat! You killed my brother!"

Without thinking, I cupped my hands like a megaphone and shouted at the police officer.

"Heyyyy, copper!" It was the same voice I used for my James Cagney impression.

Before I even finished yelling, Mama, who walked slowly and complained about aches and pains in her knees and feet, popped out of nowhere. She scooped me up in her arms and ran as fast as she could, holding me tight, past her house, past the neighbor's backyard, and into the backyard of a neighbor two doors away. She crouched us down by the cellar doors and ducked behind a bush out of view.

"Shhh," she said, over and over again. She panted. I panted too, even though my feet never touched the ground.

We stayed like that, me on Mama's lap, her large breasts pressed against my back, her arms wrapped around me, her voice, which was usually loud, a whisper in my ear. She spoke fast but her words were clear.

"Why'd you do it, baby? You can't do that! Didn't nobody teach you how to be with the police?" Nobody had. Not my Jewish mother or my Black father.

How did Mama know what to do? I'd never seen her scared of anyone. What happened to make her so afraid of the police?

Years later I learned that she'd had several run-ins with the cops, which was understandable given the family business. But she had also been arrested for protecting her son Buck, my grandfather, when he was a little boy. In the late 1920s, he walked into a local candy shop in Decatur, Illinois, and the white lady who owned the place called him the n-word and slapped him across the face for walking into a white-only store. At a time when Black women were expected to bow their heads to white women, Mama beat up the woman and got arrested for it. Mama may have used her fists with her own family and even called them the n-word, but she refused to tolerate a white woman doing it.

As I hid with Mama in the bushes, I didn't know the story of how she'd risked everything for her family, but I felt her courage as I rested against her chest.

"Promise, promise, you'll never do that again," she said, more tenderly than I'd ever heard her speak before.

"I promise," I said, and I meant it.

It was the closest I ever felt to Mama.

Whenever my father wasn't on set in Georgia, he was fishing. He stocked the pond in front of the rental house with catfish and bragged about it to everyone. My favorite thing to do was to spend time with him by the water because I figured out early on, if you really wanted to be a Pryor, you needed to learn how to fish.

Even in Los Angeles, when Mama and Aunt Mexcine came to

town, they made sure to cook my dad fresh fish they had caught and prepared themselves.

"We're going to Paris," Mama said one morning at the Parthenia house.

Then she and Aunt Mexcine put on blue jeans and rubber boots, and packed up my dad's orange-and-white Ford Bronco with a picnic lunch, rods, a tackle box, and a few Styrofoam containers stuffed with nightcrawlers. When they got back, the truck stank of dead fish and worms and earth. Water sloshed around in the grooves of the truck bed. Then Mama gutted and cleaned the fish and deep-fried every morsel she and Aunt Mexcine caught.

"You drove all the way to France?" I asked, biting into a piece of flaky, deep-fried whitefish that tasted clean and crunchy.

Mama looked at me like I was speaking a different language.

"You said you were going to Paris," I clarified. My dad shook his head but had a huge grin on his face.

"No. Perris Lake. It's two hours away," he said, gently pulling on my ponytail.

I loved being one of the crowd.

When we were in Georgia, he sat for hours in his orange, green, and yellow lawn chair smoking cigarettes and fishing. Insects zipped and buzzed above the pond, and I danced around him while he consulted me about every choice he made.

"Dizzy," he said, "what you think about a minnow?" He opened up his stinky tackle box and hunted around for a little metal fish. After considering all kinds of bait, he settled on a nightcrawler, jabbed the worm onto the hook, and cast out his reel.

Something tugged the red and white ball under the murky pond.

"Liz," he whispered loudly to get my attention, "check out the bobbin."

"You got a bite!" I said, following his lead and whispering back.

He yanked up on the rod with all his strength to hook the fish.

"The motherfucker's putting up a fight!" he shouted, and leaned back even harder. "Grab the bucket!"

As soon as I placed a tin pail at his feet, he plucked a fat whiskered catfish out of the water, unhooked it carefully, and dropped it in the water-filled bucket.

When he finally decided it was time for me to learn how to fish, I couldn't wait to be initiated into the family tradition. He pulled up a lawn chair next to his and handed me a container of worms.

"Grab one," he said, pulling off the lid.

I loved that he wanted to share his favorite pastime with me, but touching worms was out of the question.

"No way," I flat-out refused.

His body grew taut.

"Pick it up." He wanted to pass down lessons he'd learned as a child and toughen me up. Lessons he'd learned the hard way, growing up in a brothel in segregated Peoria where being too soft could hurt your body and your pride.

I hid my hands behind my back.

"No, Daddy." I knew defying him in any way was likely to make him angry, but touching anything slimy or smelly ruined my thumb sucking experience.

He pulled my arm from behind my back, opened my fist, and dropped a live nightcrawler into my palm.

Big tears fell from my eyes as he guided my fingers to pick up the wriggling worm with my other hand and shove the worm's head over the hook.

Moments later, I reeled in a huge catfish, and he said, "Dizzy Liz!" in a voice filled with pride. When we showed Mama the fish, she was impressed too.

"That's the biggest one anyone pulled out of the water all day!" Mama said. "We gonna eat that one." Then she asked me, "You have fun?"

"Yes," I said, my voice still wavy with tears. "But next time can I try fishing with a minnow so I don't have to touch a worm?" Mama laughed, but when I turned around and looked at my father, his face was stony.

The night after I caught the fish, I smelled the aroma of something so delicious in the house my mouth watered. Mama had made catfish for every other meal—fried, broiled, baked, and smothered. I could barely stomach it. I followed the yummy new smell to the kitchen and found her stirring something at the stove.

"What's that?" I asked, peeking into the pot.

"Chicken and dumpling soup." Little balls of floury wet biscuits floated in a broth. It looked like thick matzo ball soup. My stomach growled.

The cast and crew were over hanging out with my dad when he caught me hovering around the stove.

"Dizzy!" he called out. Everyone in the room got quiet and turned to me. "What you want for dinner? Catfish or soup?"

I was so relieved he was warming up to me after the worm incident.

"Soup," I said. "Soup!" Even I could hear the desperation in my voice. He flashed me a wide, mischievous grin.

"Catfish it is!" he said grandly, as if he was giving me exactly what I asked for. Laughter rippled throughout the room. Sometimes there was no way to win with my dad, especially if he was going for a joke. In that moment, I felt the same powerlessness he must have felt as a little boy.

The day before I left Georgia, Mama and Aunt Mexcine invited me to follow them through the brambles behind my dad's house to go fishing at a bigger lake for bass.

"I'm tired of those catfish," Mama said. A wave of joy swept over me. Not just because Mama was inviting me to be with her, but for a chance to not eat catfish, I would have followed her anywhere.

As my great-grandmother and great-aunty hiked through the woods, I chased after them, dodging dragonflies and swatting away mosquitos, shaking my head like a wet dog. After a while, they found a small spot to set up on the shore and plopped down on the ground to prepare their bamboo rods. Mama passed me a rod with a live minnow already dangling from the hook. My gratitude knew no bounds.

After a few minutes, Mama said, "You come from a great people." She wasn't looking at me, she was keeping her eye on the bobbin.

I thought Mama was talking about my grandfather Buck, who died when I was a baby. I'd never even seen a photograph of him and my dad hardly ever brought him up. I couldn't wait to hear her stories.

But then Mama said, "The Jews are a great people." *The Jews are a people?* I had no idea. My mom and I spent most Jewish holidays sitting on the couch watching reruns of *I Love Lucy*, eating matzo meal latkes and drinking glasses of chocolate milk with giant globs of Hershey syrup on the bottom.

Mama's rod squealed as she reeled it in.

She turned to me as she baited her hook.

"The Jews are a great people," she said again. "But you do know they killed Jesus."

Twelve

"You Trying to Kill Me?"

1978–1979

Hundreds of people—the men in nice suits and the women in black dresses with fancy hats—sat on wooden pews that stretched from one side of a huge church all the way to the other. I was eleven years old, and it was the biggest church I'd ever seen, even bigger than the ones on Sunday morning television. Sad, beautiful music rang out over the loudspeakers as a choir of men and women in dark robes sang. There were big bouquets of flowers everywhere—on the podium and on the pews along the aisles—and a big polished casket on the stage. When the preacher stood up, everyone got quiet.

"Mama. Grandma Marie. Mrs. Bryant," he said, in a voice that was deep and holy. "She was a mother, a grandmother, and a great-grandmother to everyone she met. To Marie, there were no strangers. She looked to ev-er-y-body like they were her own." Salty tears stung my cheeks even though I had so many complicated feelings about Mama.

"Preach, Pastor!" a woman sitting behind us shouted as other people called out, "Amen."

It was the first Black funeral I'd ever been to and it was exactly like my father described in his act.

Black funerals are different than white funerals, right? I mean, you love your dearly departed as much as we do . . . but Black people let it hang out at the funeral.

So many people talked back to the preacher they almost drowned out my father, who moaned and sobbed throughout the whole service. Everyone around me openly expressed their sorrow, but none as loudly as he did.

I noticed how people were watching him, not just because he was a heartbroken man who had just lost the grandmother who raised him, but because he was Richard Pryor at the height of his fame.

He'd had his own sketch comedy show on NBC—*The Richard Pryor Show*—but told me he quit after four episodes because the network kept censoring his jokes. He'd starred in *California Suite*, a movie with Bill Cosby, Alan Alda, and Jane Fonda, superstars in their day; and he'd played the wizard in the film version of *The Wiz*.

Everywhere we went, people recognized him. Everyone wanted something from him too: his attention, a handshake, an autograph, money.

"Marie was a strong woman who knew how to handle her business," said the preacher.

A few people hummed. "Hmm, hmm." My dad sobbed. Aunt Mexcine and Aunt Dee took turns holding him in their arms until he got quiet.

"She was a woman who climbed to the top of the mountain just like Moses did to receive the Ten Commandments."

"Amen!" people shouted, holding their heads high, some raising one hand in the air, some raising two.

•　•　•

Earlier that morning, Rain, my father, and I landed in Peoria and the cold December air smacked us in the face as we stepped off the plane.

"It's freezing," I said.

"Don't worry," my dad said. "We won't be staying long."

On the way to Uncle Dickie and Aunt Betty's house, the limo drove us through my dad's childhood neighborhood. Everyone I saw walking on the streets was Black, just like the people in Canaan where Mama stayed in Georgia. He pointed out his old school, the community center, and the house on Washington Street where he grew up. When I looked over at him, he was choking back tears.

My father's childhood had not been easy. As we drove past his old haunts, it seemed like the painful memories came flooding back. His mom, Gertrude Thomas, worked as a prostitute in Mama's brothel. By the time he was five years old, he had been exposed to more sex and violence than most people see in a lifetime. Every day he watched as the women who made him breakfast and got him ready for school had sex with strange men. He also saw his father, Buck, beat his mother, kick her, slam her into walls, throw a chair at her face. Their violent relationship ended in divorce and an ugly custody battle when my father was ten. Mama and Buck used Gert's sex work against her and told the judge she was an adulterer. She couldn't defend herself with the truth or they all would have ended up in jail. Buck won custody, and my dad never stopped blaming himself. He remembered testifying in court that he didn't want to live with his mother because that's what Mama told him to do.

For the rest of his childhood, Mama was like a mother to him, and Buck was part of the deal. My dad was terrified of him.

My father was scary, boy. I'd piss on myself sometimes, he'd call my name.

A former boxer, Buck disciplined his son with his fists. At least once, he punched my father so hard in the chest he couldn't breathe. Onstage, he called Buck "an eleven o'clock n***er," because his dad insisted he get home by eleven.

The n-word had nuance when my father used it to describe Buck, closer to the way the men spoke it at Parthenia Street than the harsh version Mama used with me. Calling his dad an n-word was like rewriting history and taking control in a way he never could as a child.

It was still pretty early in the morning when we arrived at Uncle Dickie's house. Aunt Betty answered the front door, still wearing her nightgown and pink spongy curlers in her hair. She got right to work making us all a full breakfast: potatoes and eggs and toast and fried chicken and ham.

While he ate, my dad cried so hard I thought he might get something caught in his throat. I was still finishing up my eggs and toast when he reached into his pocket and handed me a piece of paper. I looked at it and recognized my own handwriting.

"Read it?" he asked, with a little smile on his face.

He had turned thirty-eight years old on December 1, about a week before Mama passed. For his birthday, I wrote him a poem. He must have liked it because he kept it with him and asked me to share it in front of everyone.

"Now?" I asked, my voice a little shaky.

"You think of a better time?" he said.

I shook my head no and started to read.

"Stand up, baby," he said, "so everybody can hear." I pushed my chair back so fast it made a loud scraping sound against the floor, and then I straightened out the folds of the wide-ruled notebook paper.

I cleared my throat. He was giving me the stage.

"My daddy is the famous Richard Pryor
Yes, how famous, how famous.
Of course I love him

And I will always be proud
But I really get sick of all the crowds.
I think he spends all his day long
Trying to help someone who started out wrong
He never seems happy though always so sad
Now they remember him that he's cool and he's bad
He's got the money to do what he wants
Some people want the money to do what they want
They hurt him, they slap him, inside out
But that doesn't matter 'cause he's Richard Pryor, no doubt
It doesn't matter it's the money that counts
This a story so sad and so true
He has trouble picking his friends
And that makes him blue
My daddy."

Nobody made a sound while I read, and they clapped as soon as I finished.

"Yay! Liz!" Rain said, and stood up and hugged me.

Uncle Dickie slapped his knee and laughed too loudly. He asked my dad for money all the time, and everyone in the family knew it. I thought of him when I wrote the poem.

"You know I love you, right?" my dad asked as he pulled me into his lap and kissed the top of my head.

"I do."

He took the poem, folded it up, and stuck it back into his pocket.

Two weeks after Mama's funeral, my father filmed *Richard Pryor: Live in Concert*, the first stand-up comedy movie ever made, and a genre he helped invent. He said the n-word more than forty times in front of a massive mixed-race crowd. Critics loved the movie. They called it "comedic gold," and said he could "use almost any topic, intrinsically funny or not, to introduce the brand of physical comedy that is especially his own." Audiences flocked to the theaters and the movie made fifteen million dollars, catapulting him to a whole new level of fame.

The more well known my father became, the more drugs and alcohol began to take over his life, and his drug-fueled behavior began to make the national news. One New Year's Eve, I was sleeping at the Parthenia Street house when he got into a drunken fight with Deboragh, his wife at the time. When she tried to drive away, he shot a gun at her car. Nobody was hurt, but in the morning, there were police and reporters crowded at the front gate. He was becoming as famous for his missteps as he was for his comedy.

In *Live in Concert*, he worked the negative publicity into his act.

I am really personally happy to see anybody come out and see me. Especially as much as I done fucked up this year.

As honest about his problems as he was onstage, when he was out of the spotlight he couldn't stop messing up. He always had a glass of Courvoisier in his hand and mounds of cocaine all around the house. Every night, Mercy put a wastepaper basket by the side of his bed so he wouldn't throw up on the floor.

He passed out all the time. Waking him was nearly impossible. Once, he brought Renee, Richard Jr., Rain, and me to D.C., and in the middle of the night, there was a hotel fire. Our rooms were on the fourteenth floor. I woke up to the sound of a blaring siren and red flashing lights. We banged and banged on my father's door, but there was no answer. We didn't know what to do, so we followed the hordes of people down the stairs, hoping to find him outside. But he was nowhere to be found. Rain and I panicked and couldn't stop crying, sure he would die in the fire. A few minutes later, he tapped me on the shoulder. "So that's how it is?" he said, arms crossed at his chest. "You just up and leave your old pops behind?"

Waking him during the day was even harder than waking him

at night. At home, none of his girlfriends wanted to do it. "Your father wants you to get him up," said a new girlfriend who'd only been around for a couple of weeks.

Rain and I tiptoed as quietly as we could into the living room where our father lay passed out on the couch. He snorted but he didn't wake up.

I pushed Rain to go first. "Daddy said he wanted you to wake him up," I said.

"No. He. Did. Not. Dizzy. Liz," Rain said, spitting out my name.

"Don't you call me that!" I hissed. He snorted again.

As much as I wanted to keep fighting, we still had a job to do. Rain and I crept up to him, tapped him on the shoulder, and ran backward as quickly as we could.

"Daddy," Rain whispered, and I pushed a little harder on his back. Then we ran away again.

Nothing.

Finally, Rain shook his arms, and, in a loud voice, I said, "Daddy." And jumped back.

He woke up swinging his arms like a boxer and almost punched me in the face. "What? What?" he yelled, still swinging. "Where am I? What time is it?"

After a while, he blinked and opened his eyes wide and smiled.

"Babies," he finally said. "Hey."

Then he stretched his long body over the whole length of the couch.

With a wink and a winning smile, he said. "Thanks, little mamas. Your daddy needed to get his ass up."

The times we had the most fun together were the days and nights when he wasn't drinking or doing drugs. One Saturday night when Mercy was off, I went over to the Parthenia house for leftover Chinese food and a movie night. It was our favorite thing to do together because we both loved the movies. His face lit up as he told me every detail about how the director crafted each shot and what the actors were like in real life. He knew all the ins and outs of the movie-making process, long before Google or IMDB put all the information at your fingertips.

"You get the food, and I'll pick a movie," he said, plopping down on his king-sized bed.

He had a giant TV in his bedroom so that's where we watched. I jumped up to get the food, but I was scared. The Parthenia house was huge with a big, open atrium in the middle. At night, it felt dark and haunted. The thought of going all the way across the house to the kitchen by myself was terrifying.

But I didn't want to risk disappointing him.

"Chopsticks or a fork?" I asked.

"Fork," he said.

I pushed my bare feet against the flat, rust-colored carpet and dashed to the kitchen. When I got there, I flicked on all the lights, slammed open the cabinets, and looked for dishes. I made up two plates of fried rice, moo goo gai pan, one ultra-thin flour pancake each, and drizzled them with plum sauce. I stuck two knives and two forks into my back pocket and, balancing the plates, walked as fast as I could back to his room.

"Dizzy. Here," he said, patting a spot he cleared for me on the bed. I put down the plates, straightened out the blankets, and sat down. Then I handed him his knife and fork and dug in.

About one second into his first bite, he spit out the food.

"You trying to kill me?" He looked at me in horror, like I was the Hillside Strangler. "It's still cold!"

I put my hand on my hip and laughed. "My mom and I always eat leftovers cold." It was true. We never reheated our food.

"Well, I don't," he said with a pout. "Go heat this up in a frying pan." He handed me his plate.

With my head hanging low, I took the plate and started to walk back to the kitchen.

"Wait!" he said, when I got to the door. "You know, your mother tried to kill me once too."

His voice was so joyful, I knew he was kidding.

"She never told you about the time she stabbed me?"

I shook my head no.

"Hmm, tell Macky to tell you about it."

"Okay." I rolled my eyes, relieved we had made up.

"Now go heat up my food. And get me a Pepsi."

The next day, I went home and asked my mom. Pink rose to her cheeks, and she looked out into the distance. She bit into a fresh bulky roll and cream cheese squeezed through the space between her crooked front teeth.

Finally, she pointed a butter knife covered in cream cheese at me, and said, "I can't believe your father's still talking about that." Her voice sounded girlish and flirty.

It was true.

From then on, my dad brought up the stabbing story a lot. Each time he did, I'd run home and tell my mom just to see her blush and giggle. She always said the same exact thing.

"Your father," she said, with a private little smile on her face, and that's all she would say.

Thirteen

I Couldn't Stop Thinking About It

2012

After Ife came to my office and admitted how deeply she was affected by the n-word, I couldn't stop thinking about it. What made the word so powerful that hearing it caused indelible points of encounter for so many people?

For months I immersed myself in everything I could find about the word. Journalist Farai Chideya called it "the nuclear bomb" of racist slurs.

In his 2002 book *N***er*, Harvard legal scholar Randall Kennedy revealed he'd found that nearly every famous Black figure in American history had been called the n-word by a white person, especially when they tried to break barriers. At a 1947 baseball game, the crowd shouted at Jackie Robinson, the first African American major league baseball player: "We don't want you here, n***er." Malcolm X's white teacher discouraged him from becoming a lawyer: Be realistic, he said, "about being a n***er."

In his 2004 book, *The N-Word*, cultural critic Jabari Asim explained how the word represented deeply ingrained ideas about Black worthlessness—that African Americans were intellectually, biologically, immutably inferior to white people. The n-word was all about keeping Black people down, and it helped enforce a social contract that endorsed white supremacy.

Even the dictionary was complicit in the oppression. Until 1998, Merriam-Webster's defined "n***er" as "a black person," as if the slur and the person were the same thing. It wasn't until a Black activist from Michigan named Delphine Abraham and the NAACP publicly denounced Webster's that they changed the definition to "an insulting and contemptuous term for a Black person."

How could I have taught slave narratives, novels, movies, and history books that quoted it without educating my students about the word itself?

The more I learned, the more I realized how layered and controversial the word was, even among Black people. In Chris Rock's 1996 HBO special, he did a whole routine about how there was a difference between Black people and the people he called "n***ers." According to Rock, n-words loved being ignorant, stole from their friends, and pulled out guns at the movies. The joke was edgy, but it relied on racist stereotypes and got a laugh by using the n-word as a slur.

As I tried to consolidate all the information into a lesson plan, I couldn't ignore two names that were always at the center of any conversation about the n-word: Mark Twain and Richard Pryor. They were the two most celebrated humorists of their respective generations, and both used the n-word to illuminate deeper truths about racism.

Twain was a satirist whose 1884 novel *The Adventures of Huckleberry Finn* condemned slavery, but his repeated use of the n-word made teaching the book a hot-button issue. My father was one of the first Black comedians to embrace the n-word in his comedy, taking a racist slur, reclaiming it, and setting in motion a revolution in Black self-expression.

I wasn't ready to tell the students I was Richard Pryor's daughter, but there was no way to talk about the enduring legacy of the word without touching on his work.

When the new semester started, I was armed and ready with a whole new plan. We would devote an entire week to studying the n-word. My hope was that talking about the word and all of its ugliness would defuse its power in the classroom so when we encountered it in our history books or film, everyone would feel safe and prepared.

We started with *Huck Finn*. The novel follows Huck, a teenager on the run from his abusive father, and Jim, an enslaved man running to freedom. I knew the book would be hard to stomach—the n-word appears more than two hundred times—but I wanted to use it to spark discussion.

"The constant repetition of the word was distracting," said Shayla, an African American junior who always chose her words carefully. "I couldn't absorb anything else."

She echoed the concerns of Black parents and educators who had fought to have *Huck Finn* removed from public schools since the fifties, largely because of the word. At the time, it was still one of the most assigned books in American high schools.

"What would you say if I told you there was a version of the book without the n-word?" I asked, referring to a 2011 edition that replaced the n-word with the word "slave." "Would that fix the problem?"

"That's ridiculous!" May scoffed. She was a tiny badass with elaborate tattoos winding up each of her delicate pale arms. "Cutting the word out of the book just sanitizes history."

A handful of students cautiously nodded.

"Why do we have to read it at all?" asked Shayla. Her voice had an edge.

"The book is complicated, but I think there's value in it," I said. "Twain used Huck and Jim's story to show the faulty reasoning behind slavery and the inhumanity of it. But relying on nineteenth-century dialect, especially the n-word, establishes a racial power dynamic. White person on top. Black person on the bottom."

I flipped off the lights and pulled up a 1975 *Saturday Night Live* clip starring Chevy Chase and Richard Pryor. It perfectly illustrated the power dynamic we were talking about, but I didn't mention that one of the performers was my father.

In the sketch, he plays a man interviewing for a job with Chase, who uses word association to vet candidates. It starts off innocently enough. "Dog," Chase says. "Tree," my dad answers. But Chase quickly progresses into using increasingly offensive terms. "Negro?" he asks. "Whitey," my dad answers, meeting Chase's increasing aggression head on.

Chevy Chase: Colored?
Richard Pryor: Redneck!
Chevy Chase: JUNGLE BUNNY!
Richard Pryor: HONKY!
Chevy Chase: SPADE!
Richard Pryor: HONKY! HONKY!
Chevy Chase: N***ER!
Richard Pryor: DEAD HONKY!

As soon as my dad says, "dead honky," Chase backs down and instantly hires the applicant, making him the highest paid janitor in America. The provocative humor was daring for 1975. It exposed the racial tension churning just under the surface of any interracial encounter and made a bold statement: It's racist when white people say the n-word, and Black people aren't going to let them get away with it.

Throughout the three-minute sketch, the studio audience howled, but hearing my dad called the n-word made me uncomfortable. When I looked around, everyone in my classroom was laughing too. But not Shayla.

She didn't come to class for the rest of the week. Maybe she had the flu or maybe she needed a few personal days. But a little voice told me she didn't show up precisely because we were talking about the n-word.

The next week, Shayla came to my office hours. She took a seat across from me on the other side of the desk. Before she started talking, she tucked her hair—thick twists that fell just below her shoulders—into a black scrunchie at the top of her head.

"Last week," she said, her beautiful brown face tight and anxious, "I skipped a few days of class."

"I know. We missed you."

She took a deep breath and looked me in the eyes.

"I couldn't talk about the word anymore. I couldn't. I was getting angry and wanted to walk out."

I'd considered pulling Shayla and my other Black students aside before we talked about the n-word in class to have a conversation about how that might go. But in the end, I wasn't really sure what to say, and I didn't want anyone to feel singled out.

"Was there something I might have done to make you feel more comfortable?" I asked her.

She let out an awkward little laugh. "Honestly? No. I know the skit was saying it wasn't okay to say the word, but it was really hard to hear white students laugh at a Black person getting called the n-word."

It was jarring for me to hear too, but I thought that was because it was my father.

"My Black friends and I say the word to each other all the time, but it's different. I couldn't talk about the n-word with white students. I didn't want them to ask why they can't say it, and we can. It's too much. I didn't feel safe."

My stomach dropped.

I'd missed the big picture. Not everyone was going to feel safe in the same way. My Black students could not put the word behind them just by talking about it in college. There were too many layers of painful history.

For Shayla, seeing the word over and over again in *Huck Finn* and hearing it out loud in the *SNL* sketch re-created a racially charged power dynamic with her white classmates. By assigning those works in a mixed-race classroom and not acknowledging the tension, I'd inadvertently manufactured a point of encounter with the n-word. Even a thoughtfully constructed educational discussion could trigger anger and fear and shut people down.

The n-word wasn't simply a relic of the past. If you were Black and living in the United States, it had the power to terrorize you wherever you went.

Interlude Five

I went to jail for income tax evasion. I didn't know a motherfucking thing about no taxes. I told the judge, said, "Your honor, I forgot." He said, "You'll remember next year, n***er."

Richard Pryor,

. . . Is It Something I Said?,

1975

In the fall of 1901, Theodore Roosevelt invited Booker T. Washington, a former slave who was now his advisor on race relations, to dinner. Washington was the first Black person to dine as a guest of the president at the White House.

The backlash was swift and scathing. Only five years after the U.S. Supreme Court rubber-stamped Jim Crow segregation across the country in *Plessy v. Ferguson,* the public was outraged that an American president had shared a meal with a Black person—even someone as accomplished as Washington—in the heart of the nation's capital.

Several politicians capitalized on the anti-Black sentiment. Senator James Vardaman from Mississippi, one of the president's loudest and harshest critics, used racist language as a weapon. "Roosevelt takes this n***er bastard into his home, introduces him to his family, and entertains him on terms of absolute social equality."

At a moment when sharecroppers and tenant farmers in the South—Black and white—found themselves in relentless debt, Vardaman incited a new kind of Southern white nationalism, pitting white workers against Black ones. He vowed that white people, even those with nothing, would always be superior to Black people.

Poor white farmers in the South flocked to him. They showed up at his rallies decked out with red ties around their necks and proudly called themselves a name that had long been used to demean them: "rednecks."

Senator "Pitchfork Ben" Tillman from South Carolina harnessed the redneck ideology and whipped up anti-Black rage. "Entertaining the n***er will necessitate our killing a thousand n***ers in the South before they will learn their place again."

The violence was unrelenting. From the 1880s until the 1960s, more than forty-four hundred Black men, women, and children were lynched in the United States.

Fourteen

"Nobody Will Ever Love You"

1979

One morning, not long after Mama died, I woke up to the sound of trucks backing up, men shouting and stomping through the house, and the whir of an electric drill. Barbara Walters, a famous TV journalist, was coming to the Parthenia house with her crew to interview my dad. I was the only one of his children with him at the time.

All morning, a cameraman followed us around. My father and I held hands and showed Walters the new tennis court where a private coach gave me lessons, and the pool house where my father threw me two giant birthday parties, including the most recent one for my twelfth birthday with ponies and a skywriter.

As we walked by his miniature horse Ginger, I caught a whiff of my dad's breath and thought, underneath the cinnamon scent of Dentyne, I smelled Courvoisier. I gripped his hand tightly, hoping I was wrong.

Inside, the crew made the living room look like a set. Tall lamps bathed the white couches in warm light, thick electrical cables and construction paper were laid out on the floor, and huge pieces of black felt blocked the sunlight from coming through the windows. For the whole interview, I got to sit next to the camera and watch.

Walters smiled at my dad and touched his knee flirtatiously. Everything about her seemed girlish and bubbly, the way so many women acted around him, like every word out of his mouth was funny. She had stiff, blond hair and pinkish skin. She wore a silky pink blouse and pink lipstick and she smelled like pink powdery flowers.

My dad was flirting with Barbara Walters too. But his voice swung between his real playful voice and his fake playful voice, an SOS signal telling you to run away as fast as you could. I was getting a little better at telling the difference. The real playful voice was easier to recognize. When I was nine, he co-hosted the Oscars and took me as his date. While he worked onstage, Muhammad Ali looked after me. During a commercial break, my dad found me backstage, laughing and sitting on Muhammad Ali's lap. My dad made a mad face and pretended to be jealous. He held up his fist and said, in the real playful voice, "You better watch out, Champ." I couldn't stop giggling.

After Mama died, though, he started speaking in the fake playful voice more and more. It was harder to tell if he was serious or kidding, but he made a snarly sound when he spoke that usually gave him away.

As they talked, Walters flitted around him like a bird until she came to a question that made her nervous. My dad's body got stiffer the longer it took her to spit it out.

"When you're onstage," she said, "you talk about . . ." She swallowed like she needed a glass of water. "See, it's hard for me to say." She touched his knee again and smiled, but my dad's body was pulled taut, like a slingshot.

She said, "See, I was going to say you talk about n***ers." She said the actual word and stopped herself. "You can say it. But I can't say it."

"You just said it," he said, with the fake-playful voice. The bad one.

"Yah, but I feel so uncomfortable."

"You said it very good," he said, almost singing. "It's not the first time you said it."

He snickered. So did a few people in the crew, but not me. I knew he wasn't happy that a pretty-pink lady said that word. When his friends said the n-word sitting around the pine table, he acted like he didn't mind at all. Was it different now because she was white and a woman?

At the time, the phrase "the n-word" hadn't been invented yet. People either said the actual word or they didn't. I'd watched *Roots*, a 1977 TV miniseries based on Alex Haley's bestselling book about slavery. In the show, white people called the main character, Kunta Kinte, the n-word. I understood the series used the word to make a point about how horrible slavery had been.

Hearing the word on television made me uncomfortable, like seeing a tiny spider on the wall. I was conscious of it, but it felt far away enough not to be threatening.

When Barbara Walters said the word and my dad called her out for it, it felt like a spider dropping from the ceiling onto my neck.

During the hour-long interview, my dad got kinder, and they didn't talk explicitly about race anymore. Perhaps it dawned on him what a career-defining moment this interview could be. Walters usually interviewed presidents and only the most famous movie stars. Whatever the reason, he started to reveal very intimate details about his childhood. He said Mama raised him and he loved her, but it was also hard for him as a little boy to see his aunties have sex at home with strange men. He was telling the world the painful truth behind some of his most outrageous comedy.

His voice grew quiet, like it always did when he got serious.

"It messed me up sexually for a minute," he said. "'Cause I'm afraid sexually."

"Who believed in you?" she asked, her voice sincere. "Who cared about you?"

He looked her in the eyes and answered. "Richard Franklin Lennox Thomas Pryor the Third. And magic dust." The journalist in Walters looked thrilled she had gotten the scoop; the woman in her looked devastated for my dad.

After a while, she asked him about his love life.

"I've only been in love once," he said. "With Deboragh." She was the only Black woman my father had had a serious relationship with since I was born. Even though they were only married for a year, and Deboragh divorced him after he shot at her car, they were always close. Young and pretty, with dark-brown skin she kept moist with Vaseline, Deboragh also had a way of teasing my dad that lifted him out of his foul moods.

That didn't stop me from wanting to yell *Cut!* so my mom didn't have to hear my father say he never loved her.

He went on to talk about his girlfriends and wives. I knew he'd been married four times. To Deboragh, to my mom, to Rain's mom, and to Richard Jr.'s mom. He was divorced from all of them, and none of the marriages had lasted very long.

"How many times have you been married?" Walters asked.

"Three," he answered.

A little smile broke through my lips. He'd been married so many times, he got the number wrong.

At the end of the interview, Walters asked him about drugs. It wasn't a secret that he used them a lot. He admitted it all the time in his comedy and had been arrested for his erratic behavior several times.

She asked if he still did them.

"I love drugs," he said, "I do, I really do. But I can't do 'em a lot because it messes my life up."

I thought I knew exactly what he meant. More than once, when he was high on drugs, he'd destroyed the kitchen by throwing every single item from the drawers and cabinets, every single plate, pot, pan, and drinking glass, onto the floor.

•   •   •

After Walters left and the crew finished packing up their gear, my dad walked back and forth through the house as if he were possessed. He mumbled to himself and paced from one room to another and back to the living room. When he passed me, he acted like he didn't see me.

"That was bad!" he said to himself. "I said too much! Why did I talk about the drugs? Why did I talk about them?"

In the seventies, people didn't go on television and talk about their drug habits. Especially not ambitious Black men. At that moment, he was the most famous Black comedian of all time, maybe even the most famous comedian. If a producer or movie studio or public opinion turned against him, he could lose everything.

I had never seen him so agitated. Afraid to leave him alone and afraid to be alone with him, I stood in the living room, hoping he would stop moving while I tried to figure out what to do.

He kept pacing and mumbling, walking from room to room.

"I fucked up," he said. "I fucked up! I said too fucking much."

When he walked through the living room again, I tried to lighten the mood like Deboragh would, making a joke about a silly mistake.

"Daddy," I said. "You said it wrong." He looked at me for the first time since the interview ended and finally stopped moving. I pushed ahead. "About how many times you were married."

He said nothing.

"You said you were only married three times, but you were married four times."

It was late in the day, and the living room was getting dark. The only light was the glow from a big, round, saltwater fish tank with lionfish and clownfish and small sharks that stuck out from a set of cabinets like the Pop-o-Matic in the board game Trouble.

"Talk to your mother," my dad said. He wasn't smiling.

I was sure he hadn't heard me, so I tried again. "No," I said. "I mean, you said you were only married three times, but you meant to say four."

He paused and looked at me.

"I was never married to your mother," he said, baring his teeth like a dog. "Ask her about it. She's always playing games." And then he walked away.

Part of me wanted to believe he was just being cruel, but another part knew he was telling the truth.

Had my mother lied to me? Had my whole life been a lie?

My mom told me they were divorced. When I asked her how old I was when it happened, she said six months. She told everyone she was Richard Pryor's ex-wife. She called herself Maxine Pryor. It was the name she had on her checks and her stationery. All this time was she just playing games?

I dropped down on the couch and broke into tears. My father came back and sat down next to me. He gently pulled my hands away from my face and used the bottom of his silk shirt to dry my eyes. Looking at me, he gave me a little smile, wrapped me up in a big hug, and whispered in my ear.

"Nobody will ever love you," he said. "Do you hear me? No one. Will ever. Love you."

I felt my body split down the middle on the inside from a point below my belly button all the way up to my throat.

It took me forty years to realize he was talking about himself.

Fifteen

"You're Exactly Like Him"

1979

"You're a liar!" I roared at my mom as I stormed into the family room the morning after the Barbara Walters interview.

"What happened? What did your father do?" Her eyebrows wrinkled as she dropped her Kent cigarette in an ashtray and sat up.

"He didn't do anything!" I yelled.

I wanted to confront her about the fact that they'd never been married, but I couldn't get the words out. My mouth felt dry and sticky.

She watched me carefully.

"Then what is it, Liz?" Her voice was a smoky whisper.

I took a deep breath and tried again.

"Daddy said you were never married to each other."

For a second, she looked so shocked and offended I started to think it had all been a lie. Then her face changed. She squinted her eyes, put her hands on her hips, and looked ready for a fight.

"Did your father tell you to say this to me?"

"No! I'm the one who's mad. Not him!" My chest felt hot and empty.

Chewing on her bottom lip, my mom took her time before she spoke again. Finally, her shoulders relaxed.

"He was already married. To Pat." Pat was Richard Jr.'s mother.

He was married to someone else when I was born?

She walked toward me, her eyes gentle and sorry. "Liz. I swear. I didn't know. He didn't tell me he had a son."

The news hurt even more than finding out my parents were never married. In the hours since the revelation, I had tried to convince myself my parents chose not to marry. Maybe they were hippies who thought marriage was for squares. My mom once told me he proposed to her with a cigar band, and I made myself believe things like diamond rings and wedding dresses and justices of the peace were for people who weren't as hip as they were.

My mom reached out to hug me. I pulled away. My mind swirled with questions, like little needles under my skin. Why was my brother a secret? Was I kept secret from Rain's mom too?

I wasn't sure I wanted to hear the answers.

"I thought we were best friends!" I shouted.

"We are," my mom said. "Liz. You know I love you more than anything in the world." She reached for me again, but I backed up.

"You said we tell each other everything. You said not telling each other something is the same as a lie!" My voice echoed against the bare white walls even though the family room was small.

"I was waiting for you to be old enough to understand."

She bit her lip and gripped her arms tightly.

I knew she was telling the truth, but I felt so betrayed, I couldn't forgive her. A hot teardrop landed on my cheek.

"Daddy said you like to play games." And not the kinds of games I knew she loved: backgammon and gin rummy at the little wooden table in the kitchen, crossword puzzles she finished with a pen. He meant my mom was manipulative and dishonest.

Angry tears filled her eyes.

"He's the one who plays games," she said, and we locked eyes. Suddenly, I knew exactly what she meant. My dad did like to play games. He pretended to be nice when he was angry. He liked to pit one girlfriend against another. He didn't try to stop it when Rain and I got into arguments. Like the boxing matches he watched on TV, he liked seeing someone get knocked out.

My mom put her hand on top of mine.

"Lizzy," she said. "He's trying to turn you against me. He can't stand how close we are."

On a gut level, I knew there was some truth in that, but I wanted to be close to him so badly, I wasn't ready to face it. I wanted her to hurt. Mean words came tumbling out of my mouth even before I knew what they were going to be.

"You're a liar, and you don't know anything about him!" I screamed.

She stepped back to get a good look at me and her face changed from open and loving to determined and fierce. When my mom was a little girl and got upset, her mom punished her by locking her in dark closets and spanking her with the cord from an iron. Instead of making my mom behave the way my nana wanted, though, it made my mom into an even tougher fighter. I could see that now as her face turned hard like she was going into battle.

"Did he teach you to talk to me like that? Did he?"

She reached above my head and slammed the family room door against the wall. It bounced back and hit me on the arm. "Ow!" I said, even though it didn't hurt.

Pointing her finger in my face, she said, "You've got a cold, black heart, Elizabeth. If you loved me, you wouldn't let anyone talk to me the way you just spoke to me!"

I wanted to run across the room and smash her record collection. She's the one who lied to me! Now I was the one who didn't love her? I was supposed to apologize?

I cried so much the mucus in my nose and throat made it hard to breathe.

"Don't blame Daddy! You're the one who told everyone you were married! You're the one who said you got divorced!" She looked away. "You're the one who lied to me! That's the same as playing games!" I yelled right in her face so loudly my voice was hoarse.

She stood up straighter. Her body was shaking. "Oh, I get it. Once again, Miss Elizabeth Anne Pryor. Your father can do no mother-fucking wrong." She moved her head back and forth like a bully teasing a little kid at school. "You act like his shit don't stink."

Her eyes said, *Gotcha!* And she did. I never blamed him for anything.

Confused and frustrated, I lashed out.

"I hate you!" I screamed, bending my body forward as if I were pumping the words out of my stomach.

She cackled like she'd lost her mind. "You're exactly like him, Elizabeth." She walked toward me and stared into my face.

"I! Am!" I shouted.

The words hit my mom like a slap. She stumbled backward. Her face was lit by the sun as it streamed in through the sliding glass doors that opened to our backyard. Reflections from the swimming pool moved across her face, making patterns of waves on her blushing-red cheeks. The sun looked like a crown around her head. She looked beautiful, even though she was angrier than I'd ever seen her in my life.

Then her face turned ugly, and she put her hands on her hips.

"You're a n***er!" she said, like she meant it.

The fight floated out of my body like a ghost. She'd said terrible things before, but never that word. My legs felt rubbery. How was I still standing up?

Mommy. Please. Say you're sorry right now.

But my mom was still in the fight.

Even as I waited for an apology, the word formed a hard pebble in my heart that would stay with me forever. The moment she said it, I realized no matter how much she loved me, she was capable of breaking my heart. She'd taken the word my father spent his career reclaiming and turned it against me in a way only a white person could.

Sixteen

"The Etymology of N***er"

2013

N***er. N***er. N***er. N***er. As I wrote my first article for an academic journal, I found myself typing the n-word over and over again, all six letters, no asterisks, not even quotation marks to soften the blow.

Since I started teaching the n-word, I'd primarily focused on its painful history and how white people used it as a slur. The conversation with Shayla made me question that approach. She was too uncomfortable to discuss the n-word in front of white students, but had no problem saying it freely with her Black friends.

Of course, I knew the word took on a different meaning when one Black person said it to another as a way to build solidarity, acknowledging each other as a sister or brother. It was how my father used it in his comedy, hip-hop artists used it in music, and contemporary Black poets used it in verse. But I'd never talked about that version in class. Even when I showed students a Richard Pryor clip, he wasn't the person who said the word.

Had I taken the Black usage for granted? For months, I dug

through old newspapers, journals, and slave narratives, tracing the word's journey from a Black perspective. In the decades before the Civil War, while white people used the word to mark African Americans as primitive, dangerous, and unworthy of citizenship, Black people as far back as the 1770s used the word as a subversive weapon in satire and defiance, like my father. The historical documents confirmed what my life had already taught me: The n-word was never one thing—it could be poison or antidote depending on who controlled the mic.

The evidence was everywhere. Not only in racist newspaper editorials and farmer's almanacs, but also in oral histories and writings by African Americans themselves. Enslaved people sang a work song that described a laboring folk hero who defied the stereotype of Black ignorance and subservience. Here, they used the n-word to express pride in who they were, despite how white people degraded them by using the same word.

My name is Ran
I wuks in the sand,
*I'd rather be a n***er*
dan a po' white man.

Harriet Jacobs, a woman who escaped bondage, used the n-word in her 1861 memoir to show the bravery of another enslaved woman in the face of danger. Jacobs wrote in dialect: "If dey comes rummaging 'mong my tings, dey'll get one bressed sarssin from dis 'ere n***er."

Black people used the word to show they were strong and clever and resilient even though they were enslaved. They were people who could take some hard knocks but keep on standing. Language was a political weapon they used with skill and finesse.

As I pulled together my research, I realized I had an original take on the Black version of the word and I began to write an article. It was the version of the word my dad made famous, but artists and activists in the seventies and eighties were not the first to reclaim it. They had picked up on a protest tradition that was hundreds of years old and started during enslavement.

When I finished the article, I made the controversial decision to put the actual n-word right in the title. Inspired by the Black men and women I researched, I called it "The Etymology of N***er: Resistance, Language, and the Politics of Freedom in the Antebellum North."

I felt brave spelling the n-word out again and again, like I had finally made peace with the ghosts that told me because I was biracial and Jewish and raised in white neighborhoods, I was not an authentic-enough Black person to take on the word "n***er."

But typing those letters wasn't just an act of defiance—it was a way of using language to claim my Pryorness. My father had flung the word at American audiences like a grenade to expose its hypocrisy. I was placing it on the page as evidence, asking my readers to see it, study it, and reckon with it.

Did my father feel this empowered when he titled his album *That N***er's Crazy?*

For so long, white people had used the n-word to control the narrative, but as far back as I could find, Black people used it too, and took the narrative back.

Interlude Six

It wasn't Black back in those days because Black wasn't beautiful yet.

Richard Pryor,
"Craps" (After Hours),
1971

In the 1920's, a group of young and rebellious Black writers in New York City—Langston Hughes, Countee Cullen, Wallace Thurman, and Zora Neale Hurston—wanted to tell Black stories, for Black people, the good, the bad, and the horrid. They didn't care what white people (other than their wealthy patrons) or older African American intellectuals thought.

As Langston Hughes wrote, Black artists can "express our individual dark-skinned selves without fear or shame. If white people are pleased, we are glad. If they are not, it doesn't matter. We know we are beautiful. And ugly too."

Together this group was the literary heart of the Harlem Renaissance, a cultural explosion of modern Black fiction, poetry, theater, dance, music, and art that embraced African American themes. Their writing poked fun at the Black bourgeoisie and explored taboo subjects like sexual fluidity, gender norms, class hierarchies, and colorism.

They also said the n-word to each other and about each other, and did it with glee.

Embracing their highbrow status as esteemed authors, they dubbed themselves "the N***erati," a title that fused the n-word and "literati" to celebrate the authentic Black culture they inhabited. The foursome called Thurman's West 136th Street apartment "N***erati Manor." The name was a revolt against the elitist Harlem establishment that rejected anything that symbolized white racism.

Hurston is said to have coined the term around 1926. I am "Queen of the N***erati!" she joked, proudly calling herself a word that had been used as a slur against Black people for generations, unafraid to make it her own.

Seventeen

A Black Jewish Girl from the Valley

1979–1980

"Brillo head!" A short white Jewish kid shouted over "Hava Nagila" at my classmate's bat mitzvah.

"Dude, call her Pubes!" yelled his skinny, freckled friend.

I was the only Black girl at the party. *Were they talking about me?*

"Gail's got pubes on her head," they sang in unison. It took me a second to realize they weren't making fun of me, but they were mocking my friend Gail, a white Jewish girl with tight curly hair that framed her head like an afro. She was one of my friends from my new school, Westlake School for Girls, an exclusive prep school in Bel Air.

"Oh! My! God! Whatevs!" said Gail defiantly, like the Valley girl she was. Grabbing me by the hand, she pulled me off the dance floor and away from the party. As we walked into the synagogue bathroom, she held her head high like she was too good to care. But when I caught Gail's reflection in the mirror, she was crying.

"Everyone hates my hair," she said, as she used her fingers to pick out her tight curls.

"No way," I said, smoothing my freshly straightened ponytail and readjusting my tortoiseshell side combs. The truth was I didn't like my natural hair either. Gail was white, but we both had hair that was a very different texture than the most popular girls at Westlake had. Theirs was silky, straight, and fell below their shoulders. Ours was corkscrew curly with ringlets that kept their shape.

Gail was even more sensitive about her hair than I was. She was a mean girl who could make her friends break down in tears with a single, fluttery eye roll. But now her mascara was running down her pale cheeks because two boys called out how different her hair looked from everyone else's in front of the whole party.

I knew what it felt like to be different. Ever since I started Westlake, I was one of the only Black girls wherever I went—from the classroom to my gymnastic team to the fancy bar mitzvahs I went to almost every weekend. I was also the only Jewish kid who had no idea when to say prayers or when to stand up and sit down during the service.

"Those boys don't know what they're talking about," I said, trying to console her. "You're adorable and your hair is too."

"I hate it," she said through tears. "It's so short and nappy."

Why did she call it nappy? I'd only heard Mama use that word when she talked about hair that needed to be washed and combed. Passing Gail my lip balm, I looked at myself in the mirror and replayed what the boys said in my head. Were they trying to insult her by saying her hair looked like a Black person's hair? Were they saying Black hair was ugly and dirty?

After the bat mitzvah, we went back to Gail's house and stood around her kitchen island, gossiping about the party with her mother.

"So. Tell me everything," Mrs. Lowenthal said. "Did you like Tricia's outfit?" Tricia was the bat mitzvah girl.

"So cute," Gail said.

"Were a lot of boys there?" Mrs. Lowenthal asked. This was a standard question because Westlake was an all-girls school.

Gail started listing: "Eugene Smith, Marky Greenbaum, Brian Sacks . . ."

I interrupted. "Tell your mom what Brian said." Brian was one of the boys who'd made fun of Gail's hair.

At first, Gail glared at me, but then she rolled her eyes gently and sighed. "They said my hair was like Brillo and called it pubes."

"Brian Sacks? I play tennis with his mother. That's totally rude!" Mrs. Lowenthal said.

I nodded in agreement, but it felt like what the boys said was worse than rude. It felt like they were saying there was something wrong with being Black.

"As a Black person, I was very offended," I said. I'd never said, "as a Black person" before. In fact, I never said, "as a Jewish person" either. But it seemed like declaring I was Black was the only way I could get her to understand how awful the boys had been.

Gail's mom stared at me for a minute as if she was about to break some important news.

"You're not really Black," she said.

I blinked. Was she saying that because I had a white mother? Because my father was Richard Pryor? Because my friends were white, and I had light skin?

"I mean you're not like other Black people," she said just to clarify.

It sounded like she was trying to give me a compliment by putting other Black people down. The most upsetting part of Mrs. Lowenthal's claim was what it meant about me. If I wasn't really Black, why did my mother call me the n-word?

Westlake was a very competitive school to get into. I was the only girl from my elementary school who was accepted. I was also the only applicant who wasn't white. Angie, my best friend from sixth grade, stopped talking to me because I got in and she didn't. Her mother was so mad about it, she couldn't resist confronting my mom.

"Ran into Angie's mother today," my mom said as I sat on the couch organizing my binders for the first day of school. "She said, 'I'm sure it didn't hurt Elizabeth's chances with Westlake that she's Black.'"

Did Angie's mom think I wasn't smart enough to get in? Or because I was Black I got something I didn't deserve?

"Disgusting," I said, because I knew my mom wanted me to. But every day I went to Westlake, I wondered if I really belonged there.

Most of the girls at Westlake were white and had never met a person who had a white Jewish mother and a Black dad.

"So, you're half Jewish?" said Karen Edelstein as we did homework on the great lawn during a free period. It was a question I'd been asked many times before.

"Not half Jewish. All Jewish," I said, repeating what my mom told me to say whenever someone asked that question. "If your mom's Jewish, then you're all Jewish. There's no such thing as being half Jewish."

"But your dad's Richard Pryor," she said. "He's Black." Everybody at school knew who my father was. He appeared in three new films when I was in seventh grade: *Wholly Moses!*, *In God We Trust (or Gimme That Prime Time Religion)*, and *The Muppet Movie*, which almost all of my friends had seen. Being his daughter got me a lot of attention at Westlake, but it always took me by surprise when people brought it up.

"Yes, my dad's Black and my mom's white."

"So, you're mulatto?" I'd heard the word a few times before. The term came from slavery and referred to people of mixed African and European descent, and it was tinged with a violent history. In the nineteenth century, most children labeled "mulatto" had enslaved mothers who were sexually assaulted by white enslavers. I didn't know the history at the time, but there was something about the word that made me feel uncomfortable and dirty. Like maybe Karen was calling me a name, even if she didn't realize it.

Chewing on a No. 2 pencil, I tried to figure out how to answer. At the beginning of seventh grade, I made fast friends with the only other Black girl in my class. She lived in the most exclusive Black neighborhood in L.A. We bonded over roller skating and cute boys. She even set me up with a handsome Black neighbor who starred on a popular TV show, but she and I never actually talked about what it meant for us to be Black. By the end of the school year, we saw each other less. All of my best friends were girls who liked performing in plays and who lived closer to my house in the Valley. And all of them were white.

As Karen stared at me now, demanding an answer about whether I was mulatto or half Jewish or something else altogether, I made a snap decision.

"I'm mixed," I said, landing on the closest label I could find to express all the different parts of me without denying any of them. Even if I wasn't entirely sure if it fit.

My mom had a bunch of friends who, like her, were white women raising Black girls. Whenever they talked about their daughters, they called us "mixed." My sister Rain called herself "mixed" too. But the reason I liked the term most was because of Lisa Jones, a tall, beautiful, Black woman who was about ten years older than I was. Lisa once dated my dad and was now one of my mom's closest friends. Everything Lisa said was funny and kind. One time, when she opened her front door and saw my outfit, she let me know how much she liked it by saying, "You are try . . . ing, Miss Liz," waiting a full second between the "try" and the "ing."

Lisa was like a surrogate Black mom. She tried to teach my mother how to raise a Black child. Every few months, we drove south to Lisa's house in Leimert Park because she was the only person who my mother let straighten my hair. One day, I sat on a chair in the middle of her kitchen while she heated up a metal hot comb on the flames of the gas stove. The smell of my burning hair filled the house, and I was so excited about the transformation that I couldn't stop reaching up and touching the silky strands. Lisa kept swatting my hands away.

"You got that good hair, darling," she said, pulling the hot comb through a patch of soft curls.

My mom crossed her legs and frowned. "She doesn't get it from me," she said. "Mine is so thin and flat."

Lisa tsked. "Macky, you know you and Richard gave her that mixed hair."

I loved the way Lisa said "mixed." There was something playful about it. Like we all had an inside joke. It was also roomy and spacious enough to include both of my parents and all the different parts of me. It made me feel special instead of different.

Even so, when I told Karen I was mixed, I knew the math didn't quite add up.

My dad called me all Black. My mom called me all Jewish.

How can a person be all Black and all Jewish but also completely mixed?

A few weeks later, I jumped up and down in a ballroom as the DJ blasted New Wave music at Pamela Berman's bat mitzvah. Eight other seventh graders, all of them popular, danced in a circle with me. Casually, I tried to move as close as I could to Jeremy, a cute white boy who went to Harvard School for Boys, Westlake's "brother" school. Shaking my straightened hair all around, I danced the Pogo, hoping that if I sang as loud as I could, Jeremy would notice me.

I screamed the lyrics to The B-52's song "Dance This Mess Around."

He turned a dazzling smile my way, but when there was a short lull in the music, he started to wander off. I needed to do something to get his attention. "What school do you go to?" I asked, my palms sweaty. I already knew the answer.

"Harvard," he said, as a girl I recognized walked over. It was Angie, the girl from my elementary school who was mad I'd gotten into Westlake and she hadn't. My heart raced. Was she still mad at me? What if she embarrassed me in front of Jeremy? What if she told him I only got into Westlake because I was Black? She was tall and red-headed and confident. Jeremy was shorter than she was, and she threw her arm over his shoulder like they were best friends.

She surprised me by being friendly. "Hey! It's the KEAM team!" she said.

I giggled and Jeremy looked confused. "Kaia, Elizabeth, Angie, and Maria," I said. "We're the KEAM team. Best friends in elementary school."

"Which one are you?" he said.

"Liz," I said, and when he raised an eyebrow, I added, "E for Elizabeth."

He smiled and bumped his shoulder against mine.

When the music started up again, Angie made sure the three of us danced together. I couldn't believe my luck. We bopped up and down to Devo, Rick James, and Kool & The Gang. We took turns doing a "Soul Train" line in the middle of the dance floor. Jeremy grabbed my hand and we did the Robot together. Angie didn't look happy about that at all. There was a kernel of anger in her eye. It reminded me of the way my mom looked right before she called me the n-word. I never wanted to see that look again. All I wanted was to keep the magic moment going.

Suddenly, I was struck with a desperate feeling: I had to beat Angie to the punch.

My dad called himself the n-word and it made people laugh.

Without completely understanding what was about to come out of my mouth, I shouted over the music. "You guys should call me n***er. Or n*g."

As soon as I said it, I wished I could take it back, but it was too late.

Jeremy looked at me with fear in his eyes and dropped my hand. He shook his head no.

My heart sank. I wanted to dance and sing and jump up and down together again. But the n-word hung limply between us, like the deflated balloons that decorated the party.

"I want you to," I said, "I like it." But I did not want him to. I just wanted Angie to know I didn't think I was better than her. Yes, Jeremy had been holding my hand, and yes, I got into Westlake, and yes, I was Richard Pryor's daughter, but I was also different from everyone else at the party.

Jeremy refused to call me the n-word, but not Angie. She heard me say the word and burst out laughing. She loved the new nickname I gave myself.

"N***er!" she said over and over again as the three of us danced. She cracked up every time she said it. I laughed too, but I could feel the tears building up inside.

The next morning, I hated her for it. I also hated myself.

Eighteen

Something Horrible Happened

2014

Subject: Awful News. From: Wren Thompson.

Early one morning, I got an email from Wren, a white student of mine. The night before at a Smith College panel on free speech, a white alum said, "n***er." Wren's email included a link to the recording of the event, so I listened.

"Let's talk about the n-word," the alum said. "Let's talk about the growing lexicon of words that can only be known by their initials."

Like a preacher calling out to her congregation, she asked, "When I say, 'n-word,' what word do you all hear in your head?"

The audience responded immediately. "N***er," they said, repeating the actual slur.

"You all hear the word 'n***er' in your head," she said, repeating it too. "See, I said that. Nothing horrible happened."

The next day, the campus exploded. Students marched through the quad, held signs calling the alum a racist, and demanded a response from the administration. They were so angry at the president of the college (a white woman who moderated the panel) they chalked "Impeach!" on her driveway.

For weeks, the n-word was all anyone on campus talked about. A Black student called out four of her professors for saying the word in class. An older white student agreed with the alum and said everyone should "buck up." She blamed the uproar on "politically correct police" and accused them of blocking free speech. A Black classmate pushed back. She said the n-word was a way to police her. The faculty debated freedom of speech versus hate speech. The president admitted she was blindsided by the students' response. The conversations were passionate, but also academic and political. The idea that the personal impact of the word mattered wasn't getting through.

In response, Black faculty organized a campus event to discuss racism and Black resilience at Smith and invited me to give a presentation. It was the first time I'd ever spoken about the n-word in such a public forum.

The first draft of my speech was academic. It focused on my historical research about the Black version of the word. But as the campus uproar grew I realized this wasn't the right tone for the moment. If I really wanted to reach everyone and help them understand the devastating effects the word could have, I had to come clean and get personal.

On the day of the event, more than three hundred faculty and students crowded together in the packed auditorium. They vied for empty spots on the steps and stood in the back of the room three rows deep. Fewer than 5 percent of Smith students were Black, but looking out at the audience, I could see that Black faces made up at least half the crowd.

"I'm nervous," I said, and took a slow, deep breath.

"When my students and I started talking about the n-word in class, I thought the discussion would be formal and buttoned up. Technical. Instead, our conversations got raw. My students shared their personal experiences with the word, which I've come to call 'points of encounter.'"

The room was hot, and my voice was shaking.

"In honor of their openness, I'd like to share my own deeply personal points of encounter with the word.

"When Black people say it freely and with ease, it leaves me with a sense of longing for a part of the African American experience I do not share. When white people say it, it reminds me of a relationship to power I will never have."

I paused and took another breath.

"The word reminds me of how my white mother, in a fit of rage, called me the n-word when I was twelve years old."

A silent chill came over the room.

Then I added, "A year later, I told a group of white kids they could call me the n-word. One of them did. I feel ashamed telling you the story even now."

Until that moment, I had never told anyone about my friend Angie and the bat mitzvah.

An unexpected sense of relief washed over me. In the hours and days and weeks that followed, students and colleagues all over campus wanted to talk. They lined up after my speech, waited patiently during my office hours, and flooded my inbox with emails, wanting to share their own painful memories about the n-word because I had shared mine.

With each conversation, the shame started to lift. All those years ago, the word made me feel dirty and alone when all I ever wanted to do was fit in.

Now, the more vulnerable I was in front of an audience, and the more they embraced me, the more something inside me cracked open and began to heal.

It was the kind of truth telling my father had done onstage.

Sharing my stories changed the trajectory of my life. At Smith,

I became the go-to person to talk about the n-word, and a leading journal in American history accepted my article for publication.

Campus life changed too. The mood settled down. The administration grew more open to listening. The students felt empowered. And the next time a white professor said the n-word—and doubled down on his right to say it—half the students dropped his class in protest. Eventually he stepped down.

Speaking out against the n-word had the power to create change. What the students didn't know at the time was they were drawing on a legacy of protest that had been going on for almost a century.

Interlude Seven

In 1937, Margaret Mitchell won the Pulitzer Prize for *Gone with the Wind,* her epic novel about a resilient, spoiled Southern belle who struggles to survive the Civil War and its aftermath. According to the book, good Black people were happier when they were enslaved, the KKK were saviors, and free Black men were a threat to all white women.

The n-word appears in the book more than a hundred times.

When Hollywood producer David O. Selznick optioned the bestseller for a record sum, Black activists including the NAACP called the novel "propaganda for race hatred and bigotry." They organized a grassroots campaign to protest the demeaning portrayals of Black people in the film. They didn't want the movie to incite lynching like *The Birth of a Nation* had twenty years earlier. Selznick received so many angry letters, he opened a file he called "the Negro Problem."

After months of mounting pressure, Selznick toned down the

script's positive portrayal of the KKK, turned the novel's Black rapist into a white man, and cut the n-word from the white characters' dialogue. But he would not budge when it came to Black characters saying the n-word. In January 1939, as the movie went into production, the word still appeared in the script almost as many times as it had in the book.

When Selznick held auditions, Black actors were forced to repeat the n-word as they read for their roles. Unlike the empowering version of the word popular among young Harlem artists, Mitchell's Black characters used the word to berate other Black characters who wanted freedom. The Black press was outraged and influential film critic Earl J. Morris became the hero of the hour. For weeks, he wrote inflammatory editorials promising boycotts and picket lines. After an onslaught of negative publicity, Selznick finally backed down.

By the time *Gone with the Wind* was released in theaters, the n-word was completely scrubbed from the film.

Nineteen

"Richard Pryor Running Down the Street"

1980

Late one summer night when I had just finished seventh grade, I was lying on my bed, flirting with a boy on the phone. Anthony was from my old school, and he was Black. He had a crush on me and sometimes after school, when my mom was still at work, he came over to my house and we kissed for hours. His attention toward me was all-consuming and completely unlike that of the boys I'd met since I started Westlake. They were all white and they said the n-word around me like it was no big deal. On a bus to the beach, Randy mocked his best friend. "Dude," he said, "you look like Mick Jagger. You have n***er lips." He made it sound as if looking like a Black person was gross and had a defiant look in his eye, like he was inviting me to challenge him, but I didn't. That made me feel worse.

Anthony made me feel like a popular girl, as if everything about me—my hair, my skin, the shape of my lips—was beautiful.

"You're the prettiest girl I know," he said.

As I spun the phone cord around my wrist, a news flash on television caught my attention.

"Richard Pryor suffers serious burns at his Northridge home; rushed to area hospital. News at 11."

I rolled my eyes and sighed.

"What?" Anthony asked.

"Nothing," I said. "It's just so annoying how the news always lies about my dad." A few weeks earlier, rumors had swirled while he was filming *Stir Crazy*, his second buddy movie with Gene Wilder. The film made him the highest-paid Black actor in Hollywood and also the most gossiped about. The tabloids reported he'd had a heart attack or was on drugs. But my mom said it wasn't true.

Anthony chuckled and paused for a second.

"Is it okay if I ask you something?" he said.

"Yesssss," I said, stretching out the word playfully.

"Your dad's so funny," he said. "Is he funny at home too?" People asked me this question all the time, usually as soon as they found out I was Richard Pryor's daughter. I never knew how to answer because in real life he didn't crack jokes, or do funny voices, or act out routines like he did onstage. Admitting that to a stranger felt like I was selling out my dad. Sometimes we had fun—like when I was eleven and he let me drive his car on the freeway, me sitting on his lap and steering while he pushed the pedals—but it didn't seem as if that was the kind of story people who asked whether or not he was funny wanted to hear.

I couldn't ignore the question, though, because my father taught me to be warm to his fans. Once when a stranger yelled out of a car, "What up, Rich?" I told him I didn't like it. He looked at me seriously and said, "The only thing to worry about is when they stop."

"Last week," I told Anthony, "he had a big roller-skating party for Memorial Day and let me and Rain roller-skate inside the house."

"That's so cool," Anthony said, just as my mom barged into my room.

"Your father's been in an accident," she said.

I turned my head. My mom's hair was a mess. Her glasses were tilted on her face. She looked frantic.

"No," I said, trying to calm her down, "it's not true."

She wasn't listening. "Liz. Hang up and get dressed," she said, rushing out of my bedroom. "Daddy's hurt. We need to go."

As we raced to the hospital, my mom swerved in and out of traffic, which distracted me from worrying. For months, she had worn a black pirate patch over her eye because she had scratched her cornea with a wire wig brush. While she was recovering, I had to do everything around the house—make breakfast before school, make her coffee in the morning, cook us both dinner—and she couldn't drive. This was the first time she'd gotten behind the wheel of a car in months. To be safe, she took off the eye patch, but for the whole ride, she put her right hand over her eye and steered with her left hand while shouting orders at me.

"Check my blind spot," she said. "On the right! Behind me!"

By the time we got to the Sherman Oaks Burn Center, I was overwhelmed with anxiety. Questions flooded my brain.

"What happened to him? What's a burn center? Is he okay?"

"Honey," my mom said as she pulled over the white line, taking up two parking spots, "I just don't know."

From the moment we walked into the hospital waiting room, we were surrounded by friends and family—his ex-wife Deboragh; Aunt Dee; my sister's mom, Shelley; Lisa Jones; David Banks; Rashon, my dad's bodyguard; and his friend Prophet. Aunt Dee hugged me, and I started to shake and cry because everyone looked terrified. Their small, sad smiles said it all. He was really hurt.

An hour later, a handsome doctor with thick, dark hair walked into the waiting room.

"Mrs. Pryor?" he asked.

Five women stood up.

Aunt Dee walked over and shook his hand.

"Dick Grossman," he said kindly. "I'm Richard's doctor. The next few days are the most critical. The burns are serious. Over two-thirds of his body. Right now, we're most worried about infection, so we need to keep him isolated. It's going to be a long road."

I curled up in a chair in the waiting room and listened, half asleep. The doctor said the burns stretched all the way from his stomach to his chest and neck, and were second and third degree. My father was going to need several surgeries. He even burned off his ears. How could someone's skin catch on fire? And how could they survive? The more questions I asked, the more everyone whispered like it was a big secret. They kept calling it "the accident." All I really wanted to know was the one thing nobody would tell me: Was he going to live? I tucked myself against the back of the chair, pulled the neck of my T-shirt over my head to block out the fluorescent lights, and found the only comfort I knew, my thumb.

Each day, my mom and I went back to the hospital and spent hours there. Dr. Grossman put us in a private waiting room reserved for family and friends. People brought us food and came by to visit. News vans and reporters stood at the entrance of the hospital and shouted questions at us when we walked past. The reporters were loud, persistent, and confusing. I never knew if I was supposed to answer their questions or not.

"Are you his daughter?" "How's Richard doing?" "Is he talking?" "Was it the drugs?" "Was it cocaine?" "Is he gonna make it?"

"He's doing fine," Aunt Dee said. "The doctors are very happy. Thank God he's going to be okay."

She sounded confident, even though the news reports said he might die. I hadn't been able to see him yet, so I didn't know what to believe. I overheard Deboragh and Aunt Dee say he was in terrible shape and in pain.

One afternoon, I heard a sound like a wailing cat echoing throughout the halls of the hospital.

"What's that noise?" I asked my mom.

She looked at me so gently, I thought she was going to cry. "That's Daddy." There were no words that could comfort me at that point, but it didn't stop my mother from trying. "But don't worry," she said. "It's good for him. They're making him better. They have to put him in a jacuzzi to get off the dead skin so new skin can grow back. It hurts, but he's okay."

When I finally got to see him a week later, Aunt Dee held my hand as I walked to his room. My knees were shaking.

"Don't cry in there," she said. "You gotta be brave for him."

I took a deep breath. The room looked too bright. He was lying on an egg-crate pad for a mattress, and he smiled at me with lips that were still charred like meat cooked directly on the fire.

My lips wobbled when I tried to smile. I couldn't hold back my tears.

"Dizzy Liz," my dad said, his voice husky. "I'm okay."

I sighed with relief and stepped closer to the mattress.

He smiled again and blew me a shaky kiss. He had so much love in his eyes, but I'd never seen him look so fragile. I wanted to hold him tight. The nurse tapped me on the shoulder, reminding me not to touch.

Maybe because my dad was a comedian or maybe because he was famous or maybe because he was doing drugs when the fire started, but people treated the accident like it was funny.

When it happened, he was freebasing in his bedroom—using flammable chemicals to make it easier to smoke cocaine from a glass pipe. On the night of the accident, he was so drunk that he used too many chemicals with his cocaine. The drugs blew up. Luckily, Aunt Dee was staying at the Parthenia house and saved his life by running into the bedroom and throwing a blanket over him. After the fire was out, he ran and ran and ran. He ran out of his bedroom and out of the house and down his long driveway and out of the gate and onto the street. A police officer caught up with him a few blocks from the house, but he wouldn't stop running.

"I can't stop," my dad said to the officer. "I can't stop. If I stop, I'll die."

An ambulance rushed him to the hospital, and in the initial hours after the explosion, the police wanted to find proof he was doing drugs. A drug charge would have meant jail time because he was already on probation for shooting at Deboragh's car. Aunt Dee tried to protect him by saying the accident was caused only by alcohol. The police didn't buy the story and raided the Parthenia house, hoping to find hard proof, but I was told his housekeepers and Aunt Dee had already cleaned up all the incriminating evidence. The cops found nothing, but my dad's reputation for doing drugs was forever cemented in the public eye.

While he was fighting for his life in the hospital and facing serious drug charges, his tragedy became a national joke. All of the late-night talk show hosts and comedians made fun of it. The most famous bit had a person holding up a lit match and bouncing it in the air. "What's this?" they said, pointing to the lit match. The answer? "Richard Pryor running down the street."

A few weeks after the accident, my friend Josie invited me to a high school party in our neighborhood. I hadn't left my house for almost a month, except to go to the hospital. I didn't feel comfortable going to the party because my dad was in such bad shape, but my mom said I should get out of the house and be a regular kid. So I dressed up, wearing a brand-new Norma Kamali shirt with poofy shoulders. I even wore mascara for the first time.

Josie was my age, but a lot more experienced in everything from boys to R-rated movies. She lived a few blocks away. Her parents were hippies who thought it was better for their kids, and any kids in the neighborhood, to experiment with drugs at home. Josie took full advantage of this opportunity. The house was always full of teenagers, and we all smoked pot together in her bedroom from a six-foot-tall red translucent bong. We coughed and giggled and told silly stories. Smoking reminded me of watching my dad and Uncle Dickie. All of my troubles floated away.

Rumors about my pot smoking spread fast at Westlake. I was worried everyone would think doing drugs was for losers. But the cool girls in my grade were impressed, and they asked a million questions. I felt like a celebrity, like I finally had a shot at fitting in.

Before the party, I walked over to Josie's house. "How's Richard doing?" Josie's father asked. He'd never met my father before, but people always called him by his first name.

"Fine," I said, not wanting to think about the hospital room and his piercing screams. "Thank you for asking." The truth was he'd been in the hospital for three weeks, and we still weren't sure he would make it.

When Josie and I got to the backyard party, there were streamers and Christmas lights hung everywhere. I grabbed a soda from a big bucket with ice and noticed a few kids from the neighborhood staring at me and whispering.

I checked the waistband of my skirt to make sure it hadn't gotten twisted up.

Brandon, a friend of Josie's big sister, was the first kid to walk over to us.

"He's such a fox," Josie whispered in my ear. And he was—tall with feathered honey-blond hair, and his eyes were a kind of hazel I'd never seen before, flecked with orange and gold and green. He walked with a strut like a real surfer, even though he lived in the Valley. He was a perfect distraction from worrying about my dad.

Josie smiled at him, but he looked right at me. Nervous energy shot through my veins.

"You're Richard Pryor's daughter, right?" he asked.

Suddenly, I did not feel like a regular kid at all. Even at a neighborhood party, I couldn't avoid the spotlight.

"Yes," I said. "I'm Liz."

"Cool," he said, as a few of his friends joined us. When he pulled a matchbook out of his pocket, I didn't think anything of it. But then he looked around at his friends, ripped a match out of the book, and lit it.

"What's this?" he said, bouncing the match up and down. His friends snickered. "Richard Pryor running down the street."

They all laughed. My heart shriveled into a tiny, little ball. Tears threatened to fall. I rubbed my eyes and worried I'd gotten mascara all over myself.

I wanted to stick up for my father, but I was afraid to say anything in front of the older kids, so I laughed too.

"Hey," I said, trying to change the subject and hide my shame, "do you know where I can get some 'ludes?" I was talking about Quaaludes, a drug I'd heard Josie's big sister talk about. I knew smoking pot made me cool with the Westlake girls. Maybe asking for other drugs at this party would make me cool here too. Maybe it would help me forget how bad I felt.

"Naw," Brandon said. He didn't look impressed at all. "You need to ask Stan about that."

For the next hour, Josie and I bounced around looking for some kid named Stan and asked everyone we met for Quaaludes. I felt like a big shot. Like I was a kid who belonged at the party. I felt beautiful and popular, and for the first time in weeks I didn't think about how sick my dad was.

I had no interest in actually finding the Quaaludes. The thought of taking a drug like that terrified me. I still ate chewable Flintstone vitamins. It was the attention I loved.

By the time Josie's dad picked us up, I was so relieved nobody had the drugs that I hopped into his car with a big smile on my face. But when I got home, my mom was furious.

"Is there something you want to tell me, Elizabeth?" she asked, barely containing her anger.

"No," I said, taking off my jacket and not making eye contact.

"I got a call from Melanie Resnick's mom. She said you went to a party tonight looking for drugs."

"I did not. And Melanie wasn't even at the party," which was true.

"It doesn't matter, Liz. Someone called Melanie's mom and said Richard Pryor's daughter spent the whole night looking for drugs while he's in the hospital for freebasing."

I felt so angry and helpless and betrayed.

"They're liars!" I yelled at my mom. "Everyone's always telling lies about me!"

I wanted her to yell back at me, to call me a liar.

She surprised me, though. Taking me in her arms, she hugged me. Her tenderness was so unexpected, it unleashed a flood of salty tears.

"Those people are so fake," I said, choking and sobbing. "Why are they talking about me behind my back? They're two-faced! They said they liked me and I was their friend. They're fucking assholes!"

"Shhh," my mom said. "It's okay. It's okay. Darling, it's okay."

I leaned my head on her bare shoulder. The heat of her skin warmed my cheeks.

"You're beautiful, Elizabeth. You really are. And special. I wish you believed in yourself as much as I believe in you." But as I took comfort in her arms, a new thought popped into my head.

People are watching me now.

I knew people paid extra attention to me because I was Richard Pryor's daughter, but after the fire, while my dad was fighting for his life, I was under a different kind of scrutiny. My father wasn't just famous now, he was infamous. According to the world, he was a Black man who had everything but risked it all because he was addicted to drugs.

Six weeks later when he finally got out of the hospital, I went to a get-together with some Westlake friends. A guy I had never seen before came up to talk to me.

"Are you Richard Pryor's daughter?" he asked.

"No," I said, for the first time ever.

Twenty

"Any Relation?"

2016

For the first time in years, I dreamt about my father. He looked like he did when I was a child: round faced, skin unblemished by scars, and he still had a mole on his chin like he did before the fire. He beckoned me to follow him through a tight, grassy passageway between two brick buildings. Maybe it was the Parthenia house, maybe it was Smith College. I tried to reach him, but it felt like my shoes were stuck in mud. I couldn't catch up. He kept calling to me, saying something I couldn't make out. When I was nearly close enough to hear him, I woke up. It was the same dream I kept having every time I lectured publicly about the n-word.

In the years since I first shared my personal experience with the word, talking about it publicly had become like a second job. Colleagues at nearby high schools and colleges invited me to speak to their students. I published an essay about how teaching the n-word required self-reflection. And the historical article I wrote was finally slated for publication in the summer of 2016.

And yet, as honest and vulnerable as I was in public, there was a huge piece of the puzzle I still kept under lock and key. I had never acknowledged in any of my talks that I was Richard Pryor's daughter.

For most of my life, anytime someone caught a glimpse of my license or credit card or airline ticket or school registration, I could count on them asking if I was related to Richard Pryor. "Any relation?" they would ask. Sometimes I said yes, but since my father's accident, I usually said no. There was an intimacy to the question that made me uncomfortable. It felt like they wanted me to divulge the inner workings of our complicated relationship or satisfy their curiosity about the private life of a celebrity.

As I got older, the question stopped coming. Since he died, only one person had asked, "Any relation?" She wanted to know if I was related to a Massachusetts school teacher named Ellen Pryor. I was not.

The more I talked about the n-word, though, the more difficult it was to hide the truth. I saw signs of my father everywhere—in the history I studied, in the conversations I had, and even in my dreams.

When I heard the news that Gene Wilder had passed, I finally admitted to my husband, Jerry, that I'd never seen *Blazing Saddles*, even though I'd told my students I had.

"Get the fuck outta here," he said, playing up his Long Island accent. "We gotta watch it tonight." I plopped down next to him on the couch, and we did.

Turns out the critics are right. The movie is bold, irreverent, and very funny. In the satirical western, railroad tycoons install a Black sheriff to distract the residents from their scheme to level a small town and build the railroad right through it. To everyone's surprise, the sheriff is one of the good guys. He comes up with a plan to save the town with the help of the railroad workers—Black, Chinese, and Irish—who ask for land in exchange. The town leaders are resistant, but eventually they agree to a compromise: "We'll give some land to the n***ers and the ch*nks, but we don't want the Irish."

The line is classic Richard Pryor, subversive to its core, a laser-sharp social commentary about the absurdity of racism. Even in the face of imminent destruction, the white townspeople can't help but use slurs to describe their saviors. My student Charlotte had paraphrased the line, but she was spot on for connecting the dots between the film and my lecture that day in class. The joke was even historically accurate. In the nineteenth century, white Americans were as racist toward Irish immigrants as they were to the Black and Chinese. Historian David Roediger wrote, "Folk wisdom held that an Irishman was a 'n***er,' inside and out."

What made the joke even funnier was that the Irish eventually assimilated into white America by adopting the racist ideas and language of their white oppressors. They shouted "Down with the N***er!" when they voted against abolition and brutally attacked Black people during the 1863 New York City Draft Riots to show their allegiance. But in *Blazing Saddles*, the racist townspeople single out the Irish for being the most inferior race of all.

Once I watched the film, I realized what I should have said to Charlotte when she retold the joke: "Great point, but let's not say the word. That's a funny line, but best not to repeat it verbatim in class even if we want to talk about the meaning behind it."

At the time, I was unable to distinguish the shock of hearing the word in class from the package the word came in—my dad's biting humor. In one punchline, he exposed the historical truths I'd spent my whole career trying to figure out. He was at the vanguard of the conversation I'd been trying to have.

I couldn't really talk about the n-word anymore without talking about him.

Graduation weekend, I finally got a chance to claim him as my father and reframe the *Blazing Saddles* incident. I gave a lecture to one hundred and fifty alums and parents about the history of the n-word.

I started with a joke.

"Out of nowhere, an eager student in my class asked, 'Have you seen *Blazing Saddles*?'"

Then I leaned forward with a *pssst*. "Which was funny, because my father, who happens to be Richard Pryor, co-wrote the movie."

The audience roared.

It was the first time I'd ever said publicly that I was Richard Pryor's daughter. I wasn't just revealing a family connection. My father was an essential part of the work I was doing. He used his platform to influence public discourse about American racism. And he used the n-word to do it.

Interlude Eight

"Racism is a bitch. It's hard enough being a human being."
Richard Pryor,
Live on the Sunset Strip,
1982

In 1963 the most famous American painter of the twentieth century captured an image of a little Black girl walking to school in a starched white dress and pigtails, books tucked under her arm, head held high. Four federal marshals escort her, two in front, two behind. Spray painted on the wall behind her, in huge letters above her head, is the word "N***ER."

Norman Rockwell's *The Problem We All Live With* tells the story of six-year-old Ruby Bridges as she walked five blocks from her New Orleans home to attend an all-white school in the wake of *Brown v. Board of Education*. The 1954 landmark Supreme Court decision ruled that segregated public schools were unconstitutional.

Rockwell's painting immortalized the bravery of thousands of Black children whose only desire was to go to school in the face of violent opposition to desegregation. For more than a decade, white protesters across the South hung Black students in effigy, sprayed children with high-powered fire hoses, sicced dogs on them, spat at them, and blocked school entrances, shouting insults like "n***er go home."

As the nation watched the fight for desegregation unfold on the nightly news, they witnessed unspeakable acts of violence and the flagrant use of the n-word aimed at peaceful protesters. Until then, the word wasn't universally acknowledged as offensive, but the civil rights movement created a groundswell of resistance to the slur.

The Problem We All Live With brought that message to an even broader audience. Rockwell showed armed guards protecting an innocent child from an angry mob, which he represented with the word "N***ER" painted behind the girl. The n-word had become a symbol in the fight *against* American racism.

In 1964, six months after Rockwell's painting appeared on the cover of *Look* magazine, under mounting pressure from equal rights activists, President Lyndon B. Johnson signed the Civil Rights Act into law.

Twenty-One

"I've Been Wrong"

1981

"Hello, my dear," my dad said, picking up the phone extension in his bedroom and interrupting my conversation with a friend. "Say good-bye. Time to hang up."

"Dad-dy!" I said, my voice giggly and teasing because I was delighted. As an eighth grader, nothing pleased me more than when my father showed up as a regular parent. When he first got out of the hospital, he was quiet and withdrawn.

Now, months later, as the scars from his burns healed into marbled and discolored twists, and everything he touched got greasy from the vitamin E oil he used to moisten his skin, he seemed like a different person. Grateful to have survived the fire, he was more relaxed and a more involved father than he'd ever been. Sometimes, after school, he picked me up for a movie in Westwood Village. Other times he taught me the ins and outs of playing dominoes. Once in a while, he told me his secrets.

"I'm sober," he said as we sat in the kitchen batting around ideas for his new vanity plate because the license plate "I-M-L-U-C-K-Y" was already taken.

"What's sober mean?" I asked while I experimented with alternative spellings for "lucky" on a piece of paper.

"It means I don't drink anymore. Or do drugs." Goosebumps rose up my arms. I knew he thought drugs and alcohol got him into trouble, but I never heard of anyone giving them up.

"Not ever again?" I asked.

"One day at a time," he said. "No cognac, no wine, no pipe, no people trying to use me or steal from me. Your father's cleaning up his act."

Is this what it was like to have a sober dad? If so, I loved it.

"What about 'lucky' spelled 'L-U-C-C-I?'" I asked.

He looked at me with a silly face, making a square shape with his lips. "I'm loochy?" he said. And we laughed.

For the rest of the day, anytime something funny happened, we puckered our lips and shouted, "Loochy!"

As my relationship with my father grew stronger, my mother and I grew further apart. We fought constantly. She criticized everything I did and took each of my perceived missteps as a personal attack. If I ended a phone call with my nana abruptly, she said I was trying to embarrass her. My handwriting was too loopy for her to read, and I chewed my food so loudly that she couldn't concentrate. When I tried to defend myself, she said I had a bad attitude. If she was really mad, she told me I was fat and said no man would ever want me. That's usually when I reminded her that she called me the n-word and never apologized. I threw that fact in her face like mud.

But our ugliest fights were always about my dad.

"Your father flies you first-class to Hawaii, and I can't even buy myself a new pair of underwear?" my mom said a few days after I got back from a Christmas trip to Maui with my dad and Rain. For the last few winter breaks he'd taken us to stay at the exclusive Hāna-Maui Ranch Hotel.

"Oh, my God!" I said, in my Valley girl voice. "You're, like, so annoying." I knew my mom never went on trips or spent money on herself, even though she worked hard her whole life as a secretary. She hated the job so much, she refused to let me take typing in school. "Don't ever do it, Elizabeth, or you'll end up working for some asshole man!" I understood her frustration and felt guilty about going on extravagant trips without her, but being away was also a relief. At fourteen years old, I found it so hard to be around her. I felt guilty about that too.

"You think it's okay that your mother scrimps and saves while her daughter goes halfway around the world and doesn't even call to say 'Merry Christmas'?"

"We're Jewish," I deadpanned.

"You're missing the point, Elizabeth. Your mother doesn't have a pot to piss in and your father sicced his lawyers on me to take away the house."

I had no idea what she was talking about. When I was ten, my dad bought us a three-bedroom ranch house in Studio City. They had a written legal agreement that said each of my parents owned half of it. He had to pay the mortgage and pick up the bill for anything that needed to be fixed. The only way he could sell it was if he ran out of money.

"Yes, Elizabeth," she said, her voice dripping with sarcasm. "Apparently, your father, who you love so much, and who is building himself a second home in Maui, is broke."

"How can you say that? There's no way he's trying to take away the house."

"Is that what you think about your perfect father?" she said, her hands on her hips. "That he's incapable of doing anything to hurt you?"

She flung those words into the softest, fleshiest part of my heart. She knew he'd spanked me when I broke the vase in front of Mama and how humiliated I'd been afterward. She also knew he'd hit me more times over the years and each time I tried so hard to be a good girl for him. Several years before, when he took all his kids to Paris, he spanked me with a belt for turning up the radio too loud in the limo, even though Rain was the one who did it. He spanked me once when I spent the night at his house and he thought I spoke rudely to his housekeeper Mercy. The next day, I showed my mom the black-and-blue marks on my back. She brushed me off and said she'd had it a lot worse when she was a kid.

Now, marching over to the kitchen table and rifling through a stack of papers, she pulled out an official-looking letter.

"'Pursuant of the agreement between Richard Pryor and Maxine Pryor dated . . .' blah blah blah," she said, waving around the letter. "He wants to sell the house."

The whole time we were in Hawaii, he'd never mentioned it. Did he really need the money from our house to clean up his act? It didn't seem like he was struggling financially. The movie *Stir Crazy* set box-office records. One of the first things my dad did when he came home from the hospital was buy two Rolls-Royces, one for himself and one for his friend David Banks.

The questions spun around in my head so quickly that when my mom put her hands on my shoulders, I let her.

"Liz," she said, her eyes pleading. "I'm terrified. What are we going to do if he sells the house? What if we wind up on the streets? I haven't slept a wink since I got the letter."

She looked desperate and scared, with big, dark circles under her eyes. I knew she saved every penny she could, clipping double coupons from the Sunday newspaper and buying all my clothes at Marshalls. There was no way she could ever afford to get us another house.

My mom took a loose strand of hair from my ponytail and tucked it behind my ear. Then she gently rubbed my neck and shoulder. "You have the power to fix this," she said. "All you have to do is crawl into your father's lap and be a daddy's girl. Tell him you can't stand to see your mother so upset. Tell him when he hurts your mother, he hurts you."

I cringed. If I asked him about the house, he might think I was one of the people who was using him and trying to steal his money.

"Why are you putting me in the middle?" I shouted. "You just want to turn Daddy against me! You want me all to yourself!"

Fire lit up her eyes.

"Is that what you think? You don't see that everything I do is for the sake of your relationship with your father? You don't see what I sacrifice? And you can't do this one thing, not just for me, but for yourself?"

Ranting now, she paced up and down the hallway like a trapped tiger in a cage.

Finally, she walked back into the family room and pointed her finger in my face. "If you think your father's so great, why don't you go live with him!"

"Maybe I will!" I used my snootiest, hardest voice.

She snorted.

"You're delusional, Elizabeth, if you think your father gives that much of a shit about you or anyone to take you in! Your father cares about one person. Numero uno." She pushed her finger into my chest. "That's another thing you both have in common."

That weekend at my dad's, he called me into his bedroom for a talk. The room had been redecorated since it was damaged in the fire and felt more open and inviting now. Tall, wooden sculptures of African men and women stood in the corners and there were framed textiles hanging on the wall. The art was from Kenya, where he'd traveled before the accident. Like many other African Americans in the 1970s, he became fascinated with tracing his roots to Africa and visiting the motherland. The trip and the people he met had a huge impact on him, and he talked about it all the time. He also brought home presents for me and Rain, including intricately beaded Maasai wedding necklaces.

Now he sat on the edge of his bed, waiting for me and looking nervous.

"Have a seat," he said, taking a puff of his cigarette and inhaling deeply. Webs of white scars covered the back of his hand, but his fingers still looked long and elegant like a piano player's.

"I got a few things I need to tell you," he said. "Part of being sober is that I have to come clean to the most important people in my life about all the things I did wrong."

I nodded, even though I had no idea where he was going.

"I'm not gonna call anybody n***er ever again." That seemed even more impossible than not drinking anymore. The word was such a staple in his life—around the kitchen table, on his album covers, in his stand-up.

"Not even Uncle Dickie?"

"Nope," he said with his throaty chuckle, "not even Uncle Dickie."

Then he looked me in the eye and took my hand.

"And I ain't never gonna hit you again. Not ever."

I didn't know how much I'd longed to hear him say that. The last time he tried to spank me, I ran. With my feet bare, I zigged and zagged across the yard and through his fruit trees, dodging him like a quarterback avoiding a blitz. Eventually, he stopped chasing me and put his hands on his knees and panted. "I'm not running after you no more. So, get over here." I looked him in the eye, then turned and kept running.

"I'm sorry I ever hit you," he said. "You never deserved it. I love you."

The tightness in my chest loosened up. He looked shy and open-hearted. My mom was so wrong about him.

"It's okay," I said.

"Thanks, Dizzy." He reached into a drawer of his bedside table. It was stuffed with scraps of paper, notes he compiled of everything he'd read and considered using onstage. He shuffled through the bits of paper in every size and shape and pulled out a pack of Dentyne, unwrapped a piece, and offered me one. The cinnamon flavor burst all over my tongue.

"I gotta say something else," he said. "About the fire. It's hard to talk about."

We had never discussed the fire. He walked around without a shirt sometimes, and his scars looked messy and puckered. There were neat scars too, rectangular patches of skin missing from his legs that looked like a dressmaker's sewing pattern. The doctors had removed the skin and grafted it onto his torso and chest. Several times a week he went to physical therapy and every day he complained about how itchy his skin felt. But we never talked about how he got the scars in the first place.

"That night, I was so tired," he said. "I kept trying to stop doing the drugs and no matter how much I wanted to, I couldn't. After a while, I just gave up."

He looked me right in the eyes. Tears welled up before I even understood what he was saying.

"It wasn't an accident," he said. "I lit myself on fire on purpose. I tried to kill myself."

Why would he want to kill himself? There were so many people who loved him.

A sliver of sunlight from the windows shined on his face, and he looked more sincere and open than I'd ever seen him. "I poured alcohol all over myself and then I lit it with my lighter. I didn't know it was gonna catch quite like that." He reached over and hugged me. "Don't cry, Dizzy Liz. I'm telling you now because I never want to do anything to hurt you, and that means I don't lie to you. I'm sorry."

I had so many questions. Was he okay now? If he drank or did drugs, would he hurt himself again? But it seemed too forward to ask when he was being so vulnerable. At the same time, his confession made me even more eager for his love and affection. I thought of a horror movie he took all of us kids to when we were younger, about a parasite that takes over a fancy apartment building and infects people with lust. Rain and I didn't get that part, but for years we put on funny voices and repeated a line from the movie to crack each other up: "I'm hungry. Hungry for love."

"Can I live with you?" I asked him. I wanted to show him how much I loved him. I wanted to feel his love in return.

"Lizzy," he said, his smile so sweet I knew he was going to say no. "How's that gonna work? How are you gonna get to school every day?" Westlake was pretty far from his house.

"I can be in a carpool," I said. "My friend lives a few houses away and her mom drives."

He smiled. "Your father does not drive carpool."

I could picture my mom laughing at me and saying I told you so.

"My mom and I fight all the time."

"About what?" he asked, looking curious and a little surprised.

My shoulders slumped. I didn't want to admit to the things she accused me of. And how could I tell him we fought about the house? He might think I was on her side and not his.

"Nothing," I said, utterly defeated.

"Look," he said, gently touching my chin and turning my face toward his. "Your mother's a good mother. She gives me hell. She gives everyone hell. But she does it because she loves you. You know what the problem is? You guys are too much alike."

My whole body deflated. He saw my disappointment and grabbed my hand. "If it was horrible over there, we'd make it work. But you're lucky. Macky takes good care of you."

I wanted him to know he had it wrong. It was the two of us who were alike. My mom made me feel terrible about myself. She even made me feel awful about being Black.

"She called me a n***er," I said.

"She called you what?" His voice changed. It got quiet. He wasn't playful anymore.

"When I was twelve," I said. The tears started up again. I had thought about telling him since it happened, but the only reason I told him now was to get what I wanted. The shame made me shiver. If Mama was alive and had seen me shake like that, she would have said somebody was stepping on my grave.

He put his hand on my chin. My face felt warm where he touched it, but the rest of me was cold.

"Dizzy. Why didn't you ever tell me?"

I wiped my eyes. "I didn't want you to be mad at me." I didn't want him to think I'd done something to deserve it.

"Mad at you?" He paused again. "You can tell me anything. Anytime." He reached over and hugged me tight.

I moved in with him that day. When he took me to my mom's house to pick up my stuff, they had a conversation without me. Afterward, her eyes were red, but she didn't try to stop me from leaving.

"Be a good girl, Liz," she said. My stomach felt so twisted, I thought I might throw up.

I spent the rest of eighth grade and part of ninth living at my dad's. I didn't see him much. He was working out new material at The Comedy Store. Most mornings the neighbor's rooster crowed long before he made it home, and he slept a lot during the day. Mercy made great school lunches with sandwiches cut on the diagonal and filled with bologna and cheese. She also gave me stubby cans of soda wrapped in tin foil to keep them cold.

I had everything I thought I wanted, but I missed my mother terribly. For all the constant criticism, she was my fiercest advocate and was always around to eat dinner, watch old movies, and gossip with. She was so much easier for me to love from afar.

The good news was my father never did end up selling her house. The bad news was he was so angry she called me the n-word he never again invited her over to the Parthenia house, not for holidays or parties or even just to hang out. He never really spoke to her again. And I never forgave myself.

• • •

Not long after I moved in, my dad filmed his comeback concert, *Richard Pryor: Live on the Sunset Strip*, at the Hollywood Palladium. Watching him from my mezzanine seat, I was mesmerized. He talked about the fire, about how the cocaine pipe spoke to him in a seductive voice and tricked him into thinking he wasn't hooked. He smoked so much cocaine, he said, that drug dealers didn't even want to do business with him.

The very last line of the concert addressed the jokes people told about the fire. He lit a match and said, "What's that? Richard Pryor running down the street," letting everyone know he was in on the joke.

In the middle of the show, he talked about his four-week trip to Africa that had such a profound effect on him. He called the time he spent in Kenya "magic." On his last day there, he said he was sitting in the lobby of the Hilton Hotel in Nairobi when a little voice in his head whispered in his ear.

"Look around," it said. "What do you see?"

"I see all colors of people doing everything."

"Do you see any n***ers?"

"I haven't even *said* it. I haven't even *thought* it."

The little voice told him the most important news of all. "That's because there aren't any."

The word was obsolete and it hit him like a lightning bolt. "I started crying and shit. . . . Oh, my God, I been wrong. I got to regroup my shit."

For years, he had used the word to express himself and reshape modern comedic performance and the parameters of Black artistic expression. The n-word was in big bold letters on the cover of two of his albums. Audiences knew him as the comedian who made jokes using it. In just a few years, generations of hip-hop artists, inspired by him, would use the word in their music to change the course of American culture.

Now Richard Pryor, the man who made the Black version of the word a part of the American lexicon, was disavowing it in his art and in his life.

"I ain't gonna never call another Black man 'n***er,'" he said, standing under a spotlight on the Palladium stage. He was ready to let the word go. Just like he told me he would.

It felt like my father was taking a stand for every Black person in the world. Not saying the n-word was as radical and revolutionary as when he started saying the word onstage in the first place.

I never heard him call anyone that word again.

In the show, the last thing he said about the n-word felt even more personal to me: "I don't want those hip white people coming up to me and calling me no 'n***er' or telling me n***er jokes. I. Don't. Like it."

I didn't like it either.

He was drawing a line in the sand, but what did that mean for my mom?

My father had cut her out of his life because she called me the n-word. Did that mean I was supposed to cut her out of my life too?

Twenty-Two

The Scam Odds Chart

1984–1985

"Dime, dime, dime. Indica, homegrown, sensibud," yelled the man selling weed on the corner. He approached my car as I drove through a rundown neighborhood with stucco bungalows, peeling paint, and bars on the windows.

"Roll down the car window," I said to my best friend Jules, a pretty Jewish girl with gorgeous hair and a smile so warm my dad called her "sexy Julie." Awkward, I know, but it fit.

"P," she said, short for Pryor, her favorite nickname for me. "I don't think this is a good idea." She wasn't wrong. We were sixteen-year-old girls in our private-school uniforms—short gray skirts with white button-down blouses—driving around in a part of town we'd never been to before and that didn't feel very safe. My friend James told me about it when I called him looking for pot.

"I'm dry," James said. "Try East Hollywood. Bring your Thomas Guide," He gave me the cross streets and hung up.

Jules agreed to be my copilot, and we set out after school. "Where's the 'stang?" she asked. I usually drove my mom's yellow

Mustang, but today I was in my dad's favorite car, his black VW Rabbit convertible.

I let out a big sigh. "Maxine accused me of sneaking out. I called her a pain in the ass. Per usual, she lost her shit and sent me to stay at my dad's."

I had moved back to my mom's in the middle of ninth grade, but never stayed for long. We constantly blew up at each other—over money, my bad grades, my lousy attitude—and then she'd kick me out. I spent all of high school going back and forth between my parents, and was a regular in detention for breaking the dress code because I never knew whether I'd left my uniform at his house or hers.

Fiddling with the map book, Jules asked, "Did you sneak out?"

"Of course. That doesn't mean my mom's not losing it."

As we drove deeper into less familiar parts of Hollywood, Jules called out directions from the map, but we had no idea where we were going until we found ourselves in a neighborhood where emaciated men stumbled into the street, shouting out the names of different kinds of pot and their prices.

Adrenaline surged through me. "We should leave," I said, but Jules had already reached out the window and handed a guy ten dollars, and he tossed a folded tinfoil packet into the passenger side of the car and ran off.

"Julie!" I said, as I sped up and drove around the corner. "You gotta open it up before you give him the money."

Sure enough, when we unfolded the foil, it was not marijuana.

"What?" Jules said when she saw my face. She hadn't smoked much pot and was clueless.

"Can't you smell it?" I said. "It's oregano."

She threw the packet out the window, and I floored the gas pedal. We giggled nervously until my car merged onto the 101.

By the tenth grade, my friends and I called each other "the Westlake girls." Each of them was like family to me, which was good because things at home were pretty awful. Jules was smart as a whip and my best Westlake friend, but there was also Andrea, pronounced the European way, who was flirtatious and ditzy but smarter than she looked. There was Wendy with the long black hair, who loved the Rolling Stones and always had a horde of theater boys trailing behind her. And Sara, my only other friend whose parents were no longer together. She was a tall, pretty girl, wise beyond her years, who always had a cigarette in her hand and said things like "It pays the bills" when I asked if she liked her job at the bagel shop. I spent most of my time after school and on weekends with my friends, smoking pot, drinking wine coolers, and gossiping about the guys from Harvard School for Boys.

Jules and I were blasting *Purple Rain* and driving over to Wendy's to talk about boys, when Jules turned down the music.

"I have a theory," she said.

"I'm listening," I said.

"Guys in high school only notice girls with blond hair, blue eyes, and big boobs."

I interrupted. "Is this a make-me-feel-crappy theory?"

"No!" she said. "Listen! They're too immature to recognize we're a different kind of pretty, *and* also funny and interesting and super smart, which actually makes us even prettier!"

She was trying to group us together, but in her theory, the only girls high-school boys had crushes on were white.

"So, how long do I have to wait for guys to figure out how awesome I am?" I asked, side-stepping the issue.

"I'm thinking college," she said.

"We're totally screwed!" It seemed like a long time to wait.

Later, as I sat on the floor of Wendy's bedroom with Jules's head on my lap while Andrea doodled on her philosophy homework, Sara presented that week's Scam Odds Chart. It was a list that predicted which one of our friends would make out with a given guy over the weekend. The girls made the list, and it provided hours of matchmaking gossip, but in retrospect, it was kind of degrading. Guys scammed on girls, not the other way around. The list was our twisted attempt to take control.

I reached up and snatched it out of Sara's hand, accidentally knocking Jules to the floor. I wanted to know the odds of making out with Richie Rothenberg, a golden, Jewish guy I'd had a crush on since eighth grade.

"Thirty to one odds I end up kissing Richie?" I asked. "Ouch." That stung. On top of that, there was only one other guy in my column. Two to one I end up with Phil, a smart guy from the debate team. He was a year ahead of me, and I barely knew him.

"Why would you put me with Phil?" I asked. None of the other Westlake girls were matched with him. Just me.

Sara looked at me and raised an eyebrow. "He's a cutie," she said. "So nice." It was true, but it felt like there was something she wasn't saying.

"We've never even had a real conversation."

"I've never talked to Scott Stevens," Andrea said about one of the most popular football players. "But I'm two to one odds with him."

"That's because you're easy," Wendy said, and they all cracked up as I felt a pit forming in my stomach.

As far as I could tell, the only thing Phil and I had in common was we were both Black.

I didn't like the thought of being matched romantically with another Black person just because of the color of my skin. Besides, I was mixed. What made them think I had a better chance of kissing Phil than Richie? Did being Black outweigh my Jewishness? Wasn't I a Westlake girl above everything else?

I pulled a pen out of my pocket and scratched Phil's name off the chart so hard, I poked holes in the paper.

"Re-lax," said Sara sternly at the same time Wendy said, "It's 'otay.'"

Wendy was quoting Eddie Murphy playing Buckwheat on *Saturday Night Live*. Buckwheat was a Black character from a fifties' television show called *The Little Rascals* who wore rags and spoke in dialect. Murphy's Buckwheat was a huge hit and made fun of the racist way *The Little Rascals* portrayed one of the show's only Black characters. But when my white friends and everyone else said "otay," which they did all the time, it didn't sound like social commentary. It sounded like they were making fun of Black people.

I had no idea how to talk to my friends about how I felt about Buckwheat or the Scam Odds Chart or being paired with Phil. Usually, I told the Westlake girls everything—about my mom's latest outburst, the boys I had crushes on, and how I wanted to be an actor when I grew up—but I never talked about how I felt about being Black or even mixed. Those were subjects I protected like tiny, microscopic aliens placed inside an impenetrable force field.

As much as my dad talked about race onstage, and my mom blurted out her questionable observations about Black people in our living room, neither of them ever had a direct conversation with me about what it meant for me to be Black. At least not since I was seven years old when my father told me it was my job to stand up to anyone who called me the n-word.

There was one guy in high school I was more obsessed with than anyone else, a senior with dark-brown skin and big, brown eyes. By the end of sophomore year, nobody drew my attention more than Aaron Payne. I saw him for the first time at a Harvard football game. When he walked by me, leading a flock of equally beautiful boys like geese in V-formation, he gave me the wryest smile I'd ever seen. In that moment, my life spanned out in front of me like a montage in a romantic comedy.

My infatuation soared when I realized every popular girl at Westlake wanted him too. He was smart, confident, and artsy, but a huge part of the attraction was my furtive belief that if a Black guy who dated white girls chose me, it would somehow prove I was cool and beautiful exactly the way I was.

For months, I imagined Aaron's soft lips pressed against mine. Every outfit I wore, I wore for him. When I saw him making out with a popular girl at a party, I did what any self-respecting Westlake girl in 1984 would do. I made out with one of his closest friends.

Still, he never asked me out.

"Why doesn't he like me?" I asked Jules one night as we stretched out on the floor of my father's home gym, stoned and listening to Pink Floyd's *The Dark Side of the Moon*.

"He's going to college in the fall," she said. She knew I meant Aaron. Lately, he was the only guy I ever talked about. "And he's a dick."

We giggled, but as I took another hit, I felt uneasy.

"Am I totally hideous?" I asked.

"What?" she said. "No way!"

"Then why doesn't anyone want to go out with me?"

"None of us have boyfriends," she said, which was true, but she was dodging my question.

"Guys chase after you. They have crushes on you," I said. "Nobody chases after me. Am I that weird?"

She reached over and played with my hair. "We're all a little weird. I mean, I asked Mrs. Barrett for extra geometry homework last week, which is objectively weird."

I passed her the joint carefully, so she wouldn't burn her fingers.

"It's good to be different," she said.

"What's good different about me?" I could hear the desperation in my voice and hoped she didn't hear it too.

"You're funny. You've got the best curls. You ask the best questions." But she was talking around something. I was talking around it too. I didn't know how to say what I really meant, or ask the questions I really wanted to ask.

Is it okay that I'm Black? Will you accept me if I say it out loud? Can any of these boys ever love a Black girl?

Even though I knew Jules loved and supported me, I didn't think she knew how to read between the lines or really hear me.

Instead, I asked, "Fatburger?"

"Carneys," she said, choosing the burger place that competed for the best in L.A. at the time. The conversation was over. We got up and headed out.

Even as my awareness of the differences between me and my friends grew, it didn't stop me from going to Harvard-Westlake parties every weekend. They were the place to be, and by junior year, I was quasi-popular, a medium-big fish in a small pond: stylish, cool, and good friends with some of the cutest guys at Harvard School. So, when I got separated from Andrea and Sara at a huge rager, it wasn't a big deal. I did a few laps around the party until I spotted them outside.

Andrea was standing with Sara at the bottom of the driveway, flipping her short black hair and smoking a clove cigarette. I headed over, but between us was a group of popular Harvard football players, all of them white. The guys were so high up on the social scale that even though I saw them every weekend, knew where each of them lived, and gossiped about the girls they dated, I'd never spoken to any one of them before.

My mind was a whirl. Would it be awkward to walk by without saying hi? Do I just ignore them like I always did? Do I shout out to Andrea and Sara and hope the boys notice me?

As I considered the possibilities, I moseyed by, careful not to look over because nothing could be more embarrassing than getting caught checking them out. As I walked closer, their energy was infectious—they were cracking up and heat radiated off their bodies like a bonfire. Out of the corner of my eye, I saw they were all gathered in a circle around Clay, a senior. They hung on his every word.

Suddenly, the volume dropped. The boys stopped talking.

A little thrill moved up my arms and chest like a tickle. *They're gonna say hi.*

I mustered up my biggest, most confident smile and looked right at them.

Clay was looking right back. His lips were moving, but I couldn't hear what he was saying, so I took a tiny step forward.

Before my foot hit the ground, he spoke up.

"I was gonna say 'n***er,'" he said to his friends, "but then she walked by."

The words were a full-palm slap that almost knocked me off my feet. I was too stunned to react.

Clay hadn't actually called me the n-word, but he may as well have. Even worse, he called me "she." Did he even know my name? Somehow, that compounded the hurt even more.

"Harsh, dude," said one of Clay's friends.

Snapping out of my daze, I made a beeline for Andrea and Sara. With each step, I realized something even more painful than what Clay said. There was no way I could tell my closest friends about what just happened. What if they said it wasn't a big deal? What if they thought I was being oversensitive? What if bringing up the n-word put it in their minds? What if they associated me with the word?

There were no more than three or four yards between the boys and my friends, but by the time I reached them at the end of the driveway, I had tucked the memory deep down and pretended it never happened.

"Hey, chica," said Andrea. "Where ya been?"

"Dude," I said, sounding like the Westlake girl I so wanted to be, "let's blow this popsicle stand. This party sucks."

"You're Black, you know," said Hayden Colorno, my closest guy friend senior year. He didn't look at me, but instead sat intently at his bedroom desk with a bright light and a magnifying glass, inspecting a half ounce of weed.

I knew I was Black, but his words were a shock. It was the most direct any of my friends had ever been about my race.

Hayden went to the public school in my neighborhood. He was also adopted and told me he never felt like he fit in. I'm not sure if it was because he always felt like an outsider or because he was always stoned, but Hayden Colorno was deep.

My body buzzed with questions I couldn't fully formulate. Hayden waited patiently. He was quiet while he used a pair of tweezers to separate the red and purple hairs from his recent haul of sticky Indica bud.

Eventually, I said, "No. My mom is white. So I'm mixed," which had been my stock answer since middle school when my friend Karen asked if I was mulatto.

Hayden turned to me then, his blond, newly shorn curls standing upright and his bright eyes tender and open.

"If you go shopping on Rodeo Drive, there is nobody who will see you and say, 'That girl is mixed.' You're Black, and no matter what you call yourself, Black is exactly what people are gonna see."

Part of me was furious. How dare Hayden insist I could only be one thing. When my father told me I was Black, it opened up a world of possibilities and explained so much. But since then, I'd gotten so many negative messages that told me there was something wrong with being Black—from my mom, from my friends, from movies and television. It seemed like, from the perspective of anyone white, being Black was the same thing as being an n-word. I couldn't relate to that thinking at all.

Another part of me understood Hayden was trying to be a straight shooter and maybe even protect me, bravely saying what none of my other friends ever had. And I knew it was true. No matter how I struggled to find the right word or label to describe how I identified myself, the world was still going to see me in one way.

Twenty-Three

The Word Is Two Words

2017

"What about how your dad uses the n-word in his stand-up?" asked a Black English teacher from Springfield, Massachusetts, during one of my public lectures about the n-word.

At each of these workshops, I asked the audience the same question: Why is it so hard to talk about the n-word? An emotional dialogue always unfolded. In upstate New York, a white teacher shared that he called a Black classmate the n-word when he was ten years old, even though he didn't know what it meant. He never forgot how ashamed he felt when he found out. In Richmond, Virginia, a Black professor stood up in the audience and shared how in the second grade three white boys chased her home after school every day and called her the n-word. She teared up as she recounted the experience. So many people had so much to share, I could never get through my entire lecture.

Their candor encouraged me to open up too. Every time I gave a workshop, I told the audience Richard Pryor was my father, but I had never talked about the specific way he used the n-word. When the teacher in Springfield asked the question, it threw me. I had no idea how to answer. Instead, I focused on the bigger issue: the Black version of the word I'd been researching.

"The word is two words," I explained. "It's a homonym. Young people understand this distinction. They'll talk about the white-racist version with the hard 'er' that means 'you are the word and I'm not,' and the Black version like my father used with the soft 'ga' that means 'I am this word, I'm part of this community, I'm better than enough.'

"Context is everything. Novelist Gloria Naylor differentiated between the white racist version and the warm, familiar way it was used in the living rooms of Harlem. Black intellectual Ta-Nehisi Coates explained why white people should never say the word and why it was okay when he did it by comparing it to how his wife and her girlfriends could call each other 'b*tches,' but he'd get clobbered if he tried to say it.

"I never want anyone to say either version of the word in my classroom, but I won't tell another Black person not to say it. It's a form of protest against racism, and I'm not going to stand in the way of that."

Heads nodded throughout the packed room, but I'd also side-stepped the part about how my father used the word. The teacher wanted to know how I felt about it, and twelve years after his death, I didn't really have an answer. I'd seen almost all of my father's movies and was in the audience at several of his live performances, but I hadn't really examined the n-word in his stand-up because I still hadn't listened to any of his albums.

Throughout my life, I met people who felt like they were his intimates because of how well they knew his comedy. I was committed to knowing him as a real person who loved playing with dogs and eating Mama's catfish, whose favorite artist was Pissarro, who got loud when he smacked his dominoes and quiet when he fished.

By the time I was a teenager, I realized why his records deserved their X rating. On each album, he revealed raunchy details about sex.

No one wants to know anything about their parents' sex life or even talk about sex with them. When I was fifteen years old, my father took me to see the movie *Fast Times at Ridgemont High*, a coming-of-age comedy. We sank down in our seats, mortified, as the main characters talked incessantly about their sexual fantasies and had explicit sex. Slinking out of the theater, we rushed to the car and never spoke of it again. After that, listening to his comedy was out of the question.

I reached out to my sister Rain to ask about her memories of his early comedy. She was five years old when she first saw him perform at The Comedy Store, but she had never listened to his records either. His albums weren't on her radar as a kid, and after he died, the thought of listening to them was just too painful.

Even as an adult and historian, I avoided my father's earlier work. The Richard Pryor I related to most was the man who said he was never going to call another Black person the n-word. His rejection of the word felt like an affirmation of my own experience. It bonded us. I was afraid hearing him say the word over and over again would threaten that connection.

But the more I processed the n-word personally and professionally—the hurt it caused me throughout my life, its impact on so many people, and the subversive way Black people used it anyway—the more I realized how integral his comedy was to the history of the word. I couldn't ignore his influence anymore just because he was my father. To be a true scholar of the n-word, I had to listen to his work.

That night, I picked up the phone and called one of my oldest friends who was also the biggest Richard Pryor fan I knew: Richie Rothenberg, the same Jewish guy from Harvard High School I'd had a crush on since eighth grade. We'd stayed friends for decades and I loved him. While most of my childhood friends prided themselves on seeing beyond the color of my skin, Richie always embraced me as a Black Jew.

"The Right Honorable Reverend Elizabeth Stordeur Pryor," he

said playfully, because a few years before, I became a Universal Life Minister and officiated his wedding to my best girlfriend Jules.

"I need Richard Pryor recommendations," I said.

Before the words left my mouth, he rattled off a list. "'Mudbone,' 'Funeral,' 'Wino and Junkie,' 'Wino Dealing with Dracula,' 'Just Us,' 'Africa,' 'Rumpelstiltskin,' 'Shortage of White People,' 'Black Women v. White Women,' 'Cops and Cars' . . ."

"Wait! Rich," I said. "Slow down! I need to know where to start!"

"What do you mean 'start'?" he asked.

"I mean, I've never heard any of his albums."

"What? Never?" Richie sighed. "Okay, start with *That N-word's Crazy. Bicentennial N-word's* next."

With my friend's recommendations, I set out to immerse myself in the comedic stylings of Richard Pryor.

Interlude Nine

I was a negro for twenty-three years. I gave that shit up. No room for advancement.

Richard Pryor,
Live and Smokin',
1971

In 1964, Black comedian and activist Dick Gregory published an autobiography titled *N***er*. He dedicated the book to his mother. "Wherever you are," he wrote, "if ever you hear the word 'n***er' again, remember they are advertising my book."

For a hundred and fifty years, the predominant African American philosophy argued that if Black folks acted politely, got educated, worked hard, and stayed in their place, they would be treated as equals in America. In the sixties and early seventies, the Black Power movement challenged so-called "respectability politics." They argued there was no way for Black people to get ahead without being bold and outspoken. And they used the n-word to express themselves.

In literature and film, Black intellectuals called out the inherent racism in American society that made it impossible for them and others to be truly free. Telling their raw, personal stories, proponents of Black Power showed how inequality was deeply ingrained, systemic and inescapable, no matter someone's accomplishments. As Malcolm

X asked: "Do you know what white racists call Black Ph.D.'s?" His answer: "N***er!"

The n-word became a symbol of their opposition to injustice. Writer Robert H. deCoy published *The N***er Bible*. Activist H. Rap Brown titled his memoir *Die N***er Die!* Novelist Cecil Brown called his book *The Life & Loves of Mr. Jiveass N***er*. In 1971, a rising star in stand-up comedy introduced himself onstage like no one had before. "I'm Richard Pryor," he said. "I'm a n***er."

Their in-your-face use of the n-word changed America's relationship with the word. In 1981, Lee Atwater, a white Republican strategist, highlighted the impact on politics: "In 1954, a candidate for office in the South could win by saying 'n***er, n***er, n***er.'" By 1968, a candidate "can't say 'n***er,' that hurts you, [it] backfires."

Refusing to be subdued by the n-word, Black Power intellectuals transformed the slur into a fighting word and a rallying cry for liberation.

Twenty-Four

Uncle Toms, Sambos, and Sellouts

1986–1989

"I can't stand the Uncle Toms on this campus!" said Huey, a Black student in black fatigues and a black beret. "I can't stand the Sambos with Black faces and white souls who walk by other Black folks without saying hello! Or even nodding! I'm sick of the sellouts!"

I slumped in my chair and avoided eye contact with everyone. *Was he talking about me?*

Huey and I were both in a class at Tufts University called "Race Awareness in America," an experimental course that attracted students of all racial backgrounds. It was the center of Black intellectual life on the mostly white campus. The class asked students to think about how race and racism affected their daily lives. The energy in the classroom was electric, and by the time it was over, it had completely changed everything I thought I knew about being Black.

When I first got to college, I tried to embrace my Blackness, even though I wasn't exactly sure what that meant. I went to the African American students' orientation and met interesting people, but I connected more with the kids I met on the first day of drama class. My new friends loved theater and fashion and were mostly white. I also landed my first real boyfriend, Daniel, a beautiful Jewish guy I met one night singing songs from *Hair* in a friend's dorm. He came home with me for the holidays, and both of my parents adored him. My dad even got him a job working on one of his films.

Then I enrolled in "Race Awareness in America." The course was taught by a Black community activist named Jim Vance who encouraged students to speak their minds and have difficult discussions. Each class was a revelation. Turns out, I wasn't the only Black person on campus who had white girls sticking their fingers in my hair and tugging at my curls, got sucked into conversations about affirmative action and grilled about my SAT scores, or who'd been called the n-word while walking down fraternity row.

The class introduced me to a new world where Black students opened up to each other about what it was like being Black. I was intrigued by it. But at the time there were some things Mr. Vance said that didn't quite sit right with me.

"This is real, people," he said, a few weeks into the semester. "There's a war going on. What side are you on?"

Was the war between white people and Black people? Did everyone have to choose sides?

The white students insisted there wasn't a war at all. They admitted there were isolated incidents of racism but the solution was simple: follow the golden rule and treat everyone the way you want to be treated. I knew in my heart that wouldn't solve the problem. But if the choice was between the white side and the Black side, I didn't want to choose a side. What about me and my boyfriend Dan?

I raised my hand.

"Can't there be a third side?" I asked. I looked at Dan, who I had convinced to take the class with me, and saw his big brown eyes get huge. "Dan and I are an interracial couple. We're on our own side."

The classroom exploded in laughter. Dan shifted uneasily in his seat. One Black student slapped his forehead and dragged his hand down his face.

A short Black woman sitting next to me leaned over to her friend. "Mixed-up and confused," she said.

Another Black woman said, "Black folks always accept and take in interracial couples. White folks reject them."

"People!" Mr. Vance said, trying to quiet the classroom and help us better understand. "Listen up. What's the quickest way for a Black man to die in the United States?" Just like that, he had everyone's attention. As I scanned the room, all the students looked as unsure as I felt. When no one said anything, Mr. Vance answered his own question. "The quickest way for a Black man to die in the United States is to walk down the street holding the hand of a white woman."

A few of the Black students nodded their heads, but a white student sitting across from me looked shocked. Mr. Vance softened his tone. "It doesn't matter if a Black man and a white woman love each other. Or a Black woman and white man do. They still live in a society that draws racial lines and values white lives over Black ones. The war isn't about individual behavior but about a system of power. If you're not part of the solution, you're part of the problem."

Mr. Vance was trying to teach us that the more we were able to acknowledge and recognize racism in all its forms, the better equipped we were to fight against it. But it wasn't until Huey went off about Sambos and Uncle Toms that I realized that even though I wasn't white and didn't want to be, I was part of the problem too. I had never in my entire life said "hello" to a Black person I didn't know just because they were Black to show my solidarity. I'd blown off events at the African American student center because I didn't want to be defined only by my race. Now I understood how that seemed like a rejection of all Black people and why Huey might think it made me a sellout. The realization made me sick and ashamed.

My whole life I'd tried to act like and talk like and fit in with my friends who were all white. I didn't realize that beyond my father and

Mama and my mom's friend Lisa Jones, there existed a vibrant Black community that already considered me a member.

A few weeks later, I was lying on my bed writing in my journal about Mr. Vance's class when the phone rang.

"Hello, dear!" It was my dad. His voice was excited. I was surprised to hear from him because his life had gotten even busier since the fire. He'd starred in smash hits like *The Toy*, *Superman III*, and *Brewster's Millions* and made another concert film, *Richard Pryor . . . Here and Now*. He'd also fathered a whole new generation of Pryor kids, my youngest siblings Steven, Franklin, and Kelsey, who at the time were all under three years old and all called me "Wiz."

He had taken on the most challenging role of his career too. He wrote, directed, and produced a semi-autobiographical story about growing up in Mama's brothel, his difficult relationships with women, his alcoholism and drug addiction, and the suicide attempt that almost killed him. The movie was called *Jo Jo Dancer, Your Life Is Calling*. I flew home from college to attend a screening and cried throughout the whole film. The critics panned it. They said it lacked the honesty and authenticity that made his comedy soar. He was crushed and had been a lot more subdued since *Jo Jo Dancer* underperformed at the box office.

It was great to hear him now sounding so upbeat on the phone.

"I saw Bill Cosby at an event yesterday," he launched right in. "I told him you go to Fisk University. He said that's a really good school." I loved hearing him talk about college. He paid for it, but he rarely asked me about it.

"It's Tufts, I go to Tufts University." I hated to correct him but couldn't help myself. Fisk is an historically Black college. Tufts is a predominantly white one.

The line got quiet. Why had I made it so awkward? I needed to find a way to connect again.

"I'm Black," I said, my voice shaky and my eyes tearing up

unexpectedly. "I mean, obviously I always knew that, but I guess I didn't understand how much it mattered. Like, did you know you're supposed to say hi to other Black people when you walk down the street?"

Chuckling, he said, "I was supposed to teach you that, Boston Blackie. Remember when I used to call you that? Your old man fell down on the job."

A few days later, a package arrived at my dorm. I tore the box open, and found an audio cassette and videotape inside.

There was no note, so I called him. "Did you send me a package?" I asked.

"Yes! It's for your real Black education. Make sure you listen to the whole album and watch the film."

Thrilled, I dug in as soon as I hung up the phone.

The audio cassette was a 1970 album by The Last Poets, with four Black men on the cover—two in dashikis, one in a black turtle-neck, and the other a conga player who kept the rhythm in check. It was spoken-word poetry, a precursor to rap music; songs that were confrontational and deep. Like the first track on the album.

*N***ers shouldn't be scared of revolution*
Because revolution is nothing but change
*And all n***ers do is change*

It was a call to action, and I was so touched that my father had shared it with me. He was inviting me into a secret Black world, the one where Black people get real with each other and build a coalition for change.

The videotape was even better. It had a handwritten label—*Malcolm X*—the title of a 1972 documentary. Watching the movie over and over again, I cried every time Malcolm was murdered. My dad and I didn't really talk about what it all meant, but it felt like he wanted me to make Black liberation the center of my life, and I was eager to make him proud.

. . .

For the rest of my time at college, I immersed myself in Black culture. I read *The Autobiography of Malcolm X* like it was a bible and listened to jazz music like Miles Davis's *Bitches Brew* and John Coltrane's *Blue Train*. I never missed an episode of the television show *A Different World*, and I went to the Reggae Sunsplash Festival in Jamaica twice. I was making up for lost time, and there was so much left to do.

The more I read and learned, the more I began to openly identify as a Black woman, and the more conscious I was that I didn't have any close Black friends. I even broke up with Dan. The relationship had probably run its course, but a white boyfriend didn't fit my new vision of myself.

The first close Black friend I made was a brown-skinned, Puerto Rican punk rocker from English class named Sabina Sepulveda, who turned me on to Toni Morrison. We spent hours in Sabina's Somerville apartment smoking weed, talking about books, and playing dominoes. I taught her how to smack the dominoes hard against the table and shout, "Tenderloin!" whenever she scored ten points, like my dad taught me.

Sabina accepted me right away. So did Francesca, who became my guide into the Black student community. She was an almost-white-looking woman who grew up around her father's family in Harlem and put me in my place almost every day.

When I tried to show how enlightened I was by insisting I loved wearing my curly hair natural and would never straighten it again, she pounced.

"That's light-skinned privilege," she said. "You know that, right? Like only a mixed girl with wash-and-go hair like yours would ever say that. Most Black girls need to press their hair just to get a job! You need to think!"

One of the biggest insecurities I had around my new friends was whether or not I was Black enough to be part of their inner circle. My anxiety spiked whenever they said the n-word, which they did a lot. Using the word was like the ultimate symbol of their self-acceptance, and I envied them for doing it with such ease. Whether they were from the Bronx or Dallas or Oberlin, Ohio, they said it to each other, affectionately or to tease, but it was always the inclusive version with the soft "ga"—the one my dad used for years in his stand-up. Even after he rejected the n-word, it continued to take on a life of its own in Black culture.

My new friends revered the early comedy of Richard Pryor—sneaking into their parents' record collection as young teens to listen to his X-rated albums—and many of them adopted the version of the n-word he made famous. The word seemed to roll off their tongues, a defiant stance against racism, and it connected them to one another. I longed for that sense of kinship, but the thought of saying the n-word like they did made me feel like a fraud.

Still, I gave it a shot. One afternoon, Francesca and I were hanging out at my apartment and goofing about a musician friend of ours named Mike.

"You know that n**ga thinks he's looking like a Bob Marley motherfucker," she said, making fun of Mike's hair, which he had styled into long locs that didn't really suit his nerdy personality.

"Too bad that n**ga sings more like a Bobby McFerrin-don't-worry-be-happy motherfucker than a revolutionary," I said, trying to say the n-word as effortlessly as she had, even though it sounded forced and artificial to my own ears.

Before I finished my sentence, Francesca put her hand up to my face and looked at me sternly, perhaps hearing the shakiness of my voice and picking up on my discomfort. "No," she said. "Sister, no." Then her own voice got gentle and she laced her fingers in mine. "You don't have to say that, Liz. You're one of us without it."

When she first called me out for using the n-word, shame washed over me. The word was not authentic to the person I was or the experiences I had growing up, despite my father's relationship to it or the fact that I was Black. People who grew up around family and friends who spoke the n-word in their homes and communities could see this clearly. In the end, I came to appreciate how Francesca tried to redirect me with such familiarity and love. A barrier between us had broken, and I never used the n-word that way again.

Even as my relationships with my new friends grew closer, I felt embarrassed about having my Black awakening so much later than everyone else. Everything about me—my record collection, my favorite movies, the dance moves I knew best—suddenly seemed so white, like a bright white beacon flashing from my forehead, advertising to everyone I was a sellout. I needed to make a change.

I called Jules, my best friend from high school, who was now a junior at Swarthmore.

"I broke up with Dan," I said when she picked up the phone.

"Oh no," she said. "I love him!" That hit me hard. If Jules was on Dan's side, how could she be on mine?

"We moved apart," I said.

"What happened?"

"Well," I said, feeling a little sorry for her for not catching on, "I'm Black."

"I know!" she said, trying to suppress a laugh. But I wasn't sure she really understood.

"I mean, being Black is important to me. It's like the center of my life now."

"Oh, wow!" she said, and sounded so genuinely interested, I told her how *Controversy* was my new favorite Prince album and all about the best parts of Toni Morrison's *Song of Solomon*.

"I've made so many good friends," I said. "I feel like they really get me."

"P," she said, "I'm so happy for you."

I believed her, but it didn't change the fact that I'd never been able to have a deep conversation with her or any of my high school girlfriends about race.

"So, you get it?" I asked.

"Get what?"

"Why you can't be my best friend anymore."

She got quiet.

I said, "'Cause I need to be around people who understand what it's like to be Black."

"Of course," she said, still trying to sound supportive, hiding how sad she felt. I knew I was hurting her, but my worldview had completely shifted, and I didn't have the words to describe all the thoughts churning inside me.

And I would miss her too. Who else would answer my phone calls at three in the morning after I woke up shaking from a terrible dream? But at the time, I was convinced the only way to fully commit to being my authentic self was to let the friendship go.

My resolve only lasted a few months. Over time, we started an uneasy and intermittent dialogue about how to navigate an inter-racial friendship that continues to this day. The conversations have been hard, but they've been worth it. Jules is still my best friend and our discussions about race have deepened our relationship and my understanding of myself.

Around the time I broke up with Jules in college, I broke up with my mom too. I refused to speak to her for over a year. I couldn't forgive her for not preparing me for life as a Black girl growing up in a white world.

Many years later, I found a note in a stack of my mother's papers. I wrote it more than a year after I stopped talking to her, when I was finally ready to welcome her back into my life.

Dear Mommy,

This letter is long overdue, but I wanted to be my own person before I wrote it. Thank you for accepting my newly found pride in myself as an African American, Jewish woman. As much as my language may seem to exclude the only person who took the time to care about me growing up, you misunderstand, and I misarticulate. You are wholly and singularly responsible for giving me a space to find this part of myself. From keeping your cynicism about my father to yourself, to bringing in other Black women to mess with my hair, everything— and finally accepting me today, listening, even when my words may hurt. For a woman who couldn't have possibly known how to raise a Black child, I think you did a better job than you think. Thank you for always giving me confidence that I have a great mind, which could only be the gift of a woman with an even greater mind.

> *I love you,*
> *Elizabeth*

At the time, she told me she loved the letter, and our relationship fell back into a familiar pattern. We talked on the phone every day, fought over everything, but we were never able to have a deep conversation about race or the time she called me the n-word when I was twelve years old. She couldn't. For me it represented all the ways she didn't understand my experience as a Black person or see me the way I wanted her to. In the end, I chose to be grateful for everything she did and sacrificed, including bringing my father into my life when I needed him most.

My mother loved me the very best she could, and she did it with more love and tenderness than she'd ever been given.

I met Kenny the summer after my senior year of college. He was a Black student at BU a few years younger than I was, good looking and just under six feet tall. A popular frat boy and a jock, he loved playing baseball, watching football, and debating radical politics with his more conservative Black friends.

One July night, Sabina and I packed him and two other friends into my two-seater Toyota MR2 to go see Spike Lee's *Do the Right Thing* on opening night. During the movie, Kenny held my hand.

There was something about him that felt off—he wasn't obsessed with movies, he never laughed at my jokes, and he said mean things about his friends—but in every other way, he seemed like a perfect fit for my new life.

Overnight, I had a new boyfriend. He brought me to Black fraternity parties, he introduced me to step-team competitions with thousands of Black participants, and we even started a business together selling Black Greek merch, including little slippers my nana knitted by hand. He showed me a world I'd never seen before. An all-Black world, and I loved it. But whenever I laughed too loudly or got silly, he'd knock me down a peg.

We'd been together for almost four months when I brought him home for Thanksgiving. We stayed with my sister Rain since I wasn't talking to my mother. After we dropped off our bags, the first thing I wanted to do was introduce him to my father.

Kenny nibbled on his fingernails as we pulled into the gated community in Bel Air where my father now lived.

"Does he know how fat you got?" he asked on the way up the driveway.

My stomach lurched. I'd put on thirty pounds since we started dating. He often said belittling things that made me feel bad about myself, but at the moment, I chose to ignore the signs. I was sure my father would be so proud of me for accepting my Blackness and having a boyfriend with radical politics to boot.

When I rang the doorbell, my father's housekeeper, a white woman named Georgia wearing a uniform, answered and said, "Your daddy is in the living room."

We followed her into a cavernous room with huge windows and almost no furniture where he was lounging on the only couch, smoking a cigarette.

"Do you need anything, Mr. Pryor," Georgia said.

"No," he said, and she left the room.

He looked more exhausted than I'd ever seen him before, but

he still rose from the couch to shake Kenny's hand. My boyfriend returned the gesture limply. I'd forgotten to tell him my dad judged a person by the strength of their handshake.

"He was born in Newark, New Jersey," I said, trying to cover for Kenny's faux pas, and showing off that I was dating someone who hailed from such a Black city.

"I been to Newark more than once or twice," my dad said, sounding not at all impressed by Kenny's hometown, but trying to find some common ground.

"Oh," Kenny said, without making eye contact, "I actually grew up in Orange." It was a more upscale suburb two miles from Newark, but quibbling over neighborhoods rebuffed my father's overture.

Nervously, I reached for a bowl of mixed nuts in the middle of the coffee table, and grabbed a handful.

"You sure you wanna eat those?" Kenny asked.

I let the nuts slip out of my fingers and into the bowl without answering. My father studied me for a long beat, eyed Kenny, and took another puff of his cigarette.

"Liz," he said, "on your way out, tell Georgia I need a Pepsi."

He had dismissed us.

When I got back to Boston, I called him to see if maybe the visit with Kenny hadn't been as awful as I thought.

"What happened to Daniel?" my dad asked.

"We broke up."

"Too bad. I liked him."

I was crushed. I thought trading in my white boyfriend, getting rid of my white friends, and shutting out my white mother would mean I'd really and truly embraced my Blackness. By rejecting Kenny, my father let me know that's not how it works. A lifetime of emotional turmoil with inappropriate women gave him a superpower: He could spot toxic relationships at five hundred paces, even if he never followed his own advice. He knew instantly Kenny wasn't the guy for me, no matter his politics or the color of his skin.

Twenty-Five

He Made the Word a Universe

2017

"Thank you. Good evening. Hope I'm funny."

I wandered through my rural Massachusetts neighborhood, listening to *That N***er's Crazy* on repeat, blasting Richard Pryor through my earbuds.

After a lifetime of avoiding my father's early comedy, I was finally embracing his influence on the history of the n-word. He sounded young and energized on the album, like he had before the fire. Memories came rushing back: his sweet, clean smell; the way he chuckled at his own jokes; and how the framed gold record of *That N***er's Crazy* hung near the entryway of his office at the Parthenia house. Until that moment, I'd forgotten the time I'd snuck a listen to the album as a little girl and was lulled to sleep by his voice, even though I didn't understand the humor.

He recorded it at a San Francisco nightclub in early 1974. Instead of leading the mostly Black crowd through a series of punchlines, he told stories, embodied characters, and put on voices, switching them up at breakneck speed. His father; a preacher; a simpering white husband politely asking for sex; and in a particularly prescient moment, a Black man who is harassed by the police, which throws him off his game on a date. Then there was the wino who meets Dracula.

Say, n***er. You with the cape!
What your name, boy? Dracula? What kinda name is that for a
n***er?

I laughed out loud and choked back tears as I dodged overgrown hedges and little black flies. It was the same Dracula routine he performed the first time I ever saw him do stand-up when I was six years old.

For most of the album, he compared how Black people moved through the world in contrast to how white people did. Black folks were no-nonsense realists: direct, unapologetic, and funny. White ones were gullible, uptight, subdued, and passionless. Like how *The Exorcist* could never have been made with Black people.

N***ers would have handled that movie differently. They would
have walked into that house and said, "What in the fuck is that
funky smell?"

He also singled out Black women for their particular brand of straight talk. Under the guise of mocking himself for his "white women disease," as he called it, he showed respect for the Black women who took him to task. "Don't ever marry a white woman in California," he said, but caught himself mid-joke. "A lot of sisters probably [thinking], 'Don't marry a white woman anywhere, n***er.'"

As I cranked up the volume and listened to him turn Black stereotypes into strengths, there was no way to avoid how often he used the n-word. He used it to refer to other Black people, to imitate white people, even to imagine how Black women might refer to him—but it didn't affect me in the way I thought it would. It wasn't alienating or an inside joke I wasn't in on, and it didn't feel like a bomb going off the way it had in my classroom.

After two days of immersing myself in *That N**er's Crazy*, I moved onto his 1976 album *Bicentennial N***er*. By the time he recorded it, his sense of humor had become even more overtly political. One of my favorite jokes on the album, if you can call it that, had him imagining a conversation between two enslaved Africans in the hull of a slave ship, not the most obvious setting for stand-up comedy. When one of the men laughed, the other asked what was so funny. "Yesterday," the first man said, "I was a king."

The audience on the record tittered uneasily, as if they didn't know whether or not to laugh. His understanding of the African diaspora and slavery made it clear he had deepened his knowledge of Black history since his Berkeley days in the early seventies. In one of the routines, he painted a picture of slavery that was poignant and historically accurate. His enslaved characters came from Dahomey in West Africa, suffered through the Middle Passage, endured new diseases that went untreated—"I used to could live to be a hundred and fifty, now I die of high blood pressure by the time I'm fifty-two."

Three hours later, I had listened to the album five times and walked so far from home, I needed to call my husband to pick me up.

"You gotta hear this," I said, queuing up the album before I even kissed Jerry hello. "He's light-years ahead of his time."

We'd been sitting in the driveway for twenty minutes when the album wrapped up with a two-hundred-year-old man recounting the horrors of slavery while the "Battle Hymn of the Republic" crescendoed in the background.

"You all probably done forgot about it," the old man says wistfully about slavery. Then my dad breaks character and uses his own voice for the last line of the album, "But I ain't gonna never forget it."

Jerry and I sat quietly for a few moments.

"He loved breaking down history just like you do," he finally said. "Maybe," I said, hoping he was right.

"No," he said, "he did. Your dad was an historian. Just like you."

Over the next few weeks, I worked my way through every one of my father's comedy albums and concert films. Of all his performances before he disavowed the n-word, the one I felt the most connected to was his 1979 film *Richard Pryor: Live in Concert.*

He took command of the entire stage with the elegance of a dancer and folded powerful political statements into the vulnerable and self-deprecating way he processed his troubled life. I recognized all of the references. He whipped his hips back and forth as an over-sexed monkey, trembled all over as a neurotic Doberman, and buckled to the floor as his angry heart clenched during a heart attack. The monkey was a pet we had for six weeks at Parthenia Street. The Doberman was around for years, and growled at everyone who tried to leave the house. The heart attack was one of many he'd had since I first visited.

It was also the first time he brought his children into the act. "My kids think everything I do is funny," he said about the time he almost drowned in the pool at the Parthenia house, and Rain, Richard Jr., and I couldn't stop laughing because he was swimming with flippers and a snorkel and we thought it was a joke. I remember hearing the routine as a little kid and being so excited to be part of the show. Watching it again as an adult and as a mother, it hit me in a new way. He was talking about the kind of parent he wanted to be. "I don't wanna fuck my kids up like I'm fucked up."

As I watched and rewatched the film, I kept coming back to the story he told about the fateful night when he and his then-wife Deboragh had a New Year's Eve party and got into a huge fight. It was December 31, 1977, and they'd only been married for three months, but he'd been drinking and doing drugs more than usual. The intensity of their arguments had been building. I was asleep in the guest house when the fighting got out of control. She jumped into the new Mercedes my father bought for her, threatening to leave, and he pulled out a .357 Magnum and started shooting at the car to stop her. The sound of gunfire and screaming woke me up. No one was hurt, but the cops came to the house, and he was charged with assault with a deadly weapon. By the next day, the story was all over the tabloids.

In the concert film, he owned up to his bad behavior.

> I don't want to never see no more police
> in my life
> at my house
> taking my ass to jail
> for killing my car

His candor and self-awareness allowed people to laugh with him. But as I listened to the story, I realized he was also setting the stage for something bigger.

> . . . the police came
> I went in the house
> 'cause they got Magnums too
> And they don't kill cars
> They kill n*g-gars

When I heard the joke, I spluttered out the kind of laugh that makes milk shoot out of your nose. Long before organizations like Black Lives Matter existed, my father called out police brutality and abuse of power poetically, rhyming the n-word with car, twisting the very sound of it into an indictment of anti-Black violence. Like a linguistic Robin Hood, he took the racist stereotype of the word—that Black people were ignorant, dishonest, dangerous, oversexed, out of control—and turned its negative connotations into Black empowerment.

In the opening moments of the show, he joked that Black folks trampled over white ones to get into the theater.

We saw about eight dead white people when we was coming in, still had tickets in their hand. N***ers are just running over them getting in here.

At first glance, it sounded like he was echoing the racist stereotype that Black people were violent and aggressive. But in reality, he used the n-word to amplify something much more complex and nuanced about racial dynamics in the United States: When it came down to it, white people weren't as tough as they made themselves out to be, and Black people didn't get enough credit for their determination, resourcefulness, and swagger.

Listening to my father's albums over and over again, I realized I'd gotten something very wrong about the n-word.

In my research, I argued that the n-word was two separate words with two separate meanings depending on who said it and why—the version Black people used with each other, and the white version, which was racist. The article I published about it even won a prize.

My father made me rethink everything I thought I knew about the word.

The white version I was right about. It was a singular, vile, one-track, disgusting slur, the word he mocked with his white-guy voice and always said with a crisp "er."

But the Black version of the word? It was a universe.

My dad used it to mean "Black," "huckster," "trickster," "badass," "father," "uncle," "brother," "downtrodden," "revolutionary," "fighter," "asshole," "person," "guy," "slave," "drunk," "junky," "fine fellow," "rule breaker," "rule follower," "friend," "enemy," and even a person who was Vietnamese, like he did on his 1975 album . . . *Is It Something I Said?*: "White folks tired of our ass too. They're getting them some new n***ers. The Vietnamese." He was making a political statement about what lay in store for Vietnamese refugees when they came to America.

His version of the n-word combined his personal pain with the history of trauma experienced by all Black people in the United States. He mixed that anguish with pride and culture and panache, and, of course, humor. In *That N***er's Crazy*, he used the word to talk about Black resilience in the face of American racism. If a white man came face to face with a Martian, he'd be terrified, my father said, but a Black person would think nothing of it. "Nothing can scare a n***er, after four hundred years of this shit."

He walked the same tightrope I'd been trying to walk in the classroom, only he did it with balance and grace. His Black characters weren't pure heroes, and his white characters weren't pure villains. Mocking the very idea of a stereotype, he called out the absurdity of racism and made it impossible to ignore. And he made it funny. "We'll give some land to the n***ers and the ch*nks, but we don't want the Irish," he wrote in *Blazing Saddles,* the very line that rocked my classroom.

In that moment, listening to his comedy and finding connections between his work and my own, I felt close to him in a way I hadn't since he died.

How had I missed the fact that my obsession with the n-word had everything to do with him?

His comedy and his innovative use of the word allowed him to distill the ugliest aspects of American culture, making hard truths easier to digest and laying the groundwork for a whole new generation of artists.

Interlude Ten

Hope I'm funny. 'Cause I know n***ers are ready to kick ass.
Richard Pryor,
*That N***er's Crazy,*
1974

In 1987, a young visionary from South Central Los Angeles started Ruthless Records in his parents' garage and launched the multimillion-dollar gangsta rap industry. Building on the massive success of East Coast hip-hop, Eazy-E assembled an L.A. "supergroup" with his favorite local rappers, including Ice Cube and Dr. Dre.

They called themselves N.W.A, or N**gaz Wit Attitudes, a callback to the Black Power movement and a protest against the injustice they faced growing up. In the 1980s, Ronald Reagan's War on Drugs disproportionately targeted Black people, who were five times more likely than whites to be incarcerated for similar drug offenses. Police in riot gear treated drug busts in Black neighborhoods like military incursions, breaking down doors with battering rams and imposing lengthy mandatory minimum sentences for possession.

N.W.A's album *Straight Outta Compton* went platinum. Their controversial lyrics exposed the violent realities of their neighborhoods and bragged about how they survived it. They rapped about joining gangs, dealing drugs, brandishing AK-47s and sawed-off shotguns, using women for sex, and kicking ass. In a song that infuriated the FBI, "Fuck tha Police," they unapologetically promised to take down cops in retaliation for police brutality.

And they peppered their songs with the n-word.

Until 1988, the word was a rare feature in hip-hop, but once N.W.A burst onto the scene, it was everywhere and had a new spelling. By writing the word phonetically, with an "a" at the end, N.W.A codified what African Americans already knew and what Richard Pryor made famous. There were two separate n-words, and the one with the soft "ga" contained a multitude of possibilities as a tool for political change. And it belonged exclusively to Black people.

From that point on, artists from Tupac Shakur to Kendrick Lamar made the word "n**ga" a hip-hop staple in music so powerful it influenced culture, politics, and public discourse around the world.

"That's our word now," Ice Cube said about the n-word in 2017, "and you can't have it back."

Twenty-Six

"You Got It, Toyota"

1991–1992

"I was a little kid, about five years old," my dad said, as we sat on his bed at the Bel Air house. "I had on my little cowboy suit, and I stepped in some dog shit. And I just kept slipping like I couldn't get up."

"On purpose?" I asked, pushing a tiny tape recorder closer to him on the bedspread. He looked so frail and gaunt and spoke slowly and carefully, like he wanted to be sure I heard every word.

"Yup. I was covered with shit, but they were all laughing. My dad, my mom, Mama, even some of the ladies that worked at the whorehouse was laughing."

I was captivated, afraid to move a single muscle or do anything that might make him stop. As honored as I was to listen, it was hard to hear about my father as a little boy who needed to slip in shit to get attention. Suddenly, his all-consuming drive to make people laugh made perfect sense.

"Did you know you were funny back then?" I asked.

"I knew nothing else. But that I knew." His eyes locked with mine, like he'd just revealed his deepest secret.

After college graduation, I realized the simplistic way I'd tried to embrace my Blackness was misguided, so I ended things with Kenny, moved home to L.A., apologized to my mom, and reconnected with Jules. I even started listening to Elvis Costello again. But the sense of belonging and acceptance I'd felt with my Black friends in college was missing and left a gaping hole. My father got me a job working as a production assistant on his final film with Gene Wilder, *Another You*. Carrying a walkie-talkie made me feel like a big shot, but my heart wasn't in it, and I never got promoted past fetching coffee for actors. I felt insecure, isolated, and lost, eating triple orders of fast food, drinking too much red wine, and waking up in the morning next to people I didn't know.

Spending time with my dad talking about his life was one of the few bright spots.

"Liz, your father has something he wants to ask you," said Deboragh, my dad's ex-wife. They were still best friends, fifteen years after he shot her car. The three of us were sprawled out on his massive bed because there was still almost no furniture in his house, and the bed was the only place to sit in his bedroom.

While I waited for him to say what was on his mind, I adjusted the pillow behind his back.

Very slowly, he said, "I want you to please help me write my book."

My heart was fluttering. I was pretty sure he meant his autobiography.

His eyes were turned downward and he looked shy, but he was grinning.

Deboragh said, "You went to that fancy college and studied writing, right?"

"Yes," I said, but I wasn't sure writing poems about growing up in Los Angeles and smoking weed under the Hollywood sign qualified me to write Richard Pryor's memoir. "You sure you want me to do this?" I asked him, barely containing my excitement. This was more than writing. It was a chance to hear about his life in his own words.

"You got it, Toyota," he said. "I'm an American," two of his newest catchphrases that usually meant yes.

"He's a little touched," Deboragh said, and we all laughed.

His face sparkled, which made my heart soar because lately he was more likely to be sleeping than smiling. He'd been so depressed since he got sick.

In 1986, my father was diagnosed with multiple sclerosis, a degenerative illness that attacks the central nervous system. There is no cure. For my entire life, he moved through the world with the grace of a dancer and the magnetism of the most charming man in the world. But the MS made him unsteady when he walked. He seemed more defenseless and vulnerable every time I saw him.

The first sign there was something wrong was his weight loss. His pants hung too low on his hips, and he lost his gusto for food. He treated the MS like a secret, so he didn't come out and tell me about it. Some tabloids published rumors that he was thin because he was back on drugs. Others speculated he had AIDS. He denied both, and I believed him.

I found out about his diagnosis accidentally. In 1988, my exboyfriend Dan was working as a production assistant on my dad's movie *Harlem Nights*. Dan called me from the set.

"Liz," he said, "your father's sick."

"What do you mean?" He sounded serious and so worried.

"You need to call him," he said. "He fell in his trailer, and really hurt himself. At first, everyone thought he was drunk, but he ended up going to the hospital. I overheard the wardrobe person tell someone it was MS."

I immediately dialed my father's number, but wasn't sure I had the right one. He had just broken up with another girlfriend, which likely meant he had a new phone number—he changed it whenever he ended a relationship or fired an assistant—but I called the only number in my phone book that wasn't scratched out, and his secretary answered at the house.

"Yes, he has MS," she said, "but he's going back to the set on Monday. He tripped. It was a minor accident. He's fine."

I wanted to believe her, but deep down I knew something was seriously wrong.

As he got sicker and less confident in his body, it was clear that he was no match for MS and his film career was coming to a close. By the time *Another You* came out in 1991, he looked like a too-thin shadow of himself on the screen. He still had glimmers of his comedic timing, but none of the energy and life force that made him glow. The critics panned the movie, and it flopped at the box office, which seemed to accelerate his physical and mental decline.

The rapid and unpredictable ways the illness hit him made me feel more anxious and insecure every time I saw him. When he stumbled over the Mexican tiles in the front hall, I wasn't sure how to help. I tried to offset the uncertainty by finding familiar ways for us to connect, like taking him to the movies every few weeks. One Friday afternoon, I took him to see a matinee at a multiplex in the heart of West Hollywood.

He didn't have a cane yet, and he used me as a crutch. Walking as slowly as I could, I tried to stabilize him, but if I miscalculated, he'd get frustrated and growl at me. So, I let him navigate the theater on his own. He used the seats to hold himself up and pushed from one row to the next until we got all the way to the second row. It was so close to the screen it hurt my neck to look up, but he was losing his eyesight because of the MS and couldn't see if we sat any farther back.

Within the first few moments of the movie, he got up to pee.

"Do you need help?" I asked, wondering if I should go with him.

"No," he snapped, "I can handle going to the bathroom by myself." I wasn't convinced, but didn't challenge him.

Ten minutes later he still wasn't back. I was about to go looking for him when someone whispered in my ear.

"Are you Elizabeth?" Startled, I turned around to see an older white woman crouching down next to me. "Your father says he's gonna be at the car."

Panicked, I bolted out of the theater.

I found him wandering around the sprawling parking garage looking for my blue Acura. Sweating as he rested his weight on one car after another, his face was pinched in pain and he looked terrified.

"Where were you?" There was an anxious edge to his voice I'd never heard before.

"I'm here. I'm sorry. It's okay." He grabbed my shoulder and leaned all of his weight on me.

I got him into the car and buckled him in.

"Don't ever leave me alone like that!" he said, his body shaking.

"I promise I won't." I hugged him until he started to relax. It was the last time I took him out by myself.

Slowly, the MS destroyed his body and his hope. He walked less, stopped taking care of himself, and even though he'd always been vain, he let his hair get gray and matted. Depression gripped him, and so did the pain. I visited him often, but he was usually lost in his own world. If I slipped out of the room, he rarely noticed.

Connecting with him over the book at a time when I was drowning in my own life—drinking too much, smoking too much pot, and isolating myself from people—felt like he was throwing me a lifeline, giving me purpose. Every day, I'd show up at 10:00 a.m. with my tape recorder and my notebooks, flop onto the bed next to him, and we'd dive right in. One time, he spent the entire morning describing a long meandering dream he had about catching a magical trout with Sammy Davis Jr. and an Irish nurse named Rose.

At lunchtime, he'd call his housekeeper on the intercom and ask her to cook something gourmet, like lobster ravioli or French onion soup or homemade cheeseburgers with fancy cheese. He never ate much, and sometimes he was too exhausted to continue into the afternoon. On those days, we'd rewatch his favorite movie, *The Silence of the Lambs*, a newly released film he had on videotape along with hundreds of other VHS screeners lining the walls of his bedroom in huge, neat stacks. As the movie played on repeat from his giant rear-projector television, he pointed out different elements he wanted me to see, like how the set decorators sewed swastikas onto the serial killer's quilt to show how unhinged the character was. "Do you see that, Liz? That's how you make a brilliant movie. Attention to every detail."

Over time I grew braver, tossing out questions I wouldn't have dared ask when we started.

"How did you first know when you were unhappy?" I asked one day after he, Deboragh, and I finished eating salads with goat cheese and candied pecans.

"Geez maneez!" he went off. "I've got to talk about my life in this fucking recorder. And it scares me to death. 'Cause I got two people here who know me *fairly* well. And they're not gonna agree with anything I say. They're gonna push me to the iceberg. Ah shit . . . What's the question?"

We let him off the hook, even though he'd skirted the answer. His eyes glazed over and the corners of his mouth sagged.

The hardest stories to hear were about his childhood. I knew the facts: Mama had raised him in her brothel. His mother, Gert, hadn't been around. Buck had been dead for twenty years now, and my father didn't seem to miss him much. What I'd never known were the ugliest stories, especially the ones that were hard for him to revisit about the nasty and violent relationship between his parents. Buck, who'd once been a professional boxer, manhandled the women in his life the same way he did his opponents in the ring and the johns in Mama's brothel. He hit Gert frequently, and one day she defended herself against the constant beatings by cutting open his testicle with her fingernail.

As my father told the story, he grew more animated than he'd been in weeks, slicing his finger through the air and grabbing at his crotch as if he were in pain. "He ran out of the house screaming for Mama, who lived two doors down. 'Mama! Mama!' he yelled and there was blood everywhere." He imitated Buck's voice in a way that sounded almost comical. But then Deboragh's beeper went off.

His eyes got wide. "That's my dad telling me not to talk about him anymore," he said, looking truly spooked, like he was reliving the fear he must have felt growing up in such a violent house.

Until the beeper went off, as horrifying as the image was, he almost had me believing the story about my grandparents was funny. Watching the panic take root behind his eyes helped me see, in a way I never had before, the layers of his pain, physical and emotional, still haunting him. He had been beaten, neglected, lonely, and afraid.

Growing up as Richard Pryor had been terrifying. Trauma formed the building blocks of his worldview. His incredible life force allowed him to kick and claw and scrape his way free. Confronting his demons and broadcasting them to the world was ultimately how he made his way out. But he never completely escaped the pain of his childhood. His whole life had been a constant tug-of-war—the kind of man he so wanted to be on one side and his self-destructive behavior on the other.

"The army was the first time I felt truly free," he said one morning after I settled next to him on the bed. "I got out of Peoria, I got away from Mama's house, and I got away from my father."

I couldn't imagine the army as a liberating experience. Deboragh must have agreed because she hopped off the bed and crossed her arms.

"Except all those times the white sergeants called you n***er," she said.

He looked affronted. He never liked being corrected, although Deboragh was one of the only people who could get away with it. "Yes, Debbie," he said in a fake stern voice, "except when they called me that." Slowly, he shimmied his body toward the pillows so he could sit up. "I said I *felt* like I was free, not that I was. They treated me no different in Germany than they had in Peoria."

"What happened?" I asked.

"The white guys always wanted to fight us Black dudes. I tried to stand up for a friend of mine one of them was beating on, and when I did, they kicked me out." Years later, I learned he had actually stabbed a white soldier with a switchblade to defend his friend. The soldier was fine. There were no repercussions for the constant beatings by the white servicemen, but my father was discharged for protecting the Black soldier.

As we were nearing the end of the interviews, news broke that the four LAPD officers who were caught on film beating a Black man for a traffic violation had been found not guilty. The Rodney King verdict shocked all of us. The graphic video of King getting pummeled by the cops seemed like more than enough evidence for the jury to convict. As news of the not-guilty verdict spread, the city erupted. For five days, buildings burned and businesses were destroyed, especially in the Black parts of Los Angeles where anger over police corruption and brutality was highest.

The uprising was broadcast live all day. My father shook his head and asked over and over, "How are they still getting away with beating down a brother like that?"

It was the first time I had ever personally witnessed an incident of such blatant police violence, but my father had known that kind of racism since he grew up in Peoria during the height of Jim Crow segregation. Throughout his life, he used the stage as his platform to stand up and fight against the injustice he saw everywhere.

I felt called to action.

The news reported that the First AME Zion Church in West Adams was looking for volunteers to help out, and I hopped in my car the next day and went. I joined other young Black people to help clean up the city—storefront by storefront. I made friends with Black filmmakers and writers who were passionate about rebuilding the community. For the first time in a while, I felt like I belonged. When I visited my father after shoveling out a burned-out grocery store, my clothes still reeking of smoke, he beamed at me with pride.

Once we finished the interviews, my dad set me up in an office at Columbia Pictures, the studio where he once had a film company, Indigo Productions. Hauling my microcassette recorder and my Macintosh SE into the small space, I spent weeks playing back the recordings and transcribing each and every word. As I listened, I tried to keep up with the conversation, but sometimes I'd get so lost in his voice and his stories I'd forget what I was doing and have to rewind the tape.

Finally, I made it through all the material and printed out forty pages of single-spaced transcripts. I put them into brand-new manila folders, lined them up neatly on my desk, read through every page, and made detailed notations on each one. I felt so organized and accomplished.

But as I looked at the thousands of words spread out in front me, I realized something I'd overlooked. I had absolutely no idea how to tell my father's story. There was so much to process: his brutal childhood, his desperate search for love, and how brilliantly he used his trauma to fuel his groundbreaking career in comedy. How was I supposed to craft the complex, nonlinear, and heart-wrenching journey of Richard Pryor?

Every week my father called to ask how it was going. Part of me wanted to tell him how anxious I was and ask for help. But I was afraid. Working on the book together had provided our deepest connection in years. I didn't want to risk losing it. I kept putting him off by telling him I'd show him something soon.

Day after day, I stared at the blinking cursor on an empty page, smoked Camel lights, drank bottles of Barolo, and curled up in a ball on the floor under my desk and went to sleep.

Three months later, my dad's newest assistant called me and told me I should gather up my things and move out of the office.

"We'll send your last paycheck to your apartment," she said, "and don't worry about writing the book."

My dad had fired me.

Twenty-Seven

"Take Me Home, Country Roads"

1994

"My name is Jerry. I'm grateful to be here and to be sober," said the man I would eventually marry on the very first day I met him.

The Long Island accent was as thick as an Irish brogue. I swiveled my head to see who was speaking and saw a working-class white guy in his early thirties who sounded like Ray Romano, only more New York. He looked tattered, with shy eyes, a puffy face, and a Hickory Stripe engineer's cap on his head. He was indistinguishable from a lot of the guys who came and went in the recovery meetings, so once I'd checked him out, I turned around and instantly forgot about him.

After I screwed up my father's memoir, my self-destructive behavior spiraled out of control. I stuffed my face and drank alone in my apartment every night. With no job, no sense of purpose, I felt completely stuck. In rare, quiet moments, I admitted to myself that whenever I drank, I woke up in the morning filled with shame and regret. At a party, I barfed into a trash can mid-conversation. I knocked over wine glasses. I banged on the door of a good-looking set electrician at 2:00 a.m. Every night before I fell asleep, I told myself I would never do it again, but the next day I always did. When a friend's brother died from an accidental drug overdose and I arrived at the funeral trashed, her utter disdain got through to me in a way nothing else had.

My father had gotten sober going to recovery meetings. Maybe I could too.

The next morning, I dragged myself to a meeting in the basement of a church in Hollywood. When I arrived, I peeked my head through the heavy wooden door and saw only one empty chair in the crowded room. It was next to a woman my age whom I recognized from middle school, a girl I'd been jealous of back then because all the boys liked her and said she was pretty.

She caught my eye.

Embarrassed, I pretended not to see her and looked away. When I lifted my head, she did one of the kindest things anyone had ever done. The generosity of it brings me to tears even now. She waved and then patted the empty seat next to her, inviting me to sit.

I haven't had a drink since.

Getting sober cleared up the fog and set me on a new career path. I immersed myself in the study of Black literature and history, especially Black women's studies, and followed my passion to the Africana Studies Program at Cornell University in Ithaca, New York.

One of the first people I met at Cornell was Leslie Alexander, a Ph.D. student in the history department who was a year ahead of me. She had light skin and tight ringlets that fell to her shoulders, so I asked if she was mixed.

"My mom is white and my dad is Black," she said, lifting her eyebrow. "They raised me on a commune."

"Stop it! You're joking!"

"Nope. My parents believed in a future without racism." She was smiling.

"How'd that work out?"

"Girl," she said, chuckling, "if you have some time, I'll tell you the story of little me, the tragic mulattress." I had no idea whether or not she made the term up, but I could relate. It was the first time I ever met anyone with a mixed-race sense of humor. We were instantly inseparable.

Leslie took me under her wing, and I followed her everywhere. She introduced me to other Black graduate students on campus and helped me choose classes, including a Black women's history course that traced the activism of twentieth-century revolutionaries like Angela Davis and Assata Shakur to their radical, enslaved ancestors like Sojourner Truth and Harriet Jacobs. The class was so eye-opening and insightful, it inspired me to become an historian.

The most magical thing about Leslie was she made no assumptions about what it meant to be Black. We were zipping through town in her red Ford Escort and listening to a mixtape she'd made with her mom when a track blasted through the speakers. Leslie belted out every word.

"'Almost heaven, West Virginia, Blue Ridge Mountains, Shenandoah River . . .'"

I turned down the volume.

"John Denver?" I gasped in shock.

"My mom loves her some John Denver," she said. "What's not to like about 'Take Me Home, Country Roads?'"

Leslie made it seem possible to like John Denver and be Black. It was something I realized a friend of mine had tried to tell me years before. Christopher was a Black friend I knew from college. Right before I got sober, when I was at my lowest, I took him as my date to a black-tie party for my dad. Overweight, depressed, and feeling ridiculous in a flouncy, purple velvet dress that made my boobs look gigantic, I felt so unattractive standing next to Chris, who looked dashing in his tux. As we were about to step into the limo, Chris reached over and threw his arms around me.

"Liz," he said, "you have no idea how cool you are."

Speechless and close to tears, I leaned my head into his chest. I really didn't think I was cool at all.

"I hope one day you'll be able to integrate," he said, lifting my chin to meet his eyes.

Integrate, integrate, integrate. The idea stayed with me. Maybe I didn't have to choose one thing or another. I was Black *and* Jewish *and* mixed *and* a whole lot of other things, and I could embrace all of those parts of me at the same time. I'd never really been able to do that, because I'd never truly accepted all of those different aspects of myself.

It was Leslie who made me feel like personal integration was possible because she was an integrated person.

You can be wholly and fully yourself. Be Black and like John Denver.

Her faith in her Blackness and mine made me feel, perhaps for the first time, like whatever I was, however I was, it was enough. She accepted me for being a fake vegan, dizzy for boys, a neophyte student, a lover of Black history, clueless about Anita Baker, and a person who talked way too much in class. She loved me even though I was moody, fought with my mother on the phone almost every day, was intensely private about my father, and most important, was in the tender adolescence of my Black awakening.

Leslie gave me the confidence to love my whole self, and being able to do that opened up the door to loving someone else.

While I was embracing my Blackness at Cornell—studying with other Black students and renowned Black professors, staying up into the wee hours talking about what it means to be a Black woman in a racist world, even taking Swahili—I was also immersing myself in my recovery, which meant spending time in some of the whitest spaces in all of Ithaca, New York.

And that's saying something.

Jerry and I started hanging out as sober friends with a bunch of other sober friends, drinking way too much coffee at the State Diner.

He was sweet, and he was funny, but I didn't think about him romantically because we could not have been more different. He never
went to college; spent years working on oil rigs in a Wyoming boom
town; went camping and canoeing; and when he wasn't working, he
followed the Grateful Dead all over the country—from Nassau Coli-
seum to Oakland Auditorium—and had the letters "GD" tattooed on
the inside of his lower lip.

My feelings for Jerry changed the night of my twenty-seventh
birthday. At a party for me and another sober friend, he arrived with
two neatly wrapped gifts, the extra layers of tape the only sign he'd
wrapped them himself. He handed my friend her present first, a thick
copy of Michael Crichton's *Jurassic Park*. The Westlake girl in me
reared her ugly head and turned up her nose at a mass market paperback.

Jerry blushed when he handed me my gift.

"You can return it if you already have it," he said.

"I doubt I do," I said, smiling smugly.

I unwrapped the package and found a hardcover copy of a newly
published edition of W.E.B. Du Bois's 1903 book of essays, *The Souls
of Black Folk*.

How did a working-class white guy who scraped by painting fraternity houses know anything about the most important book published by a Black intellectual in the twentieth century?

"I wanted this," I said, eyeing him with new interest. "We're about
to read it for one of my classes."

"Good. But if you have it, the receipt is inside." For a second, he
searched my eyes, and then his face broke out into a wide, crooked
smile. His jaw looked squarer, the cleft in his chin deeper, and his blue
eyes gleamed with mischief.

Holy shit! Jerry is hot!

In that single moment, like the late-spring air, I completely and
utterly lost my chill.

As we got to know each other better, Jerry revealed private things about his childhood, about his dreams, and about his worldview. He was the first person I ever met who imagined every human being—from a person without a home to someone living in a mansion—was as equal and as deserving as the next. The fact that I was Richard Pryor's daughter was completely unimpressive to Jerry. Not because he didn't admire my dad's comedy, he did. But because fame and success were not how he measured a person's worth.

On the outside, he was the epitome of working-class masculinity. He walked with a strut, spoke gruffly, was a problem-solver, a fixer, a get-it-done guy. On the inside, he was sensitive and intuitive. From the moment we became close friends, he used his whiteness like armor to protect me from the world, even though I never asked him to. Like when we drove to one of the villages north of Ithaca because a friend said a restaurant there had the best ice cream in town.

As we pulled into the parking lot, I got nervous. "Yikes. I wonder if Black people ever eat here." I said it like a joke, but I was worried.

Jerry told me to wait and went into the restaurant to scope it out. He came back less than thirty seconds later and shook his head.

"Lotta white people in there," he said with a big grin as we drove away.

Jerry also hated the n-word. At the time, I didn't use the word casually, but I would quote someone directly who said it as a slur. When I quoted the actual word to explain a famous scene from *Narrative of the Life of Frederick Douglass*, he stopped me.

"Don't say that," he said. I thought he was kidding, so I continued my story and said it again.

"Please stop saying that word," he said as he gently grabbed my hands. "It's offensive. I can't stand hearing it."

He was dead serious, and it stopped me in my tracks. He helped me realize I wasn't obligated to repeat the word just because it was there.

Until Jerry, I had never known anyone who listened to what I said and read between the lines. He made me feel seen and beautiful and special when I was with him. He even loved to go fishing just like my father. My crush kept growing day after day, but I had no idea how to tell him how much I liked him.

Fourth of July weekend, I invited him on a camping trip with my cousins in Maine.

The first night, as soon as we got into our tent, Jerry tossed a large duffle bag, like a fortress, into the space between our sleeping bags.

I was so embarrassed. "You're afraid of me!" I blurted out.

"I am," he said. I burst into tears.

Which was only okay because he kissed me. I never wanted him to stop.

We waited five days to seal the deal (a world record for me) and he made me dinner—mac and cheese with tuna and onions in a Tupperware container. But as connected as I felt to him, I worried our differences would ultimately be too great to overcome for the relationship to last.

What if my friends at school or back home didn't like him? Jerry wasn't from Manhattan or Chicago or Los Angeles or consumed by pop culture or Black or Jewish. He didn't even like sushi or Ethiopian food.

As it turned out, I had nothing to worry about. Leslie started asking him for guy advice the minute they met. At Jules's annual New Year's Eve fondue party in L.A., she instantly bonded with him over their mutual love of the Grateful Dead, and her mom was absolutely giddy and flirted with Jerry all night.

Even my mom liked him.

"He's very smart, Elizabeth," she said, pulling me aside the first day they met, "and classically handsome." But most of all, she loved that he hunted through her kitchen junk drawer, found a Phillips-head screwdriver, and fixed the misalignment in her sliding glass doors without being asked.

Jerry knocked it out of the park with my friends and my mom, but the real test, as always, was my father.

By the time Jerry met him at his new house in the flats of Encino, my dad was fragile. He could barely walk and mostly got around on a motorized scooter he called his Harley. His voice was breathy and strained, but he still smoked cigarettes, and he was still funny.

"Are you from Down Under, mate?" he said after Jerry shook his hand firmly.

"No, sir. I'm from Long Island," he said, not the least bit surprised his accent was mistaken for an Australian one.

Our plan was to spend the evening together at the racetrack at Santa Anita Park.

"How far is it?" Jerry asked.

"Half a horse day. As the crow flies," my dad replied.

I had no idea what they were talking about. "Ten or fifteen miles or so," Jerry said knowingly. "If it was a straight shot."

My father nodded in approval.

As we got ready to go to the races, one of my dad's round-the-clock caretakers, Violeta, pulled into the driveway in an SUV large enough to fit the Harley so she could chauffeur us to the track.

My father rolled his scooter up to the passenger-side door and just stopped. Violeta opened the car door, but he did not stand up or move or say a word.

She waited nervously.

Then she said, "Mr. Pryor? You gonna walk to the car? Or you need help?"

He said nothing. His head drooped, and his face looked exhausted and tense.

My heart rate spiked. What was I supposed to do? I'd never seen him like this.

Violeta waited.

"Mr. Pryor?" she said again, carefully.

Nobody moved a muscle, or had any idea what to do.

Until Jerry walked up to my dad.

"Mr. Pryor," he said, his voice matter-of-fact, "I'm going to pick you up and put you in the car."

Without waiting for an answer, Jerry gently lifted my father from the Harley, placed him in the passenger seat, reached over and pulled out his seatbelt, buckled it, and closed the door.

The dignity and grace with which Jerry treated my dad was a love potion. I'd never seen anyone be that confident, that humble, that brave. I wanted to thank Jerry or throw myself at him or raise his babies.

Instead, I reached over, squeezed his hand, and whispered, "I love you."

We got married the next year.

Twenty-Eight

"How Do You Get to Detroit?"

2018

One year after I listened to all of my father's work and eight years after the *Blazing Saddles* incident in the classroom, I set out to teach an entire course devoted to the n-word. For years I'd been obsessively researching everything I could find about the word, from its earliest uses, to its pop culture explosion, to the way Richard Pryor used it in his comedy.

Since I started teaching, there had been dozens of eruptions on college campuses because of the n-word. At Princeton University, a white professor had to cancel a popular course on hate speech because he said the word in class and insisted it wasn't racist. At Emory University, the New School, and Smith College, where I taught, students protested against professors who used the word, dropped their classes, and even changed majors. Students at Williams College boycotted the entire English department over it.

I'd also had my own professional run-in with the n-word. When I first wrote my article—"The Etymology of N***er"—I felt empowered using the full word in the title. But shortly after it came out, the editors of a leading Black history blog corrected my use of the word and replaced it with the phrase "the n-word." I was mortified to find I was so out of step with some of the most radical Black intellectuals in the discipline. I never wrote out the word again.

In my class on the history of the n-word, I wanted students to grapple with the kind of real-world conflict the word ignited that might seem at odds with freedom of speech. Together we'd explore music, poetry, essays, literature, current events, online debates, television shows, and Quentin Tarantino movies to trace the word's circuitous path throughout American history. We'd study how the word evolved from a description of involuntary Black laborers in Jamestown in 1619 to a slur during the birth of Jim Crow segregation, and how it led to the rise of lynching in the twentieth century. We'd also look at how Black folks made the n-word their own during enslavement, the Harlem Renaissance, the Black Power movement, and the age of hip-hop, when it became a driving force of the culture.

"Professor Pryor," said Quinn, one of the Black students, a few weeks into the class.

I looked across the huge seminar table where twenty-three students from all different backgrounds sat. Most of them had been in my classes before. There was Alicia, an outspoken Black student from the Bronx who was premed; Luna, a Mexican-Indigenous student who learned English in eighth grade and was now a bilingual poet; Esther, a white woman from Vermont who grew up around libertarians and was a very deep thinker; and Quinn, a Black man whose parents were professors at Harvard University.

"Have you seen the Jay-Z–Oprah conversation?" Quinn asked. He was talking about a frank discussion between the hip-hop mogul and Oprah Winfrey in 2009 that got to the heart of the generational debate over the n-word. Jay-Z made the case for using it in his music. He said a younger generation "turned a word that was very ugly and hurtful into a term of endearment." The real problem wasn't the word, he said, but the racism in American society.

Oprah disagreed. She couldn't separate the word from its racist roots. "When I hear the word, even when I'm at your concert, I think about Black men who were lynched and that's the last word they ever heard."

Jay-Z was visibly moved by her point, but agreed to disagree about using it in hip-hop.

I'd watched the conversation several times, and was curious to hear what students thought.

"Has everybody seen the video?" I asked. Almost all of the students nodded their heads.

Quinn spoke up. "Honestly, I think Oprah doesn't get it, how the word Jay-Z and other Black artists are using isn't even really the same word the lynch mob used. Hip-hop has reclaimed the n-word, the soft 'ga' version, and shaped it into something different. She's saying there's only one word, the one with the hard 'er.'"

Everyone leaned closer over the seminar table.

"It irritates me," Alicia said, jumping in. "The focus is always on Black artists using the word, especially hip-hop artists. Like if only Black people stopped using the n-word it wouldn't exist anymore. As if it's their fault white people in America say the word. That's bullshit."

I got a kick out of her swearing. When students cursed in class it usually meant they were engaged.

Esther, one of the few white students in the room, raised her hand. "I'm not Black," she said, tentatively, "but I wonder if people think Oprah is caught up in some kind of respectability politics."

Several Black students snapped their fingers in agreement, but I felt compelled to stick up for Oprah.

"Come on, you guys. Don't you think Oprah's response has more to do with growing up in the rural Midwest and the South and experiencing the violence of the word firsthand than with being uptight or prim and proper? The n-word in hip-hop is subversive and can be powerful, but it's gotta be done right."

No one said a word, but the students eyed each other skeptically.

"Last spring," I said, "when Kendrick Lamar won the Pulitzer for his album *Damn*, my son, Henry, played it for me. I loved the way Kendrick used the n-word like punctuation, sparingly, thoughtfully, to make bolder points about himself, Black life, and the world. He used the n-word just a little bit, like a fine balsamic vinegar in a salad." They laughed.

"But Henry also played this other song for me by some two-letter hip-hop artist."

"YG?" Luna guessed.

"Exactly. So you all know the song? 'My N-word?' It's awful, right? He must use the n-word in the song more than one hundred times. 'My n-word, my n-word, my n-word.'"

Before I finished quoting the simple lyrics, half of the class was on me. They shouted over each other and could hardly contain themselves in their chairs. "I love that song!" said one student. "That's my jam," said another. "The party hasn't started until YG comes on," said yet another while cracking up.

I raised my hand in the air to quiet them down.

"Professor Pryor," said Quinn, "that's an anthem for our generation! It's unapologetic in its Blackness and the way it uses the n-word is everything."

"Seriously?" Could I be that wrong? I thought I was in lockstep with my students.

"If I'm totally honest, I think it's a little sus when Black folks don't say the n-word," said Alicia.

Like a team of synchronized swimmers, the whole class turned their heads to look at me.

"Except when they grew up around white people and never had the flow." She bit her lip sheepishly and smiled.

I laughed off her comment, but that night I woke up drenched in sweat and sticking to the sheets. In class the next day, we were all going to watch my father disavow the n-word in *Live on the Sunset*

Strip. Their homework was to listen to *That N***er's Crazy* in preparation. All semester, I'd been looking forward to teaching the comedy of Richard Pryor. His work was central to any discussion of the word, but I hadn't really thought about the fact that I was going to stand up in front of my class and talk about my own father.

When I was a little girl, he told me "Don't let nobody call you that" at the exact same time he was putting the Black version of the word on the map. He let his grandmother Mama call me the word, but refused to speak to my mother again when she did. He introduced me to *The Last Poets*, an album jam-packed with the n-word, years after he rejected the word onstage. His lessons were full of contradictions, like the word itself.

As I wrung out my soaking-wet nightgown, I was gripped with anxiety. What if I couldn't make the students understand how truly groundbreaking it was, in 1982, for my father to stop calling himself and other Black people n***er? That he regretted using the word as an artist, even though he was trying to say something important with it? That by giving up the word, he risked damaging his reputation and alienating his audience? What if the students dismissed his decision to renounce it in the same way they had dismissed Oprah's argument?

What scared me even more was the possibility that our discussion would drive me to say something aloud I'd never even admitted to myself: my own feelings about the word. I thought my father was the most cutting-edge voice of his generation. The way he used the n-word as a magic wand to expose American racism had an unprecedented cultural impact. But as proud as I was of how he used his voice to stand up against Black oppression, I was glad he disavowed the n-word. It had haunted me my whole life, made me feel different from white people and separate from Black people. It made me feel ugly and lonely when I was at my most vulnerable. I felt inspired and vindicated by my father's decision to give it up. What if my students lost respect for me when they found out?

• • •

"That's a word that's used to describe our own wretchedness," my father said from the stage in *Live on the Sunset Strip*. "And we perpetuate it now. That word is dead. The first people on the Earth were Black people. We the first ones to say, 'Where the fuck am I? And how do you get to Detroit?'"

I stood to the side of the projector while my students' eyes were glued to the screen, their faces lit only by the red glow of my father's suit. They watched as he described his burning-bush moment about the n-word on the very last day of his trip to Kenya. In the lobby of the Nairobi Hilton, he was punched in the gut with the recognition that in Africa he saw Black people everywhere doing all kinds of things, but none of them were n***ers. As a man raised in the United States, he'd grown up thinking the slur was synonymous with the people who were called the n-word. The trip to Africa showed him how wrong that idea was.

Watching him disavow the word made me wonder if his sudden epiphany had been something he'd been thinking about for longer than he admitted onstage. In particular, it struck me as deeply significant that he talked about the n-word as a symbol of Black people's "wretchedness." Did he choose the word "wretched" intentionally? Was he referencing Frantz Fanon's 1961 book *The Wretched of the Earth*, about the politics of decolonization? Had he read Fanon and other Black intellectuals before his trip to Africa, and had his reading helped change his mind about the n-word? I wish I'd known enough to ask him those questions when he was alive.

Rocking back and forth on my heels, I wrapped my arms tightly around my body, as he revealed onscreen he would never call another Black person the n-word again.

The students nodded their heads. It looked like they were rooting for him.

"They found people's remains five million years ago in Africa," he said. "You know them motherfuckers didn't speak French."

Everyone cracked up, including me.

"So you can take it for what it's worth. I ain't trying to preach nothing to nobody. I'm just talking about my feelings about it."

When the clip ended, I flicked on the lights and took a minute to let it all sink in. The students were uncharacteristically quiet. I took a deep breath.

"If my father embraced the n-word in the seventies in such a pivotal way that reshaped what the word meant," I asked, "what changed his mind about it?"

Alicia started to answer. "Pryor—" she said. "I mean, your dad, or Richard Pryor, or . . ."

"No worries! You can say any of them. They're all true!"

Everyone giggled.

"It's relational," she said. "The n-word only had meaning for your dad when he was in the United States imagining himself and other Black people in relation to Europeans and other white people."

Luna built on that. "By going to Africa, by seeing Black faces everywhere, he got a different perspective. He didn't need the word as a vehicle to connect him to other Black people anymore."

I was so moved by their empathy and how they understood the complexities of his decision to reject the n-word, but I wasn't going to shy away from the messiness of the conversation.

"Jay-Z spent time in Africa too," I said, "before he was on Oprah. What do you think the difference is between Richard Pryor's understanding of the n-word and Jay-Z's?"

Silence.

"Maybe it was a different time?" offered Luna.

"Jay-Z had Richard Pryor. Richard Pryor only had himself," added Esther.

I turned to the window and took a moment to catch my breath.

Their wheels were turning.

"I think," Quinn said, "Richard Pryor used the word to begin with because it was the authentic language of the Black world he grew up in. He needed to assert that to be true to himself onstage because nobody else had done that before. By using the n-word, he made the stage his own. But when his world got bigger, with the trip to Africa, he heard the word in a different way. To say it after that trip would be as inauthentic as not saying it on *That N-Word's Crazy.*"

The room exploded in snaps again.

Quinn encapsulated my father's journey with the n-word in a way that bridged the generation gap. Despite my fears, the class found a way to embrace Jay-Z's right to use the word, and Richard Pryor's decision not to.

When my father disavowed the n-word onstage, he was so far ahead of his time, he needed to say "n***er" to let the audience know what he meant. "We never was no n***ers," he said. He didn't have an alternative because the phrase "the n-word" wouldn't be invented for another decade.

Interlude Eleven

That's a devastating fucking word. That has nothing to do with us.
Richard Pryor,
Live on the Sunset Strip,
1982

In January 1995, pretrial motions began in the high-profile murder case against O. J. Simpson for the grisly stabbing deaths of his ex-wife Nicole and her friend. The case was dubbed the "Trial of the Century" and captivated the attention of the entire world. Simpson, who was Black, had once been the greatest NFL running back of all time and was still a household name.

A guilty verdict seemed like a slam dunk. A white LAPD detective had found a bloody glove at Simpson's home matching one from the murder scene.

The only problem was the n-word. Years earlier, the detective who found the glove, Mark Fuhrman, bragged about hating "Mexicans and n***ers." Simpson's Black defense attorney, Johnnie Cochran, argued Fuhrman was crooked, driven by racism and ambition to plant evidence at Simpson's home. All Cochran had to do was get Fuhrman's interviews admitted.

The Black prosecutor, Christopher Darden, fought back. He

argued Fuhrman's interviews were irrelevant. "The n-word had been introduced in this case," he said, for the sole purpose of inflaming the mostly Black jury. The word itself was so devastating that to simply hear it in court could have the power to upend the verdict. "It is the filthiest, dirtiest, nastiest word in the English language," Darden said. "It has no place in this case or in this courtroom."

He never once said the actual word during his argument.

In front of the entire world, Darden used a little-known phrase— "the n-word"—instead of saying the actual slur. It was a term that had quietly circulated in Black academic and activist circles since 1985 without catching on. "I'm not going to say the word," he said. "If you allow Mr. Cochran to use this word and play the race card . . . [the case will become] white versus Black."

In the end, the defense won the right to show the jury evidence that Fuhrman's use of the n-word invalidated his testimony, and eventually they won their case. But it was Darden who changed the American lexicon. By the time the jury found Simpson not guilty in October 1995, the surrogate phrase "the n-word" had become common parlance in the English language.

Twenty-Nine

"Papa's Hotel"

2005

"Liz," said Rain on the other end of the phone, "I'm worried about Daddy."

For the last ten years, my dad's health had been on a steady decline. He could no longer walk or use his hands, he could barely see, he was in and out of hospitals, and he needed around-the-clock care. His body had betrayed him. He couldn't even speak anymore, except for a few sputtered words that took excruciating effort to get out.

"What's going on?" I had my suspicions. As hard as it was to watch the MS overtake him, the circumstances of his care had gotten very complicated and difficult to navigate. He lived alone in a small ranch house in Encino, except for the shifts of caretakers who tended to all of his basic needs. He couldn't eat and relied on a feeding tube for nutrition. He slept in a hospital bed and needed to be moved every few hours so he didn't get bed sores.

"He's so isolated," Rain said. "I want to see him more. And I know he wants to see us too."

As soon as our father was incapacitated, his children received a letter with guidelines written by a psychiatrist who was treating him. I never met the doctor, but the letter said our visits caused too much stress. The visitation restrictions were heartbreaking to all of us, especially my sister and me because we lived closest to him.

Rain and I always had a deep connection, even though we were very different. Our father had us pegged since we were little girls when he gave her the clown wig for Christmas and me the Shakespeare books. Now, she was an actress and comedian who wrote and performed a one-woman show about being Black and Jewish called *Fried Chicken and Latkes*, while I was working my way through a Ph.D. in African American history at U.C. Santa Barbara. We didn't get to see each other much, but we loved each other.

Jerry and I had moved to Los Angeles in 2000. By then, our daughter, Lilli, was two years old, and our son, Henry, would be born the next year. Jerry set up a home improvement business, I commuted to graduate school ninety miles away in Santa Barbara, and we visited my dad at least once a week. He lit up when he saw me and the kids. Lilli and Henry would sit at the foot of his wheelchair and draw him pictures with colored pencils. They'd show him their artwork, and he'd grunt with approval. His eyes, cloudy with cataracts, would widen and he'd show a hint of his loving smile, which was as much as he could muster given the way the disease had ravaged his body.

On the days I visited him alone, I held his heavy, swollen hands and talked about the kids, or the latest movies, or read to him from my history books. He seemed to especially like hearing about the enslaved figures I learned about and made an excited noise, almost like a cheer, when I read to him from Frederick Douglass's narrative. After each visit, though, it became harder and harder to ignore the fact that time was running out.

When the psychiatrist's letter arrived, the blood drained from my face. It restricted all of Richard Pryor's kids and friends to one supervised visit per month with a forty-minute time limit. As always,

Rain was my first call, and we explored ways to see him more with less restrictions. We called Adult Protective Services, a Van Nuys police detective, elder law attorneys, we even reached out to a local U.S. congressperson in the hopes they could help. But nobody could, and we didn't get anywhere.

In the process, my sister and I became closer than we'd ever been. We spent the Jewish holidays together, she asked Lilli to be the flower girl in her wedding, and we spent hours reminiscing about our childhood at the Parthenia house.

More than once, she called me out for being ridiculously naive. Like the time I told her maybe our father was a feminist because he always had female friends visit at the house. She looked at me and pursed her lips.

"Liz," she said, "those were prostitutes."

We even started visiting our dad together at his house. We laughed when Henry asked if he wanted to do a puzzle, and the two of them had a full conversation with Henry babbling and my father responding with blinks and head drops. And we hugged him a lot.

For a moment it felt normal. Rain and I joined him at the Kennedy Center in D.C. when he became the inaugural recipient of the Mark Twain Award for American Humor, and friends and family rallied around to support him as his world became smaller.

But after one of our visits, we were told coming to see him together was a violation of the visitation restrictions. After that, we were instructed to meet him one-on-one in the lobby of the Courtyard by Marriott in Sherman Oaks.

The last time I saw my father, I yelled at him.

For more than a year, I met him exclusively at what my kids called "Papa's hotel." Once a month, his caretakers drove him to the Marriott in his red retrofitted van and wheeled him into the lounge next to the lobby.

At first, the concierge and the people who worked at the front desk would line up for a chance to speak to Richard Pryor and shake his hand.

"Mr. Pryor, your work has meant so much to me," one bellhop said. My father's eyes lit up, even as his head sagged from the effort.

A year later, nobody noticed us anymore.

His caretakers looked sad and often asked why I didn't visit more often.

I told them I wasn't allowed.

On the day of our last visit, an intense Black man whom I'd never seen before escorted my father to the hotel. Standing with his hands behind his back like a trained soldier, the man looked strong and focused, his jaw hard, his face expressionless. He wasn't wearing fatigues, but he was gearing up for battle.

When I leaned in to kiss my father, the bodyguard raised his voice and barked like a drill sergeant.

"Don't touch Mr. Pryor!" he said.

He barked again when he thought I stood too close to the wheelchair. "Stand back from Mr. Pryor!"

Anxious and flustered, I called the real estate attorney from Orange County who coordinated the visits. He had no idea who the guard was.

When I hung up the phone, I turned to my dad.

"Do you know who this man is?" I asked.

"No," he said, pushing the word out with tremendous difficulty, and clearly audible for the first time in years.

Shaking and sobbing, I was frantic.

The man ended the visit as soon as I started crying.

"This is too stressful for Mr. Pryor!" he shouted as he released the wheelchair lock, tucked my father's hands into his lap, and rolled him toward the exit.

Overwhelmed, I grabbed my leather tote and stood up. Everything fell out—keys, loose change, paper receipts, a sippy cup that smelled of fermented apple juice. I shoved everything back in and ran after them.

I yelled loudly, through my sobs, not at the bodyguard, which might have made sense, but at my father as hotel guests averted their eyes.

"Do you see what's happening, Daddy? Is this how you wanted it to end up?" My voice echoed through the lobby.

He never turned back. He couldn't. And then they were gone.

Two days later, on Saturday, December 10, 2005, I was in Florida for a friend's wedding. I was driving a rented SUV down a commercial highway in Boynton Beach on a road lined with palm trees, big box stores, and national chain restaurants.

My flip phone rang. It was Jerry.

"Babe, can't talk," I said. "Driving."

"Lizzy. I'm so sorry. But your dad died this morning."

I tried to pull the car over, cutting across three lanes of traffic. I jumped the SUV over a rounded curb and nearly killed myself in the process. I was bawling.

What kind of person tells you your father died while you're driving a car?

But Jerry didn't want me to hear it from someone else, and sure enough, within half an hour, his death was breaking news on every major media outlet, and friends from around the country started blowing up my phone.

There was no escaping it. My father was gone.

A few days after the funeral, a messenger delivered a copy of Richard Pryor's last will and testament. None of his creative legacy went to his kids. I knew in my heart that was not what he wanted. I hired a lawyer and fought in court and lost. I appealed and lost again.

Soon after, I was removed completely as a beneficiary.

Disinherited. Cut out of the family photo album.

Interlude Twelve

It seems that death was quite a surprise to his ass. Didn't think you
was ever gonna die, did you, n***er?

> Richard Pryor,
> . . . *Is It Something I Said?*,
> 1975

On Monday, July 9, 2007, two white horses pulled a wagon with a
plain pine casket through the streets of Detroit. Thousands of people
followed the carriage down Jefferson Avenue, including six pallbear-
ers wearing black suits.

It was a funeral for the n-word.

At the ninety-eighth annual convention of the NAACP, organizers
vowed to symbolically "bury the n-word." But the word refused to die.

Three months after the funeral, hip-hop superstar Nas announced his ninth album, *N***er*. When it was released on July 15,
2008, the album debuted at number one on the Billboard 200 with
only the name of the artist on the cover. The label had refused to sell
it with the original title, but a frustrated Nas proclaimed, "People will
always know what the real name of this album is and what to call it."
By using the n-word openly and freely, he said his intention was to
defang the word and make it as inoffensive as the word "cracker" for
white people.

Over the next two decades, as rap dominated the charts and became the biggest-selling music genre in the world, young white suburban men became its leading consumers in the country. Despite the extensive multiracial reach of the music and the widespread use of the Black version of the n-word, the racist version of the word with the hard "er" persists.

In 2024, a white member of a Division 3 swim team at a Pennsylvania liberal arts college allegedly held down a Black teammate and used a box cutter to carve the word "n***er" into his chest.

Thirty

"Your Father's Legacy"

2014

"This is a bold request, Liz," my good friend Rhea from graduate school emailed. "You may not be the right person to ask, but I would love the opportunity to showcase your father's legacy." She had recently been appointed as a curator at the Smithsonian's National Museum of African American History & Culture and wanted to know if I had any Richard Pryor memorabilia to donate to the museum.

I racked my brain. There was the Maasai wedding necklace he'd brought me home from Kenya; some letters and cards he'd written to me over the years; and a boot jack, used to remove cowboy boots, he once gave me when I couldn't get mine off. But that was all I had. Then I remembered the briefcase. My father's beat-up leather bag from the sixties, the one my mother gave me on the day of his funeral.

I asked Jerry to climb into the attic and get it down from the corner where I'd kept it safe and hidden all these years. He handed the bag to me gently, kissed me on the head, and left me alone in our room. Unzipping it carefully, I pushed aside the vellum receipts, a nightclub flier, an invoice from The Apollo Theater, and zeroed in on the two spiral notebooks. I pulled out the more well used of them and cracked it open.

A familiar story jumped off the very first page, one I'd somehow missed years before when I first opened the bag. It floored me.

> She stabbed me yesterday. Knives look extra-long when you get
> stabbed with one. Like a great fencing master, she gave a long
> thrust and found her mark in my forearm.

It was my dad's version of the fight my parents had before I was born. The stabbing story. He must have written it the day after my mother stabbed him, but even in the moment, he saw the humor in it, and couldn't help but turn it into material for his comedy.

> She withdrew and struck her "I'm a killer" pose. She has quite an
> "I'm a killer" pose.

Picturing my mom with her hands on her hips, I couldn't stop laughing. She really did have quite the "I'm a killer" pose. I reached for my phone to call my mother, but then I remembered I couldn't. In May 2011, she died at home after a battle with pancreatic cancer.

When my mom first called to say she was sick, Jerry and I decided she would move with us from L.A. to Massachusetts so she wouldn't be alone when I started my new job at Smith College. Jerry stepped in as her primary caregiver between carpentry jobs and child-care duties, while I figured out how to become a professor. He spent most days driving her all over the state to far-flung doctor's appointments, filling her prescriptions, making her scrambled eggs to order, and following her around detangling the cord of her oxygen tank as she roamed the house from room to room.

Twenty-seven months after her surgeon said she only had three months to live, she moaned loudly from her downstairs bedroom in our house.

"Give me a hand," she said.

Lifting her frail body from the bed, I helped her to the bathroom. Her belly was bloated with fluid. She was fat and skinny all at once. Unable to leave her alone, I sat her down on the toilet, put my hands on the sink, and stared at myself in the mirror.

"How long is the trip?" she asked. We had a wedding in Boston the following weekend.

"Not sure. Two hours to the Seaport, I guess."

"No," my mom said, reaching over to the sink and grabbing my hand with her bony fingers. "How. Long. Is. The. Trip?" She was talking about dying.

I got on my knees, held her hands, and looked into her eyes. Her face was so sweet and open.

"I don't want to go," she said.

"Don't be scared." I was crying. "I'll be right here with you the whole time."

"But if I go, I'm gonna miss you."

The next morning, she spoke her last words. "I love you and Jerry and the children."

Then the morphine took over, and then she was gone.

Reading through my father's notebook, my mother came alive again. They both did.

"You've stabbed me," I said, not really believing it myself.

"Where's the blood?" she said, with that funny look on her face

like someone pulled a sucker out of her mouth and smacked the

taste off her lovely little tongue.

This wasn't just a fight. It was foreplay.

Be cool and calm. Cry a lot. Women can't stand to see men cry.
Are you crazy? Women love to see men cry. Crying and bleeding
at the same time? Boy she must be grooving.
Hey, this is no time to think about sex.

I never understood why my parents seemed so flirty whenever
they talked about the stabbing story. But reading the real-time chron-
icle of events gave me an up-close-and-personal view of their relationship.

"Give me the keys," she cried.
"Keys? What keys?" I said, not wanting to end the scene. I hate
being upstaged by an amateur.

They loved each other, felt passion and even compassion for each
other, despite their irreconcilable differences. Some kids get a wedding photo. I got material for stand-up comedy.

There was no way I could ever give the briefcase to Rhea, the
museum, or anyone else. It was the only proof I had of my parents'
love story.

As I dug deeper into the notebook, I realized it wasn't just doodles
and setlists, like I thought when I first opened it years before, but a
place for my father to work out his creativity, a collection of his writings that expressed his fears, loves, and inspirations. It included his
regrets, musings about his childhood, ideas for scripts about a Black
army sergeant on furlough, a Black clown, a Black funeral director,
a woman (probably my mom) sucking the very life out of a chicken
wing, love poems to my mother, and even a letter he wrote to his unborn child, who was me.

To a child unborn, to a child unseen
I am sorry I didn't treat you kind
Before your arrival. But I was busy with my hangups.

I know that's no cop out.
But it's the truth.
And if the truth ain't good enough for you.
Go fuck yourself.
Love, Dad

All the time I had been looking for something about me in his notebook, and there it was, buried in his curve-and-loop handwriting. Granted, it wasn't the recognition I was hoping for, but the letter spoke to the kind of push-and-pull tension that had always characterized my relationship with my father. He was conflicted about becoming a parent from the start, guilty about how he treated my mother when she was pregnant, and scared I would reject him before he had a chance to explain his demons. His writing made him sound exactly like the man he always strove to be: honest, vulnerable, and so unapologetically charming.

Thirty-One

"I Hope I Finish This One"

2020

Fourteen years after my father died, I stood on a makeshift stage at a pop-up café in a tiny Massachusetts town, a wireless mic looped around my ear, ready to share my experience about the n-word. The stage was lit, the room was dark. Jerry and our daughter, Lilli, who was now a senior in college, smiled up at me from the audience of one hundred people who watched from little tables sprinkled throughout the room. I thought of my father at the Cafe Wha? in Greenwich Village, where he first met my mother.

Was he ever this nervous onstage? I heard his answer like a whisper or a breath, just like I had at his funeral.

Every. Single. Time.

Gathering my thoughts, I stood next to a waist-high wooden sculpture an ambitious feminist had hand carved and painted red in the shape of the letters TEDx.

For a split second, my mind went blank. *A well-meaning white student. A slur. Blah blah blah.*

I'd been preparing to give the TED talk for months. I wanted my speech to be a synthesis of everything I had learned about the n-word—points of encounter, the word's complicated influence on the nation's history and my own, and how to navigate it in the class-room.

But when I sat down at my desk to write it, the words didn't come. I picked up my father's briefcase for inspiration. It now lived on a low shelf near my desk, and I pulled out the well-worn notebook.

It always took me a few minutes to figure out what I was reading, but as a trained historian I had acquired a quirky ability to decipher old letters and journals with scratchy, handwritten cursive. I also had a knack for decoding inventive spelling like my father's. He wrote "supishis" for "suspicious" or "payshants" for "patience," and his dys-lexia caused him to leave out multiple words and write letters back-ward. My esoteric skill set made his misspelled, multi-voiced journal come to life.

Every time I opened the notebook, I got to know him better. In his twenties, he was still beating himself up for choosing his father over his mother as a child, even though he was pushed into doing it. He gave Mama his undying gratitude for raising him, but he was also terrified of her. And he faced the impending collapse of his relation-ship with my mother with a sense of melancholy. "A puff of smoke and a Ferris wheel, children's voices and my girlfriend's shrill."

As I gently flipped through the journal, I landed on a note my father wrote to himself at the top of a random page.

I hope I finish this one. This is my six hundredth book. I didn't finish the last 599 either.

This was a memoir, or at least an attempt to write one for his com-edy, that he began when he was twenty-five years old. As I scanned his felt-tipped prose, I saw something I hadn't noticed before. The n-word. My heart raced and I steadied my breath. I'd seen the word in his setlists, but I'd never seen it in his private musings. The word appeared five more times on the same page, straight from the mind of Richard Pryor before it became his trademark. He started with a conversation he had when he was six.

My father said to me one day, "Boy, you a n***er and don't forget it." Needless to say, I was shocked. "What's a n***er?"

With shaky hands, I put on my reading glasses. Was the first person to call him the n-word his father? Buck was trying to enlighten my dad about being Black in the United States, but the only way he knew how to do it was by putting him in his place.

"You're six years old and don't know what a n***er is, motherfucker?"
I knew what a motherfucker was, but I couldn't understand why he was calling me one. I never fucked his mother, but he'd been fucking mine.

The words and ideas that shaped my father's identity and comedic voice had been a part of his life since he was a child.

"Sit down here, boy. Let me tell you a few things about life. See, boy, there's black and there's white."
Another shocker because I thought there was blue and green, orange, pink, and gray too.
"The white think they're better than the Black. But that's not true son. Don't ever think it either. You understand me?"

Buck was trying to have the same conversation about being Black with his son that my father had had with me. The tears welled up.

"Yes, sir, I understand," I lied. The only time I ever called him "sir" was when I wasn't sure of myself.

As a little boy, my dad already knew what fucking was and what sex work was. He knew his father was a dangerous man and he knew to lie to keep the peace. But he had absolutely no idea how to unravel the complexities of race or racism, and no idea how to be Black in the world.

At six years old, neither did I.

My mother was right. The notebook really did explain everything. It was the last breadcrumb leading me back to my father. It took me fifteen years to understand it held the key to the connection we'd had all along. The briefcase was a priceless heirloom. It was my inheritance.

The first time I opened it was in grief, searching desperately for any proof that I mattered to him. But as I prepared for the TED talk, I opened it in worship, a devotional of leather and zippers and spiral notebooks that would one day inspire me to start my own memoir precisely where he, as a young man, had started his: reflecting on a fraught conversation with a complicated parent, rife with lessons about being a Black child in a hostile world, and a slur.

N***er.

The way he said it. The way Buck said it.

The way I struggled my whole life to make sense of it. Because the boy on the playground, because my mother at the kite festival, because Mama and Uncle Dickie and the Reverend David Banks. Then my mother spat it out, then I spat it out, then the white guys spat it out, then my Black friends spat it out, and then the white student in my class spat it out exactly the way my father, in *Blazing Saddles*, meant for folks to spit it out, and I became unhinged.

And then obsessed. And then a scholar of the word.

Just like he was.

My dad took the word his father couldn't explain and made art out of processing it. From a kitschy super hero—Super N***er—to the quintessential expression of seventies' Black masculinity, to the cover of studio albums, to an indictment of slavery in the United

States. And then, after a trip to Kenya, he rejected it, and at the end of his life, struck by an illness that literally took his voice, he could no longer speak the word even if he tried.

In all the tender moments with him—and despite everything, there were plenty—the most tender was that first conversation in the Boston restaurant. He could have fucked it up like Buck did. But he was thoughtful and quiet. He listened. He explained. He understood. And then he gave me marching orders.

"Don't let nobody ever call you that," he said.

Steadying myself on the podium, in a quavering voice even I could hear shaking, I launched into my monologue. A story about my journey with the n-word, what I learned about its meanings, how deeply personal it was for me and so many people, and why it's so important for us as Americans to talk about it openly and honestly.

I only had twenty minutes onstage, so I didn't actually talk about my father, but I felt him with me the whole time.

On March 12, 2020, the day before Smith College and most of the country shut down for a global pandemic, "Why it's so hard to talk about the N-word" was posted on the TED Talks platform. Within hours it had hundreds of thousands of views. Soon it was over two million.

Overnight, I had become part of the national conversation about the n-word. The same conversation my father helped launch into the mainstream.

Thirty-Two

For You

As I sat down to write the final chapter of my book, I got an email from a man in Fountain Valley, California. He'd bought a copy of Richard Pryor's 1995 autobiography at a thrift store for three dollars and thought it might belong to me. There was an inscription in the front cover:

To Liz, All the hope and good wishes for your life. I love you. All my best. Your father, Richard.

It was the finished version of the memoir I started that he eventually had someone else write. He'd given me a copy when it was published, but I could never bring myself to read it. After staring at it on the bookshelf for years, I gave it to Goodwill.

The man in Fountain Valley wanted to know if it was mine and if it had any sentimental value. The moment I read his email, I couldn't wait to get it back.

When the book finally arrived, I opened the cover and saw my father's familiar curve-and-loop handwriting. It must have been one of the last times he was ever able to write. As I traced the scraggly letters with my finger, I felt a burst of love and gratitude.

I propped up his memoir on my desk and set out to finish my own.

Dear Daddy,

There are so many things I never got to tell you.

    I'm a college professor now.

    Everyone says Henry looks just like you and Lilli has your comic timing.

    I've made my career talking about the n-word.

    And I think about you every single day.

    . . . About the memoir.

    I'm so sorry I couldn't get it right the first time. It took a few decades to find the words. I hope you know this book is for you.

I love you,
Boston Blackie

Notes

Prologue: December 17, 2005

4   **At the foot of the bed, I saw a beat-up, brown leather briefcase . . .** The briefcase is in my possession. I figured out how old it is from a bankbook with notes in my father's handwriting dated 1965.

One: *Blazing Saddles*

9   **Charlotte . . .** Charlotte's real name is not Charlotte. I have changed her name as I have with many of my former students.

10   ***Blazing Saddles* was a satirical comedy my father wrote . . .** His contribution is described in Scott Saul, "On RP Writing Blazing Saddles," *Becoming Richard Pryor* (New York: HarperCollins Publishers, 2014) 281–288. A couple of good articles about him and the film: Scott Tobias, "Blazing Saddles at 50: the Button-Pushing Spoof that Could Never Get Made Today," *The Guardian US*, February 7, 2024. WEB; and Jessica Kiang, "The Magnificent '74: Blazing Saddles: The Bad Words and Good Intentions that Lie Behind the Comedy of Blazing Saddles" *Sight & Sound*, August 22, 2024. WEB. https://www.bfi.org.uk/sight-and-sound/features/magnificent-74-blazing-saddles

12   **Known as the "mention exception . . ."** Free speech legal scholars describe the "use-mention distinction," and a few are especially concerned about the n-word. Randall Kennedy & Eugene Volokh, "The New Taboo. Quoting Epithets in the Classroom and Beyond" in 49 *Capital University Law Review* 1 (2021), especially p. 10; John McWhorter, "How the N-Word Became Unsayable," *The New York Times*, April 30, 2021.

12   **Some even consider it disrespectful to Black authors like James Baldwin . . .** Pen America, "Disciplining New School Professor Would Be Threat to Academic Freedom: Professor Who Employed N-Word Did So in Service of Pedagogy, Not Hate," August 9, 2019. WEB. https://pen.org/press-release

/professor-new-school-discipline/. A white professor at the New School in New York explained to students that a documentary film about Baldwin, *I Am Not Your Negro*, was intentionally titled in a way that misquoted the famous author. The actual quotation was "I am not your n***er." While explaining this fact, the professor said the word "n***er"; Colleen Flaherty, "N-Word at the New School," *Inside Higher Ed*, August 6, 2019. WEB. https://www.insidehighered.com/news/2019/08/07/another-professor-under-fire-using-n-word-class-while-discussing-james-baldwin

Interlude One

15 **In 1619, Portuguese mercenaries kidnapped three hundred and fifty people . . .** Ibram X. Kendi discusses how European enslavers introduced slavery to British North America in *Stamped from the Beginning: The Definitive History of Racist Ideas in America* (New York: Nation Books, 2016), 38–39.

15 **Those "20 & odd" . . .** John Rolfe, a letter to Sir Edwin Sandys (January 1619/20) in Susan Myra Kingsbury, ed., *The Records of the Virginia Company of London*, Volume III, 243.

15 **In Captain John Smith's history . .** "About the last of August came in a dutch man of warre that sold us twenty N*gars . . ." in Smith, *The Generall Historie of Virginia, New-England, and the Summer Isles: With the Names of the Adventurers, Planters and Governours from their Beginning* (London: Printed by I.D. and I.H. for Michael Sparkes, 1624), 126.

16 **When the governor who originally bought . . . ; "goods debts chattles servants n*gars cattle . . ."** Virginia Governor George Yeardley's last will and testament quoted in Kendi, *Stamped from the Beginning*, 39.

16 **The n-word wasn't yet a slur.** Elizabeth Stordeur Pryor, "The Etymology of N***er: Resistance, Language, and the Politics of Freedom in the Antebellum North," *Journal of the Early Republic*, vol. 36, no. 2, Summer 2016, 203–245.

Two: "This Is Your Daddy"

18 **My parents met in New York City . . .** My mother was on a date at Cafe Wha? with a white guy named Frank. My dad was on a date with someone else. They liked each other better than their own dates. Richard Pryor with Todd Gold, *Pryor Convictions and Other Life Sentences* (New York: Pantheon Books, 1995), 77. My mother told the same story.

18 **My dad was from Peoria, Illinois, a northern city that was segregated enough . . .** City of Peoria, *Joint Commission on Racial Justice and Equity, 2024 Annual Report*. https://www.peoriacounty.gov/1276/History-of-Racism-in-Peoria; "Richard Pryor's Peoria: A Digital Companion to the Biography" by Scott Saul, *Becoming Richard Pryor* https://www.becomingrichardpryor.com/pryors-peoria/theme/segregation/

19   *Max so sweet and Max so true* . . . The poem is in my possession.

19   **"My mother's Puerto Rican, and my father's Negro . . ."** According to one of my father's biographers, Scott Saul, the joke is from a TV variety show called "On Broadway Tonight," circa August 1964. I first saw a clip of it on YouTube. Scott Saul, *Becoming Richard Pryor*, p. 131.

19   **"I'm Negro . . . I'm probably one of the few people left . . ."** My father's writing about being a "Negro" is in my possession. As for the word "Black," Stokely Carmichael is credited with introducing it into common parlance during his 1966 speech at UC Berkeley as the newly inaugurated president of the Student Nonviolent Coordinating Committee, SNCC. Stokely Carmichael, "Black Power" (October 29, 1966), *Voices of Democracy: the US Oratory Project*. WEB. https://voicesofdemocracy.umd.edu/carmichael-black-power-speech-text/ See also Sally Greene, "The Birth of Black Power: Stokely Carmichael and the Speech that Changed the Course of the Civil Rights Movement," *The American Scholar*, April 26, 2021. WEB; and Sara Marcus, *Political Disappointment: A Cultural History from Reconstruction to the AIDS Crisis* (Cambridge: Harvard University Press, 2023), 91–111.

19   **By 1967 . . . to be a star like Bill Cosby . . .** My father discussed his influences in his autobiography and specifically Cosby. Pryor, *Pryor Convictions*, 72.

19   **More political Black comics like Dick Gregory and Redd Foxx . . .** Pryor, *Pryor Convictions*, 98–100.

20   **He made Marvin Gaye's political anthem "What's Going On" his personal soundtrack . . .** Pryor, *Pryor Convictions*, 115.

22   **"Say, n***er. You with the cape!"** *That N***er's Crazy*, 1974.

Three: "Don't Let Nobody Ever Call You That"

31   **When the boys at school . . . coming to Boston to promote** *That N***er's Crazy* . . . Ernie Santosuosso, "Flip Wilson Makes Pryor Engagement at Paul's Mall," *Boston Globe*, April 26, 1974, 28. The article was published two days after my birthday. Paul's Mall was a popular Boston nightclub.

Four: A Subject Too Taboo

34   **According to Mel Brooks, he didn't want to use the n-word . . . but my father insisted.** Bob Mondello, "50 Years Ago *Blazing Saddles* Broke Wind—and Box Office Expectations," *NPR*, February 29, 2024. WEB. https://www.npr.org/2024/02/29/1234699365/blazing-saddles-mel-brooks

Interlude Two

37   **In the early 1830s, a white actor in New York City . . .** Eric Lott, *Love and Theft: Blackface Minstrelsy and the American Working Class* (New York: Oxford University Press, 1993), 22–37; Elizabeth Stordeur Pryor, *Colored Travelers: Mobility and the*

Fight for Citizenship before the Civil War (Chapel Hill: University of North Carolina Press, 2016); and Pryor, "The Etymology of N***er," 231–235.

37   **"Ven de n***er all free, do as he please"** From a "Bobalition" broadside from New York *DE GRADEST BOBALITION DAT EBER VUS BE!!! 4rt ob July, 1827, cum on de 5ft.* 285 Water-street, [New York City]: [J. M'Clelland], 1827.

38   **The Jim Crow performance . . . "Do what you will/The n***er will be a n***er still."** J.W.C. Pennington, "Speech at Freemason's Hall, London, June 14, 1843," in *The Black Abolitionist Papers, Volume 1, The British Isles, 1830–1865,* ed. C. Peter Ripley (Chapel Hill, University of North Carolina Press, 1985), 106. Pennington said he was repeating a verse he heard repeated often, and it was from the Jim Crow minstrel show.

38   **The word became a degrading slur . . .** Pryor, "The Etymology of N***er."

Five: Mulatto, Oreo, Redbone, Sister

40   **The album had just topped the Billboard R&B charts at #1.** Scott Saul, *Becoming Richard Pryor*, 336–341.

46   **"Her face was so soft and beautiful . . ."** My father's private writing in my possession.

Six: "Black Is Beautiful"

53   **"Black is beautiful" was a chant rooted in the civil rights movement.** Tanisha Ford, "Kwame Braithwaite: Black Is Beautiful," *Aperture*, Fall 2017, 46–53.

Seven: The Voldemort Theory

58   **Seventy percent of all adults believe there are no circumstances . . .** Juliana Menasce Horowitz, Anna Brown, and Kiana Cox, "Race in America 2019," *Report: Pew Research Center:* April 9, 2019. WEB. https://www.pewresearch.org/social-trends/2019/04/09/race-in-america-2019/

Interlude Three

61   **On September 28, 1841, Frederick Douglass bought a first-class railroad ticket . . .** "Eastern Rail-Road—Colorphobia—Lunch Law—Robbery—Quakerism," *The Liberator*, October 15, 1841; Frederick Douglass, *My Bondage, My Freedom* in *Frederick Douglass: Autobiographies* (New York: Library of America, 1994), 394–395; and Pryor, *Colored Travelers*, 76–102, especially 84–85.

62   **"We don't allow n***ers in here!"** Frederick Douglass to William Lloyd Garrison, Victoria Hotel Belfast, January 1, 1846, published in *The Liberator*, January 30, 1846.

Eight: "A White Woman Raising a Black Child"

63   **"What they're doing in Boston is disgusting!" my mom said . . . the 1974 Boston busing crisis.** Jane M. Hornburger, "Deep Are the Roots: Busing in Boston,"

The Journal of Negro Education Summer, 1976, 235–245; and Christina Pazzanese, "Boston Busing in 1974 Was About Race. Now the Issue Is Class," *The Harvard Gazette*, June 18, 2024. WEB.

Nine: Parthenia Street

80 **"That was a hell of a psychology,"** Pryor, Richard Pryor: *Live in Concert*, 1979.

80 **"Hello, little boy . . ."** Pryor, *Live in Concert*, 1979.

80 **"My father died fucking."** Pryor, *Live in Concert*, 1979.

Ten: Points of Encounter

83 **The feeling reminded me of how Black literary scholar Emily Bernard described . . .** Emily Bernard, "Teaching the N-word: A Black Professor, an All-White Class, and the Thing Nobody Will Say," *The American Scholar*, September 1, 2005. WEB.

Interlude Four

87 **On April 11, 1865, President Abraham Lincoln leaned out of a second-story window . . .** Doris Kearns Goodwin quotes and describes Lincoln's last speech and its impact in *Team of Rivals: The Political Genius of Abraham Lincoln* (New York: Simon & Schuster, 2005), 724–749; Terry Alford discusses Lincoln's last days from John Wilkes Booth's perspective in *Fortune's Fool: The Life of John Wilkes Booth* (Oxford: Oxford University Press, 2015), 244–269.

88 **One of them was a white actor . . . "That means n***er citizenship!"** Booth quoted in Terry Alford, *Fortune's Fool*, 257.

Eleven: "Catfish It Is"

89 **He'd also just signed . . .** Scott Saul, *Becoming Richard Pryor*, 396–400.

90 **At one point, the town's sheriff had to intervene . . .** Scott Saul's research confirms my memory of racism on the set. Scott Saul, *Becoming Richard Pryor*, 396–400.

95 **But she had also been arrested for protecting her son Buck . . .** "Boy Slapped, Woman Routs Proprietor of Confectionary," *Decatur Herald*, October 20, 1929, cited in "Richard Pryor's Peoria," WEB.

Twelve: "You Trying to Kill Me?"

101 **"Mama. Grandma Marie. Mrs. Bryant" . . .** My brother Richard Jr. helped me immensely in remembering the details of Mama's funeral.

102 **"Black funerals are different than white funerals . . ."** Pryor, *Live in Concert*, 1979.

102 **. . . the network kept censoring his jokes.** See Saul, *Becoming Richard Pryor*, 436–438 and all of chapter 22.

103   **He also saw his father, Buck, beat his mother . . .** *Gertrude Pryor v. Leroy Pryor,* Circuit Court of Peoria Count, Jan. 1946. Gert's divorce complaint outlines the violence against her. The document is featured on Scott Saul's "Richard Pryor's Peoria," WEB.

103   **"My father was scary, boy."** Pryor, *Live in Concert,* 1979.

104   **"an eleven o'clock n***er"** Pryor, *That N***er's Crazy,* 1974.

105   **Critics loved the movie.** Gene Siskel, "If Pryor isn't the funniest man on earth, who is funnier?" *The Chicago Tribune,* Feb. 18, 1979.

105   **They called it "comedic gold" . . .** Larry Kart, "Pryor film adds the vital visuals of a genius' work," *Chicago Tribune,* Feb 6, 1979.

105   **"use almost any topic, intrinsically funny or not . . ."** Janet Maslin, *The New York Times,* Feb 16, 1979.

106   **Audiences flocked to the theaters . . .** Hollie West, *The Washington Post,* February 16, 1979.

106   **. . . his drug-fueled behavior began to make the national news.** "Richard Pryor, Comedian, Freed On Bail on a Charge of Assault," *The New York Times,* January 3, 1978; Jura Koncius, "Comedian Richard Pryor surrendered to Los Angeles police," *The Washington Post,* January 3, 1978.

Thirteen: I Couldn't Stop Thinking About It

111   **Journalist Farai Chideya called it "the nuclear bomb" of racist slurs.** Farai Chideya, *The Color of Our Future* (New York: HarperCollins, 1999), 9.

111   **In his 2002 book *N***er*, Harvard legal scholar . . .** Randall Kennedy, *N***er: The Strange Career of a Troublesome Word* (New York: Vintage Books, 2002), 3–44. On Jackie Robinson and Malcolm X, pp. 15–16.

111   **In his 2004 book, *The N-Word* . . .** Jabari Asim, *The N-Word: Who Can Say It, Who Shouldn't and Why* (New York: Houghton Mifflin, 2007), especially 1–84.

112   **Merriam-Webster's defined n***er . . .** "Merriam-Webster to Focus on Sting of Racial Slurs: Publisher Refuses to Redefine Words," *The Washington Post,* May 5, 1998.

112   **. . . Delphine Abraham . . .** Courtland Milloy, "It's Defined, Now Defy It," *The Washington Post,* October 14, 1997; Sam Fulwood III, "Dictionary's Stance on 'N-Word' May Mark Defining Moment, *The Los Angeles Times,* May 11, 1998.

113   **She echoed the concerns of Black parents and educators . . .** John H. Wallace, "The Case Against Huck Finn," in *Satire or Evasion?: Black Perspectives on Huckleberry Finn,* eds. James S. Leonard, Thomas A. Tenney, Thadious M. Davis (Durham: Duke University Press, 1992), 16–24; John Alberti, "The N***er Huck: Race, Identity and the Teaching of Huckleberry Finn," *College English,* December 1995; David Lionel Smith, "Black Critics and Mark Twain," *The Cambridge Companion to Mark Twain,* ed. Forrest G. Robinson (Cambridge: Cambridge University Press, 1995), 116–128; Derek Bunting, "The Essential Discomfort of Reading Mark Twain's Huckleberry Finn," *Literary Focus,* July 29, 2024. Web.

Interlude Five

117 **Washington was the first Black person** . . . Clarence Lusane, *The Black History of the White House* (San Francisco: Open Light Books, 2011), 219–231.

117 **The backlash was swift** . . . Gary Dorrien, *The New Abolition: W.E.B. Du Bois and the Black Social Gospel* (New Haven: Yale University Press, 2015), 202–208; Mark Christian, *Booker T. Washington: A Life in American History* (Santa Barbara, CA: ABC-CLIO, 2021), 96–97.

117 **"Roosevelt takes this n***er . . ."** Vardaman quoted in Dorrien, *The New Abolition*, 204.

118 **. . . "rednecks."** Albert D. Kirwan, *Revolts of the Rednecks: Mississippi Politics, 1876–1925* (Lexington: University of Kentucky Press, 1951), especially p. 212; William F. Holmes, *The White Chief: James Kimble Vardaman* (Baton Rouge: Louisiana State University Press, 1970), 237–240; Neil R. McMillen, *Dark Journey: Black Mississippians in the Age of Jim Crow* (Champaign: University of Illinois Press, 1989).

118 **Senator "Pitchfork Ben" Tillman** . . . Stephen Kantrowitz, *Ben Tillman and the Reconstruction of White Supremacy* (Chapel Hill: University of North Carolina Press, 2000).

118 **"Entertaining the n***er . . ."** Tillman quoted in Kantrowitz, *Ben Tillman*, 259.

118 **The violence was unrelenting.** Jerrold M. Packard, *American Nightmare: The History of Jim Crow* (New York: St Martin's Press, 2002), 129–134. On lynching statistics, see "Number of executions by lynching in the United States by State and Race between 1882 and 1968," https://www.statista.com/statistics/1175147/lynching-by-race-state-and-race/

Fourteen: "Nobody Will Ever Love You"

120 **"When you're onstage . . ."** The entire exchange between my father and Barbara Walters is available as a clip from "The Barbara Walters Special," November 29, 1988.

121 **"'Cause I'm afraid sexually . . ."** "The Barbara Walters Special."

Sixteen: "The Etymology of N*er"**

132 **. . . tracing the word . . . from a Black perspective.** Pryor, "The Etymology of N***er." My article argues that the n-word emerged as a subversive weapon for Black people in the United States as early as the 1770s, if not before.

132 *My name is Ran* Quoted in Sterling Brown, "Negro Folk Expression: Spirituals, Seculars, Ballads and Work Songs," *Phylon* 14, no. 1 (1953), p. 51.

132 **"If dey comes rummaging 'mong my tings, dey'll get one bressed sarssin from dis 'ere n***er."** Harriet Jacobs, *Incidents in the Life of a Slave Girl, Written By Herself* (1861), edited by Jean Fagan Yellin (Cambridge: Harvard University Press, 1987), 103.

Interlude Six

135 . . . **a group of young and rebellious Black writers** . . . Kendi, *Stamped from the Beginning*, 324–325.

135 . . . **"express our individual dark-skinned selves . . ."** Langston Hughes, "The Negro Artist and the Racial Mountain," *The Nation*, June 23, 1926.

136 . . . **they dubbed themselves "the N***erati"** . . . Karen F. Taborn, "The New Negro Movement and N***erati Manor," in *Walking Harlem: The Ultimate Guide to the Cultural Capital of Black America* (New Brunswick: Rutgers University Press, 2018), 161–164; Asim, *The N-Word*, 139–141; "The N***erati Manor in Harlem," *Harlem World Magazine*, January 25, 2014. WEB.

136 . . . **"Queen of the N***erati"** . . . Hurston quoted in Robert Hemenway, *Zora Neal Hurston: A Literary Biography* (Champaign: University of Illinois Press, 1977), 43–44.

Eighteen: Something Horrible Happened

145 **Wren's email included a link to the recording of the event** . . . Sydney Sadur, "Challenging the Ideological Echo Chamber: Free Speech, Civil Discourse, and the Liberal Arts," *SoundCloud*. It is an audio recording of the Smith College panel held in New York City, September 22, 2014.

148 **And the next time a white professor said the n-word** . . . Destiny Wiley-Yancy, "Administration Responds to Use of Racially-Charged Language in Class," *The Sophian*, October 20, 2017.

Interlude Seven

149 **When Hollywood producer David O. Selznick optioned the bestseller for a record sum** . . . Nina Silber, "'Gone with the Wind' is also a Confederate Monument, but on Film instead of Stone: Even in its time, the Film Promoted a Racist Political Message," in *The Washington Post*, June 12, 2020.

149 . . . **"propaganda for race hatred and bigotry."** Quoted in Silber, "'Gone with the Wind.'"

149 . . . **he opened a file called "the Negro Problem."** Leonard J. Leff, "David Selznick's *Gone with the Wind*: 'The Negro Problem,'" in *The Georgia Review*, vol. 38, no. 1 (Spring 1984), 149.

149 **After months of mounting pressure** . . . Ellen Scott, "Regulating 'N***er': Racial Offense, African American Activists, and the MPPDA, 1928–1961," *Film History*, vol. 26, no. 4 (2014), 11–12.

150 **But he would not budge when it came to Black characters saying the n-word.** Leff, "David Selznick's *Gone with the Wind*"; Kristin Hunt, "Hollywood Codebreakers: 'Gone with the Wind' Goes on Trial," *Medium*, March 2, 2018.

150 . . . **influential film critic Earl J. Morris became the hero of the hour.** Earl J. Morris, "Predicts Picture will be Worse Than 'Birth of a Nation,'" *Pittsburgh*

Courier, February 4, 1939; Morris, "Race Actors Flayed for 'Gone with the Wind' Parts, *The Chicago Defender*, February 11, 1939; Morris, "Offensive Word and KKK Sequence Deleted from Film Version of 'Gone with the Wind,'" *Pittsburgh Courier*, February 18, 1939; "From Casting to Cutting the N-Word, the Making of 'Gone with the Wind,'" NPR, September 14, 2014.

Nineteen: "Richard Pryor Running Down the Street"

156 **"I can't stop," my dad said to the officer.** "Cocaine-Ether Flames Injure Richard Pryor," *The Atlanta Constitution*, June 11, 1980, 1; "'That Man Was in Sheer Agony,' Ether, Cocaine Mix Burned Comedian Pryor," *The Chicago Defender*, June 12, 1980, 4; David Henry and Joe Henry, *Furious Cool: Richard Pryor and the World That Made Him* (Chapel Hill: Algonquin Books, 2013), 232.

156 **A drug charge would have meant jail time . . .** David Felton, "Pryor's Inferno: After an Explosion at Home Sends Him to the Hospital with Serious Injuries, The Great Comic Examines His Tragic Life," in *Rolling Stone*, July 24, 1980. WEB.

Twenty: "Any Relation?"

161 **I published an essay about how teaching the n-word required self-reflection.** Elizabeth Stordeur Pryor, "Talking About the N-Word," *Panorama: Expansive Views from the Journal of the Early Republic*, May 15, 2017. WEB.

163 **"Folk wisdom held . . ."** David Roediger, *The Wages of Whiteness: Race and the Making of the American Working Class* (London: Verso, 1991), 133; Noel Ignatiev, *How the Irish Became White* (Oxfordshire: Routledge, 1995); Cheryl I. Harris, "Whiteness as Property," *Harvard Law Review*, June 1993, 1707–1791; Timothy Meagher, *The Columbia Guide to Irish American History* (New York: Columbia University Press, 2005), 214–232.

163 **"Down with the N***er!"** Quoted in Roediger, The *Wages of Whiteness*, 136.

Interlude Eight

165 **Norman Rockwell's *The Problem We All Live With* . . .** Bridget R. Cooks, "Norman Rockwell's Negro Problem," *Cultural Critique*, Fall 2019, 40–79; "The Giant Footsteps of a Little Girl," *The Journal of Blacks in Higher Education*, Spring 2002, no. 35, 23; "Resistance to School Desegregation," The Equal Justice Initiative, March 1, 2014. WEB; V. P. Franklin, "Introduction: *Brown v. Board of Education*: Fifty Years of Educational Change in the United States," *The Journal of African American History*, Winter 2005, vol. 90, 1–8; Jennifer A. Greenhill, "The View from Outside: Rockwell and Race in 1950," *American Art*, Summer 2007, 70–95.

Twenty-One: "I Been Wrong"

176   **On his last day there** He talked about his epiphany onstage, but was also interviewed in *Ebony* magazine by historian Lerone Bennett Jr. "Why Richard Pryor Stopped Saying 'N***er' and Why He Is Seeking a Special Woman to Bear His Child," *Ebony*, July 1982, 118–126.

Twenty-Three: The Word Is Two Words

190   **"The word is two words . . ."** Pryor, "The Etymology of N***er."

190   **Novelist Gloria Naylor differentiated between . . .** Gloria Naylor, "Language Is the Subject," *The New York Times*, February 20, 1986, C2.

190   **Black intellectual Ta-Nehisi Coates . . .** Ta-Nehisi Coates, "In Defense of a Loaded Word," *The New York Times*, November 23, 2013.

191   **I reached out to my sister Rain to ask about her memories of his early comedy.** Interview with my sister Rain Pryor in July 2025. I spoke to Rain many times during the crafting of the book to fine-tune my memories.

Interlude Nine

193   **"Wherever you are," he wrote, "if ever you hear the word 'n***er' again, remember they are advertising my book."** Dick Gregory with Robert Lipsyte, *N***er: An Autobiography by Dick Gregory* (New York: Pocket Books, 1964).

193   **And they used the n-word to express themselves.** Asim, *The N-Word*, 199–203.

194   **"Do you know what white racists call Black Ph.D.'s?"** Quoted in Alex Haley, *The Autobiography of Malcolm X* (New York: Ballentine Books, 1965), 284.

194   **"I'm Richard Pryor," he said, "I'm a n***er."** Pryor, *Pryor Convictions*, 117. Henry and Henry, *Furious Cool*, 119.

194   **In 1981, Lee Atwater, a white Republican strategist, highlighted the impact on politics . . .** Rick Perlstein, "Exclusive: Lee Atwater's Infamous 1981 Interview on the Southern Strategy," *The Nation*, November 13, 2012.

194   **. . . "n***er, n***er, n***er."** Quoted in Perlstein, "Exclusive: Lee Atwater's Infamous 1981 Interview."

Twenty-Five: He Made the Word a Universe

208   **"white women disease"** Richard Pryor, *Richard Pryor: Live and Smokin'*, 1971.

Interlude Ten

215   **Eazy-E assembled an L.A. "supergroup" . . .** Jeff Chang, *Can't Stop, Won't Stop: A History of the Hip-Hop Generation* (New York: St. Martin's Press, 2005), 299–304.

215   **Ronald Reagan's War on Drugs disproportionately targeted Black people . . .** Michelle Alexander, *The New Jim Crow: Mass Incarceration in the Age of Colorblindness* (New York: The New Press, 2010), 59–64; Chang, *Can't Stop, Won't Stop*,

304–329; Michael Tonry, *Malign Neglect: Race, Crime, and Punishment in America* (Oxford: Oxford University Press, 1995), 111.

215   **N.W.A's album *Straight Outta Compton* went platinum.** Jeff Chang, *Can't Stop, Won't Stop*, 320–322.

215   **In a song that infuriated the FBI, "Fuck tha Police"** . . . Tricia Rose, *Black Noise: Rap Music and Black Culture in Contemporary America* (Middletown: Wesleyan University Press, 1994), 128–129; Adam Bradley and Andrew Dubois, *The Anthology of Rap* (New Haven: Yale University Press, 2010), 233.

215   **. . . but once N.W.A burst onto the scene, it was everywhere and had a new spelling.** Asim, *The N-Word*, 219–220.

215   **N.W.A codified what African Americans already knew** . . . Pryor, "The Etymology of N***er"; Jeffrey O.G. Ogbar, *Hip-Hop Revolution: The Culture and Politics of Rap* (Lawrence: University Press of Kansas, 2007), 63–68; Bradley and Dubois, *The Anthology of Rap*, 417; Todd M. Mealy, *The N-Word in Music: An American History* (Jefferson, North Carolina: McFarland & Company, Inc, 2022), 136–141.

215   **"That's our word now," Ice Cube said about the n-word in 2017, "and you can't have it back."** Ice Cube quoted on *Real Time with Bill Maher*, episode #15.18, air date June 9, 2017.

Twenty-Six: "You Got It, Toyota"

217   **"I was a little kid, about five years old"** . . . Interviews with my father, 1991–1992.

Twenty-Eight: "How Do You Get to Detroit?"

237   **At Princeton University** . . . Maryanne Koussa, "Amid Backlash, Princeton Prof. Who Used 'N-Word' in Lecture Cancels Class for the Semester," *The Daily Pennsylvanian*, February, 26, 2018; Francesca Billington, "Classroom Clash: Professor's Words in Hate-Speech Course Stir Student Walkout, Campus Controversy," *The Princeton Alumni Weekly*, March 16, 2018.

237   **At Emory University** . . . Colleen Flaherty, "Suspended for Using N-Word: Emory Is Investigating a Law Professor Who Used the Slur in Torts Class," *Inside Higher Ed*, August 30, 2018; Paul Zwier, "Emory Law Community Message from Professor Zwier," *Emory News Center*, September 18, 2018. WEB.

237   **. . . the New School** . . . Colleen Flaherty, "N-Word at the New School," *Inside Higher Ed*, August 6, 2019.

237   **. . . Smith College** . . . Destiny Wiley-Yancy, "Administration Responds to Use of Racially-Charged Language in Class, *The Sophian*, October 20, 2017.

237   **Students at Williams College boycotted the entire English department over it.** Danny Jin, Kevin Yang, and Samuel Wolf, "Students Call for Boycott of English Department," *The Williams Record*, November 6, 2019; Colleen Flaherty, "The Williams English Boycott," *Inside Higher Ed*, November 5, 2019.

237 **. . . the editors of a leading Black history blog corrected my use of the word . . .** Ibram X. Kendi, "Colored Travelers: A New Book on Mobility and the Fight for Citizenship," *Black Perspectives*, November 28, 2016. WEB. This was a written interview between me and Dr. Kendi. In my responses, I wrote out the full word "n***er," but in the published version, the word was edited to read "the n-word."

238 **"Have you seen the Jay-Z—Oprah conversation?"** "Oprah Interviews Jay-Z," *O Magazine*, October 2009.

Interlude Eleven

245 **The case was dubbed the "Trial of the Century" and captivated the attention of the entire world.** Diane Furno-Lamude, "The Media Spectacle and the O. J. Simpson Case," in Janice Schuetz and Lin S. Lilley, ed., *The O. J. Simpson Trials: Rhetoric, Media, and the Law* (Carbondale: Southern Illinois University Press, 1999), 21–24.

245 **Years earlier, the detective who found the glove, Mark Fuhrman, bragged about hating "Mexicans and n***ers."** Fox Butterfield, "Behind the Badge: A Special Report: A Portrait of the Detective in the 'O. J. Whirlpool.'" *The New York Times*, March 2, 1996; Elizabeth Gleick, "O. J. Simpson Case: The Tale of Two Tapes," *Time*, August 28, 1995; Jeffrey Toobin, "An Incendiary Defense," *The New Yorker*, July 18, 1994.

246 **"The n-word had been introduced in this case" . . .** All of Darden's quotations are from pretrial motions. Pretrial transcript for *The People of the State of California v. OJ. Simpson*, Los Angeles, California, Friday, January 13, 1995. http://simpson.walraven.org/jan13.html; Christopher Darden with Jess Walter, *In Contempt* (New York: Regan Books, 1996), 191–208.

246 **It was a term that had quietly circulated in Black academic and activist circles since 1985 without catching on.** A'Jamal Rashad Byndon, "Twain Novel Offends Blacks," *Omaha World-Herald* (Nebraska), March 20, 1986, and I also interviewed Byndon on December 21, 2018, regarding his use of the phrase in the 1980s. His was one of the first published uses of the phrase "the n-word" in reference to the actual word; Halford H. Fairchild, "N Word Should be Odious from Anyone," *Los Angeles Times*, September 16, 1987; Jeff Chang, *Can't Stop, Won't Stop*, 366; and Jesse Katz and Andrea Ford, "Ex-Gang Members Look to Mideast for a Peace Plan," *The Los Angeles Times*, June 17, 1992. Chang, Katz, and Ford all discuss a proposed gang truce in Los Angeles that used the phrase "the n-word" instead of the actual word. Statement by the Delta Sigma Theta members from the University of Pennsylvania, 1993, in Michael Decourcy Hinds, "Blacks at Penn Drop a Charge of Harassment," *The New York Times*, May 25, 1993. A group of Black sorority sisters was harassed in an event that's come to be known as "the Water Buffalo Incident at Penn." Ayanna Taylor represented the group and read the

statement: "In an atmosphere of being called the 'N' word and sexually demeaning words . . ."

246   **In the end, the defense won the right to show the jury evidence** Henry J. Reske, "Verdict on Simpson Trial: Observers Say Prosecution Lost the Case Over a Bloody Glove, Racist Cop," *American Bar Association Journal*, November 1995, 48–48b.

Interlude Twelve

253   **At the ninety-eighth annual convention of the NAACP, organizers vowed to symbolically "bury the n-word"** Associated Press, "NAACP Delegates 'Bury' N-Word in Ceremony," *NBC News.com*, July 9, 2007; Reuters, "U.S. Civil Rights Group Holds Funeral for 'N-Word,' August 9, 2007; Dale Rich, photograph, "NAACP, Funeral, 'N-Word,' 2007," July 7, 2009, in Walter P. Reuther Library, Wayne State University, https://reuther.wayne.edu/node/8428; Valeria Reitman, "Officials Call for Boycott of N-Word," *The Los Angeles Times*, November 28, 2006; Darryl Fears, "Black Entertainers Struggle with the N-word," *NBC News*, December 2, 2006, https://www.nbcnews.com/id/wbna15997741

253   **Three months after the funeral, hip-hop superstar Nas announced his ninth album, *N***er*.** Daniel Kreps, "Nas Changes Controversial Album Title," *Rolling Stone*, May 19, 2008; Ben Westhoff, "The N-word Still Alive and Well in Hip-Hop," *The Dallas Observer*, March 7, 2008.

253   **"People will always know what the real name of this album is and what to call it."** Nas quoted in Sasha Frere-Jones, "Untitled," August 12, 2008.

254   **In 2024, a white member of a Division 3 swim team . . .** Vincent DiFonzo, "Victim's Family Speaks Out on Racially-Charged 'Hate Crime' at Gettysburg Swim Team Gathering," *The Gettysburgian*, September 20, 2024; DiFonzo, "Campus-Wide Email Provides Investigation Update on Racial Slur Cut onto Student; Victim's Family and College Release Joint Statement." *The Gettysburgian*, September 22, 2024.

Acknowledgments

Weaving together a story of the classroom, the n-word, and my father was harder than I ever imagined. Three years ago, I almost gave it up. But then came my dearest friend of forty-five years, Julie Merson, who refused to let me walk away.

Jules, when you stepped in as developmental editor, you changed everything. You are the rare person who brings a fierce intellect, unbounded energy, and an open, generous heart to everything you touch. With your magical, mathematical mind, you combed through my dense academic prose and somehow helped me unearth the living, breathing story at its core. Chapter by chapter, page by page, you stayed with me, never letting me lose sight of the beating heart of this book.

I could not have written this book without you. Truly. Your creative stewardship and love are stitched into every single page. Sharing this process with you has been one of the most rewarding and grounding experiences of my life. My darling "Sexy Julie," thank you for your problem-solving brilliance, your wisdom, and for believing in me and my story. Along the way, you cracked open my heart, and I will love you forever for it.

The process of bringing this book into being was a collaborative effort. From the start, I was fortunate to find myself in the capable hands of my brilliant agent, Tanya McKinnon, who understood the contours of this story before I did. She fielded more distress calls than she bargained for, all the while remaining a steadfast champion. I am grateful for her influence, inspiration, and sense of humor, which is evident on every page. Thank you to the folks at Simon & Schuster for believing in my complicated vision. Yahdon Israel was a devoted thought partner, encouraging me to get personal about life with my father. As my editor, Dawn Davis was exacting and demanding in the best possible way. She pushed me to dig deeper and insisted the book was not finished until the n-word and its history were front and center.

My work on the n-word grew out of a ten-year journey in the Smith College classroom, a site of constant curiosity and wonder. I am grateful to more students than I could possibly name, but I single out a few for their stories and/or research assistance: Jess Buslewicz, Andrew Cooke, Lori Harris, Ifetayo Harvey, Natalie James, Cade Johnson, Saturn Johnson, Erica Linderman, Rosa Ramirez Mazaheri, Katy Morris, Dani Paradise, Lena Santana, Caty Seger, Cai Sherley, Lili Siegel, Becca Tibbits, Kayla Yousman, and of course the real Charlotte. I am especially grateful to all my students in the first history of the n-word class. It was profound.

Smith College provided indispensable resources for research and writing, including a generous sabbatical policy, funding, and countless opportunities to workshop the book. I also received crucial funding from the Program for the Study of Women and Gender. Topnotch research librarians Esther Roth-Katz and Anna Helgeson discovered pivotal evidence. Katherine Rowe, as provost, inspired me to imagine my classroom journey as a scholarly project. Yasmin Chin Eisenhauer and Travis Grandy offered brilliant insight and friendship as they helped me build the history of the n-word course. Sam Intrator and Carol Berner encouraged me to create a workshop for teachers and opened up their classrooms for me to practice.

Smith colleagues supported my obsession with the n-word from the start, including Marnie Anderson, Carrie Baker, Ernest Benz, Josh Birk, Floyd Cheung, Jennifer DeClue, Dawn Fulton, Paula Giddings,

Sergey Glebov, Valerie Joseph, Jina Kim, Daphne Lamothe, Richard Lim, Caroline Melly, Sam Ng, Sara Pruss, L'Tanya Richmond, Loretta Ross, and Kevin Quashie. Jeff Ahlman was a dedicated mentor and friend whose Nebraska-inflected advice never steered me wrong; Darcy Buerkle read multiple drafts and offered astute feedback; Jennifer Guglielmo, Patty DiBartolo, and Lisa Armstrong are close friends who allowed me to process my story when it was just a kernel. The Junior Faculty of Color Collective provided joy and friendship that offset the conflicting demands of teaching and scholarship.

Colleagues across the country offered continuous support. Barbara Krauthamer and I spent hours walking and processing. Erica Armstrong Dunbar, Beverly Tatum, Julie Lythcott-Haims, Patricia Cline Cohen, Ilyon Woo, Martha Jones, Vanessa Holden, Jim Downs, Robin Kelley, and Randy Kennedy were advocates and guides. Thank you to everyone who invited me to speak about the n-word, especially Susan Crago, Cheryl I. Harris, Devon Carbado, Kirk J. Stark, Pam Cobrin, Miriam Neptune, Brooke Newman, George Yancy, and Brian Purnell. Talks I gave at the Massachusetts Historical Society and at Barnard College honed my thinking tremendously.

Since graduate school, Leslie Alexander has remained a stalwart champion and cheerleader. In a stroke of genius, she introduced me to her sister, Michelle Alexander, who became my daily accountability partner and dear friend. In turn, Michelle invited me to join a memoir-writing group of inspiring women including Melinda Jones-Merchant, Shantae Clayborn, Lisa Factora-Borchers, Alexis Wilson, Kay Wilson, Koritha Mitchell, and Lynette Smith. Thank you to Michael E. Woods for pointing me toward the Lincoln story. Khary Polk and Christina Proenza-Coles read drafts and encouraged me to insert historical Easter eggs. Lilli Stordeur, my daughter, stepped in as a researcher and offered indispensable insight on each draft.

Many other editors and writing coaches offered guidance. Marion Roach Smith and Dori Ostermiller helped me find the focus of my memoir. Long before we worked together, Emily Bernard was an inspiration because of her beautiful writings on race. As editor, she encouraged me to write in scenes and, above all, helped me to remember how deeply I love my students and my mother.

Interviews with Deboragh Pryor, Patricia Von Heitman, and Cheryl Bland gave me new insight into my father. Conversations with my sister Rain and my brother Richard Junior helped me put pieces of our childhood together and remember Mama's funeral. I am grateful to my Uncle Maury, Aunt Sylvia, and my Silverman cousins, especially my cousin Jill, who helped me understand my mother as a young woman.

Thank you to my generous friends who allowed me to use their names and tell their stories, especially one of my closest friends, who is like family, Andrea Meyer, who processed this story with me for over a decade and read a draft with a keen editorial eye. Other close friends have carried me through the process including Sara Berrisford, Liz Cohen, Wayne Greene, Joey Singman, Lili Taylor, Melissa Unger, Michael Williams, Aaron Payne, Phil LaMarr, Kathy Saffro, Harlan Bosmajian, Aidan Bosmajian, Richie Rothenberg, Marty Rothenberg, and Ava and Rosie Rothenberg, who offered writing tips, even when they were eleven. Some of my dearest friends offered their brilliant insights with such love and tenderness that my heart aches with gratitude for having them in my life, including Annie Hall, who read multiple drafts and was beyond generous with her time and guidance, and Fredrika Newton, Carrie Moulton, Bonnie Harrison, Kathy Carlton, Kelsey Hendrix, Vanessa Corey, Thea Coughlin, Rab McKie, Nora Kiewlich, Nathalie Franco, Judith Katz, Susan Levin, and Lisa Berndt.

In the process of writing this book, I became even closer to all of my siblings. I have loved Rain since the day I met her, and her fierce loyalty and support means the world to me. Sharing our childhood memories and bonding with her brilliant daughter, Lotus, has forged an even deeper connection between us. Richard Jr. and I have become close friends, gossiping over Mama's family recipes and his massive archive of Peoria family lore. Renee and I had a heartbreaking conversation at our father's funeral that helped shape my understanding of him. Franklin and I became best friends and pen pals when he was in boot camp. Our letters jogged important memories of my childhood. Kelsey, who lives closest to me, became a confidant as we reminisced around my kitchen table. Steven and I started weekly phone calls that I cherish. I am blown away by the type of father and husband he is. Kelsey joined Steven, his wife, Teshanna, and I for a family picnic with our kids. Theirs—Roman, Xavier, and Aurora—fell instantly in love with mine and vice versa. I think our dad would be proud.

The book would not be possible without the love and devotion of my husband, Jerry Stordeur, and our children who spent hours talking about my life and my relationship to the n-word. At times, I catch glimpses of Henry, his openheartedness and vulnerability, and see my father so clearly, I'm overwhelmed. More than once, Lilli has threatened to throw a punch in her mother's defense. Ours is the mother-daughter relationship I always dreamed about. I hit the lottery when I married Jerry. He does everything for me and carved out the time and space for me to spend years focused entirely on the book. Many years ago, when he smooched me in that tent in Maine, I never imagined we would end spending the rest of our lives together. I am lucky to call Henry, Lilli, and Jerry the loves of my life.

At the heart of the book are my parents who, as flawed as they each were, created in me hope and desire to look toward the light. Thank you, Maxine, for always believing in me more than I believed in myself. And Dad, thank you from the bottom of my heart for the gift of this story.

About the Author

Elizabeth Stordeur Pryor is a professor of history at Smith College where she teaches courses on race, slavery, and her father, comedic legend Richard Pryor. She is the award-winning author of the article "The Etymology of [N-Word]: Resistance, Language, and the Politics of Freedom in the Antebellum North" and a 2016 book *Colored Travelers: Mobility and the Fight for Citizenship before the Civil War.* Her viral TED talk on why it's hard to talk about the n-word has been viewed more than two million times. She lives in western Massachusetts with her husband, Jerry, and loves to go hiking and watch movies with him and their their grown kids, Lilli and Henry.

Illustration Credits

Front Endpapers

Top Row, from left to right

Black Slaves Loaded on Ship, 1881, Credit: Grafissimo.

Mr. T. D. Rice: [graphic] As the original Jim Crow, 1885. Courtesy of the Library Company of Philadelphia.

Frederick A. Douglass, daguerreotype, circa. 1848. Courtesy of the Chester County History Center, West Chester, Pennsylvania.

Poster warning Blacks in Boston—Kidnappers—1851. Courtesy of the Schomburg Center for Research in Black Culture, Photographs and Print Division, The New York Public Library.

Zora Neale Hurston (1891–1960) at the *New York Times* book fair, New York, New York, 1938. Photo by PhotoQuest/Getty Images.

Row Two, from left to right

Norman Rockwell, *The Problem We All Live With*, 1964. Artwork Approved by the Norman Rockwell Family Agency.

Gone with the Wind, Vivien Leigh, Hattie McDaniel, 1939. Courtesy of the Everett Collection.

Booker T. Washington dines with President Roosevelt, October 17, 1901. The Frent Collection/Photo Courtesy of David J. & Janice Frent/Corbis via Getty Images.

Blazing Saddles poster art, Mel Brooks, Cleavon Little, 1974. Courtesy of the Everett Collection.

<h2 align="center">Illustration Credits</h2>

Row Three, from left to right

Adventures of Huckleberry Finn book cover, EW Kemble-Illustrator.

"The Assassination of President Lincoln at Ford's Theater on the Night of April 14, 1865," *Harper's Weekly*, April 29, 1865.

"On Stage," Photograph of Richard Pryor performing on stage, February 1, 1974, Newark, New Jersey. Photo credit: Maxine Pryor, from author's personal collection.

Wattstax, US poster art, 1973. Courtesy of the Everett Collection.

"Murder defendant O. J. Simpson (2nd L) stands with his attorneys Robert Blasier (L), Johnnie Cochran Jr (2nd from R) and Robert Shapiro (R) as the jury enters the courtroom 26 April, 1995 in the O. J. Simpson murder trial," Vince Bucci/AFP via Getty Images.

Bottom Row, from left to right

DETROIT—JULY 9: A mock funeral to symbolically bury the "N-word" is held at the 98th Annual NAACP National Convention July 9, 2007, in Detroit, Michigan. Photo by Bill Pugliano/Getty Images.

Rapper and producer Dr. Dre of N.W.A., rapper Laylaw of Above The Law, rapper The D.O.C. (back), Ice Cube, Eazy-E., MC Ren, and DJ Yella of N.W.A. (front) pose for photos before their performance during the "Straight Outta Compton" tour at Kemper Arena in Kansas City, Missouri, in June 1989. Photo By Raymond Boyd/Getty Images.

My father and me on the set of *Greased Lightning* in Georgia, 1976, from author's personal collection.

Party of Langston Hughes on roof of 580 St. Nicholas Avenue. Courtesy of the Schomburg Center for Research in Black Culture, Photographs and Print Division, The New York Public Library.

<h2 align="center">Back Endpapers
(all photos from author's personal collection)</h2>

Top Row, from left to right

Dad with me as an infant. Photo credit: Maxine Pryor.

Mom in high school, 1959.

Dad. Photo credit: me.

Mom and me, circa 1975.

Row Two, from left to right

Rain's fifth birthday party.

Richard Jr., me, Santa, Rain in Honolulu, Hawaii, circa 1978.

Maxine and Richard, circa 1974.

First Meeting with Daddy, February 1, 1974, Newark, New Jersey. Photo credit: Maxine Pryor.

Me with "Sexy Julie" Merson, August 1993, Studio City.

Row Three, from left to right

Me, Maxine, and Uncle Dickie by the pool of the Parthenia Street house, circa 1976.

Leslie Alexander and I in graduate school, Ithaca, New York, circa 1994.

My father's open briefcase, the well-worn notebook on the right. Photo credit: Harlan Bosmajian.

Dad and me on the set in Madison, Georgia, 1976.

Bottom Row, from left to right

My father sitting in his "Harley," with me and Jerry Stordeur, Christmas 1995.

Dad and me in Baton Rouge, Louisiana. He was filming *The Toy*, April 1982.

Dad and me at the ranch house in Madison, Georgia, 1976. Photo credit: Lucy Saroyan.

Rain, Dad and me in Maui near the Seven Sacred Pools, circa 1983.